BEYOND SOVIETOLOGY

Contemporary Soviet/Post-Soviet Politics

BEYOND SOVIETOLOGY

Essays in Politics

and History

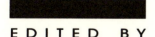

EDITED BY

Susan Gross Solomon

M.E. Sharpe • Armonk, New York • London, England

HN
523.5
.B47
1993

Library of Congress Cataloging-in-Publication Data

Beyond Sovietology : Essays in politics and history / edited by Susan Gross Solomon
p. cm.—(Contemporary Soviet/post-Soviet politics)
Includes index.
ISBN 1-56324-221-4.
1. Soviet Union—Social conditions—1970-1991.
2.Soviet Union—Politics and government—1985-1991.
3. Soviet Union—Study and teaching.
I. Solomon, Susan Gross.
II. Series.
HN523.5.B47   1993
306.0947—dc20
92-22211
CIP

Printed in the United States of America

The paper used in this publication meets the minimum requirements of
American National Standard for Information Sciences—
Permanence of Paper for Printed Library Materials,
ANSI Z39.48-1984.

BM (c) 10   9   8   7   6   5   4   3   2   1
BM (p) 10   9   8   7   6   5   4   3   2   1

Contents

Preface

This collection of essays had a serendipitous beginning. In the mid-1980s, the Joint Committee on Soviet Studies (JCSS) of the Social Science Research Council and the American Council of Learned Societies became concerned about the fact that few young students were specializing in internal Soviet politics and policy, and--even more alarming--few were staying in the specialty. At the very time when remarkable political developments in the Soviet Union itself were calling into question fundamental assumptions about the operation of Soviet domestic politics and society, the supply of young political scientists qualified to interpret those changes was dwindling. To reverse this trend, the Sub-Committee on Soviet Domestic Politics of the JCSS endorsed the holding of a series of workshops that would bring together for two-week periods faculty and pre- and post-doctoral students working in the field.

The First Workshop on Soviet Domestic Politics and Society was held in Toronto in June of 1987, administered by the Social Science Research Council and funded by the Carnegie Corporation. The intellectual freshness and excitement of the twenty young participants who had gathered to argue about the substance and method of studying Russian politics in the midst of a Toronto heat wave was contagious. The Second Workshop, held a year later, made it clear this was not a chance phenomenon: there was something qualitatively different about the way in which this generation of young scholars was posing questions, applying theories, positing hypotheses and exploiting newly-available sources of data. At that point, Dr. Robert Huber, then Staff Associate of the Social Science Research Council with special responsibility for the operation the Joint Committee, proposed the publication of a volume of papers from the Work-shops.

The present collection, drawn from presentations made at the first four Workshops, derives from Huber's suggestion. Selecting the contributions for the volume was no easy matter. The number of first-rate papers presented to the Workshops over a four-year period exceeded by many times the number of contributions included here. The commitment to getting the work of this new cohort of specialists into print with the least possible delay meant, however, that exciting research that was at a preliminary stage could not be included.

In the course of preparing this volume, I have accumulated a number of debts which I take great pleasure in acknowledging here. In the first instance, thanks are due to those institutions and individuals without whom the Workshops would not have taken place: the Social Science Research Council, and especially Dr. Robert Huber and his predecessor at the Council, Dr. Blair Ruble, for their unflagging endorsement of the enterprise; the Carnegie Corporation for understanding the importance of the effort to revitalize the field of Soviet domestic politics in North America through the nurturing of a new cohort of scholars; the University of Toronto, and especially Massey College, for its hospitality to five successive years of enthusiasts given to arguing about Russian politics long into the night; and the Centre for Russian and East European Studies of the University of Toronto--and in particular William Guest and Jana Oldfield--for assistance in preparing the Workshops and in ministering to the needs of participants while the Workshops were in progress.

The actual preparation of the essays generated a separate series of debts. First of all, we are grateful to the Social Science Research Council, which provided funding for the publication. I would also like to thank my Co-directors, Thane Gustafson and Peter Solomon, for their wise counsel in selecting the contributions; Pat Kolb of M.E. Sharpe for her forbearance with an editor who changed the title of the volume three times; the contributors who bore with amazing good humor what must have seemed like the unremitting demands of an editor for changes or clarifications. Last, but by no means least, I am grateful to Dr. Edith Klein of the Centre for Russian and East European Studies, University of Toronto, for the caring spirit in which she joined me in editing the manuscript and for her dogged persistence in mastering the technology required to convert red-pencilled flat copy to aesthetic camera-ready copy.

Finally, a special word of thanks to all the participants of the first five Workshops. The trenchant questions they raised about one another's work provoked greater clarity and rigor; but more important, the supportive way in which they raised those questions forged solidary bonds. This volume is dedicated to them.

Contributors

Jane I. Dawson is Assistant Professor of Political Science at Wellesley College. She received her PhD in Political Science from the University of California at Berkeley in 1993.

Ellen Hamilton is a Post-Doctoral Fellow at the Center on East-West Trade, Investment, and Communications, Duke University. She earned a PhD in Geography from Columbia University in 1993.

Joel S. Hellman is an Instructor in the Department of Political Science at Columbia University. He will take up an appointment in the Department of Government at Harvard University in July of 1993.

Kathryn Hendley is a Fellow at the Center for International Security and Arms Control, Stanford University. She holds a degree in law and is a doctoral candidate in Political Science at the University of California at Berkeley.

Mark Saroyan received a PhD in Political Science from the University of California at Berkeley in 1990. He is Assistant Professor in the Department of Government, Harvard University.

Joseph Schull received his DPhil from St Antony's College, Oxford, in 1990. He is a Program Officer for the International Affairs Program at the Ford Foundation.

Michael Smith is Assistant Professor of History at the University of Dayton, in Dayton, Ohio. He earned his PhD in History from Georgetown University in 1991.

Susan Gross Solomon is Professor of Political Science at the University of Toronto. Her most recent books are *Pluralism in the Soviet Union: Essays in Honour of H. Gordon Skilling* (1983) and *Health and Society in Revolutionary Russia*, edited with John F. Hutchinson (1990). She is currently writing a history of Soviet social medicine between the wars, with special emphasis on Soviet-German medical relations.

Edward W. Walker received his PhD in Political Science in 1992 from Columbia University, where he is currently Visiting Scholar at the Harriman Institute.

Beyond Sovietology:
Thoughts on Studying Russian Politics
After Perestroika

Susan Gross Solomon

In the course of the past two years, some of the leading Western specialists in Russian studies have engaged in a systematic reassessment of the evolution of their field. The retrospectives were not written as celebrations of decades of achievement. Rather, they were driven by a discontent over the "failure" of specialists on Soviet government to predict the dissolution of the USSR and by an unease about the directions in which the field ought to move in the future.[1] Notwithstanding the anxieties that provoked them, the reconstructions of the history of Sovietology that emerged are heartening in one respect: they bespeak a profession engaged (in the best sense of the term) in the effort to understand a country whose face was often hidden. At the same time, these retrospectives suggest just how heavily the past--of Soviet studies and of the country that was its focus--continues to weigh on the established generation of scholars.

Generational Change in Sovietology

The essays in this volume were written by representatives of a new generation of experts on Russian politics and history. These young scholars were trained in the early Gorbachev period and "released into the field" when perestroika was at its height. As one might expect, the timing of their professional socialization shaped their intellectual horizons. Many of the issues that bedevil their teachers preoccupy them scarcely at all. They have other--no less difficult--challenges to face.

Several intellectual touchstones characterize the approach of this young cohort of scholars. First, they share the conviction that the discipline of political science is relevant to the understanding of Russian politics. This generation of students begins with the premise that the discipline can be the source of useful questions and heuristic approaches. Arguably, the interest of Sovietologists in political science is hardly a new phenomenon. Many of the leading Western students of Russia began building bridges to the discipline in the 1960s when the totalitarian model no longer enjoyed a position of hegemony in Russian studies; and in the two decades that followed, the overtures of Sovietologists to political science multiplied.[2] But those overtures did not always meet with unconditional success; indeed, even a comparativist as interested in Russia as Joseph

1

LaPalombara expressed scepticism about the possibility of including Russia in
the family of nations suitable for comparison.[3] What is new in the current
period is that the long-standing interest of Sovietologists in being part of the
discipline is being reciprocated by some mainstream political scientists. Indeed,
political scientists with interests as diverse as the "transitions to democracy"[4]
or "post-materialism"[5] are now looking to Russia as a research site where their
theories can be tested and their conclusions assayed. And mainstream journals
in political science are beginning to carry articles on Russia written by scholars
whose training was not in the field of Russian studies.[6] To be sure, the question
of whether the new interest in including Russia in comparative research derives
primarily from the movement of Russia toward "democratization" or from the
broadening of the discipline of political science could be debated at length.
Whatever the case, it is clear that the receptivity of some mainstream political
scientists to using the case of Russia in comparative work strengthens the belief
of this new generation of specialists that political science is a comfortable
disciplinary home. This marks a sea change from Alfred Meyer's sober
assessment, issued in 1975:

> The discipline of political science obviously has not given
> many useful tools to the area specialists. In turn, the
> theoreticians of the discipline have dismissed area specialists
> with considerable disdain for their unprofessional and unrig-
> orous methods.[7]

Second, this generation approaches the study of Russia secure in the belief that
they no longer face the problem of conducting "data poor" research. Whereas
earlier cohorts in Sovietology repeatedly apologized for the quality and reliability
of their data, this generation is confronted by an *embarras de richesses*: not only
can data hitherto "unavailable" be found and retrieved; data can now also be
generated through surveys and questionnaires. The net effect of these conditions
is that researchers no longer feel compelled to use "sui generis" methods to
study aspects of politics which seem specific to Russia.[8]

New Voices, New Tones

The essays in this book have a freshness that derives from the new frame of
reference. What is particularly noteworthy--and intriguing--is the fact that the
freshness is reflected in every facet of inquiry.

To begin, there is a keen interest among the young generation in methodologies that are relatively new to the discipline of political science, not to speak
of the study of Russia. For example, Joseph Schull addresses the old chestnut
of the role of ideology in Soviet politics. In place of the traditional focus on

ideology as a belief system, however, Schull treats ideology as political discourse and examines its form and substance. Applying discourse analysis to the understanding of Gorbachev's downfall, Schull argues that it was not perestroika that spelled the death of ideology, but ideology that contributed to the downfall of perestroika. Gorbachev's commitment to maintain the ideology, he submits, deepened the divide between language and reality.

In "Rethinking Islam," Mark Saroyan takes issue with the assumption, which he finds embedded in both the Soviet and the Western literature, that Islam is an obstacle to modernization. Arguing that the meanings which Muslims attach to various practices differ substantially from the way in which those practices have been seen in the West, he urges a focus on the "culturally constructed meanings" given to Islamic practices. At Saroyan's hands, Muslim practices and institutions become a text to be read and interpreted.

The aim of these pieces is not methodological innovation for its own sake. Both Saroyan and Schull acknowledge that the case for the new methods of inquiry rests ultimately on their ability to lay bare aspects of familiar problems long obscured from view.

Second, there is clear interest in applying theories developed in the West to some of the puzzles of present-day Russian politics. In "Bureaucrats vs. Markets," Joel Hellman uses rational choice theory to explain the type of reasoning that led state bureaucrats who had been powerholders in the centrally planned economy to participate in the development of an independent commercial banking network. Hellman's findings suggest that "in some sectors at least," market reform could proceed with the active participation of those whose position in the old order might be threatened by reform. These findings are bound to intrigue not only scholars interested in Russian strategies for economic reform but also those who seek to extend the reach of rational choice theory.

The interest among this generation of young scholars in applying to the Soviet Union and its successor states theories refined in Western political science is accompanied by a commitment to conceptual clarification. Setting aside as overworked the dichotomy between state and society, Jane Dawson devotes her article, "Intellectuals and Anti-Nuclear Protest," to clarifying the concept of an autonomous public realm and to examining the scope for the existence of such a realm in "Leninist society." The strength of the article lies not only in the clarification of concepts, but also in the sorts of questions about Ukrainian antinuclear groups--in particular, their connection with nationalist groups--that are suggested by Dawson's research on "autonomous publics."

Third, as exemplified in the essays by Hendley, Smith and Hamilton, there is a new receptivity to enriching inquiry on politics and history with perspectives drawn from other disciplines. In her article on the critical problem of allocating labor in the workplace, Kathryn Hendley uses the law on labor transfers (not only the statutory law, but the published case opinions and Supreme Court opinions) as a yardstick against which to measure the extent to which enterprise managers have taken account of the latitude available to them to encourage the development of the type of work force indispensable for a competitive economy. Drawing on her interviews with management officials and workers as well as with legal scholars, Hendley concludes that there has been a disturbing level of inertia among Soviet managers.

Michael Smith contributes a historical examination of a key element of nation-building in the years following the Bolshevik revolution. Smith engages language planning at the level of the professional linguists who made the important decisions--about alphabets, grammars and orthographies--which shaped the way in which the peoples of Russia "constructed and reconstructed" their national identities. At Smith's hands, the first generation of Soviet linguists emerges as a professional group caught by the contradictions of the "Eurasian imperative"--committed both to serving the interests of non-Russian peoples and to maintaining the primacy of Russian language.

Ellen Hamilton's study of "Social Areas under State Socialism" illustrates the potential of cross-disciplinary research for some of the socio-economic questions with which students of Russian politics are currently wrestling. Among specialists on Russia, there is ready agreement that the marketization of the Russian economy is bringing in its wake unprecedented economic and social inequality. But what is the appropriate baseline against which to measure the inequalities? Using the tools of social geography, Hamilton constructs a portrait of residential differentiation in Moscow and raises the intriguing question of how it was that residential differentiation arose in a non-market economy.

Finally, for all the stress on novelty, this new generation of experts on Russia is not indifferent to its roots. In "Sovietology and Perestroika: A Post-Mortem," Edward Walker examines the field in which he and his cohort were schooled. Walker's post-mortem presents an interesting contrast with those written by his elders. As a "post-Sovietologist with no record of predictions or lessons to defend," Walker's concern is neither the perceived "failure to predict" Gorbachev, nor the dominance of the totalitarian model (whether too long or too short). Instead, he subjects to scrutiny the epistemological orientations, conceptual frameworks, research agendas and methodologies in Sovietology, disaggregating in a novel way what he sees as the strengths and weaknesses of the field. Walker uses his diagnosis to put on the agenda interesting questions for the study of the pre-Gorbachev as well as the post-Gorbachev period.[9]

Hidden Minefields

While the new circumstances undeniably create unique opportunities for young scholars, they also create unique dilemmas. First, there are problems that can be attributed to the "push" from the discipline. Political scientists who do not specialize in Russia are understandably most interested in doing cross-cultural research on those issues which strike them as significant. These issues may not necessarily be the most significant for the understanding of Russia. For specialists in Russian politics, accustomed for so long to being specialists on the "outlier" case, it may be difficult to resist the blandishments of the discipline, but it is important for the future of studies of Russia that the Russian case drive the scholarly agenda.

Close relations with political science hold yet another hazard for young scholars. As a discipline, political science is riven by a series of conflicts on methodological, substantive, and ideological grounds. So difficult has communication between proponents of rival orientations become that Gabriel Almond, in a moment of candor, described the discipline of political science as one of "separate tables."[10]

These divisions clearly play differently in different parts of the discipline. In international relations, the debate over alternative epistemologies has pitted the goal of explanation (causal accounts based on a positivist methodology) against the goal of understanding (interpretation based on hermeneutic methodology).[11] This methodological debate has not passed the sub-field of Soviet foreign policy by. In 1988, Jack Snyder proposed bridging the methods gap between positivism and what he called "holistic" approaches to the study of Soviet international relations.[12]

Within comparative politics--the area of political science that is home to most students of Russian domestic politics--the differences between the goal of explaining action in a positivist mode and the goal of interpreting action or behavior by using Clifford Geertz's "thick description" are just now being explored.[13] The distinction is extremely significant: though nominally about methodology, in a fundamental sense it turns on the issue of what is important to study.

For those who study Russian domestic politics, efforts to "bridge the gap" (not to speak of resolving the tension in favor of one orientation or the other) would be ill-advised. In the short run at least the field of Russian politics needs both studies that aim at causal explanations and studies that aim at interpretive historical understanding of Russia.[14] The new generation should avoid making choices among the competing orientations in comparative politics until it has systematically explored and profited from the alternatives.

Second, the windfall of data which now confronts students of Russian politics creates a series of new dilemmas. Long accustomed to the limitations on inquiry that flow from "data poverty," experts on Russia who now find themselves swamped with data will have to come to terms with what William Quine four decades ago termed the "underdetermination" of theory by facts.[15] Furthermore, given the rapidity of changes in Russian political and social life, the vaunted "data richness" may turn out to be more apparent than real. While their elders complained that the target was moving so slowly that change was undetectable, this generation confronts a target that is moving so quickly that there are no baselines for assessing change.[16]

The challenges confronting this generation will require strong moorings--most important among which, perhaps, may be the kind of commitment to the study of Russia that animated earlier generations.

Notes

1. See Martin Malia ("Z"), "To the Stalin Mausoleum," *Daedalus* 119, no. 2 (1990): 295-344; Martin Malia, "From Under the Rubble, What?" *Problems of Communism* 41, no. 1-2 (1992): 106-113; Frederic Fleron, Jr. and Erik P. Hoffmann, "Sovietology and Perestroika: Methodology and Lessons from the Past," *The Harriman Institute Forum* 5, no. 1 (1991): 1-12; Alfred G. Meyer, "Politics and Methodology in Soviet Studies," *Studies in Comparative Communism* 24, no. 2: 127-36; George Breslauer, "In Defense of Sovietology," *Post-Soviet Affairs* 8, no. 3: 197-238; Thomas F. Remington, "Sovietology and System Stability," *Post-Soviet Affairs* 8, no. 3: 239-269.

2. For example, see H.G. Skilling, "Interest Groups and Communist Politics," *World Politics* 18, no. 3 (1966): 435-51; Jerry F. Hough, "The Soviet Union and the Measurement of Power," in Jerry F. Hough, *The Soviet Union and Social Science Theory* (Cambridge, MA: 1977), pp. 203-221; Valerie Bunce and John M. Echols III, "Soviet Politics in the Brezhnev Era: 'Pluralism' or 'Corporatism'?" in *Soviet Politics in the Brezhnev Era*, ed. Donald Kelley (New York: Praeger, 1980), pp. 1-23.

3. Joseph LaPalombara, "Monoliths or Plural Systems: Through Conceptual Lenses Darkly," *Studies in Comparative Communism* 8, no. 3 (1975): 305-22.

4. Adam Przeworski, *Democracy and the Market: Political and Economic Reforms in Eastern Europe and Latin America* (Cambridge, UK, 1991).

5. Ronald Inglehart, "Democratization in Advanced Industrial Societies," paper presented at the meetings of the American Political Science Association, Chicago, Illinois, September 1992. Cited in Remington, "Sovietology."

6. James L. Gibson, Raymond M. Duch, and Kent L. Tedin, "Democratic Values and the Transformation of the Soviet Union," *Journal of Politics* 54, no. 2 (1992): 329-71; David Laitin, "The National Uprisings in the Soviet Union," *World Politics* 44, no. 1 (1991): 139-77.

7. Alfred G. Meyer, "Comparative Politics and Its Discontent: The Study of the U.S.S.R. and Eastern Europe," in *Political Science and Area Studies: Rivals or Partners*,

ed. Lucian Pye (Ann Arbor, MI: 1985), p. 104. The book was originally published in 1975.

8. Fleron and Hoffmann, "Sovietology and Perestroika," p. 5. Fleron and Hoffmann suggest that because the methods used by sovietologists were sui generis, their application gave unique results. They conclude, "Social science and sovietology had little to offer each other." For the argument that the data limitations of the Soviet field actually enhanced the importance of explicit attention to theory and scientific methodology, see Jack Snyder, "Richness, Rigor and Relevance in the Study of Soviet Foreign Policy," *International Security* 9, no. 3 (1984/5): 108.

9. For a post-mortem on Sovietology that argues for greater attention to Russian as well as Soviet history, see Robert C. Tucker, "Sovietology and Russian History," *Post-Soviet Affairs* 8, no. 3: 175-96.

10. Gabriel Almond, *A Discipline Divided: Schools and Sects in Political Science* (Newbury Park, CA: Sage Publications, 1990), pp. 13-32.

11. Martin Hollis and Steve Smith, *Explaining and Understanding International Relations* (London: Clarendon Press, 1990).

12. Jack Snyder, "Science and Sovietology: Bridging the Methods Gap in Soviet Foreign Policy Studies," *World Politics* 40, no. 2 (1988): 169-94. Snyder drew the distinction between the two orientations in the following way. Positivists generally explain in terms of objective causes; holists construct meaning in the subject's own terms. Positivists trace patterns across cases, holding context constant. Holists trace patterns within cases, exploring the relationship between context and action. *Ibid.*, p. 169.

13. Bertrand Badie, "Comparative Analysis in Political Science: Requiem or Resurrection?" *Political Studies* 37 (1989): 340-51. Over a decade ago, Alasdair MacIntyre wrote an article on the epistemological difficulties involved in doing comparative politics. See A. MacIntyre, "Is a Science of Comparative Politics Possible?" in A. MacIntyre, *Against the Self-Images of the Age* (New York: Schocken Books, 1971). This piece deserves more notice than it has received from those interested in problems of cross-cultural research.

14. The only mention of interpretive work among scholars doing Russian domestic politics can be found in Fleron and Hoffmann, "Sovietology and Perestroika," p. 11.

15. W.O. Quine,"Two Dogmas of Empiricism," in *From a Logical Point of View: Nine Logico-Philosophical Essays*, ed. W.O. Quine (Cambridge: Harvard University Press, 1953), pp. 28-46.

16. Sidney Tarrow, "'Aiming at a Moving Target': Social Science and the Recent Rebellions in Eastern Europe," *PS* 24, no. 1 (1991): 12-20.

The Self-Destruction of Soviet Ideology

Joseph Schull

With perestroika and Soviet ideology both having met their demise, what remains is the task of making sense of their undoing. Many people would argue that understanding perestroika has little to do with the study of ideology, because Soviet ideology was already irrelevant when perestroika began.[1] According to this view, perestroika meant the final eclipse of ideology as an effective force in Soviet politics. It seems to me, on the contrary, that ideology brought the death of perestroika; that is, the refusal of the Gorbachev regime to part with essential elements of official ideology contributed directly to the failure of its attempt to transform the Soviet polity. Insofar as it is still important to understand the demise of this historic effort, one must take account of the ideological factor.

My paper will thus have a retrospective character. It approaches perestroika via a somewhat winding path, which begins with some general comments about ideology as a concept, and about its place in the "classic" Soviet system of politics--or that which existed prior to 1985. This is because those who downplay the significance of ideology under perestroika also, in my view, misconstrue its traditional role in Soviet politics. Indeed, most analyses of ideology in Soviet studies quite simply rest on a mistaken view of the concept itself.

Ideology: Two Views

Two common and contrasting views of ideology must be distinguished at the outset: one characterizes ideology as a belief system, while the other sees it as a form of political discourse or language.[2] The first view was always more pervasive in Soviet studies, but I would argue that it is inadequate both in general and in its specific application to the Soviet case.

The belief system model measures the vitality of ideology by its success in shaping beliefs: ideology creates beliefs that, barring countervailing beliefs or circumstances, lead to a certain pattern of action. Thus the power of ideology varies with the intensity of an individual's belief in it. Adherents form a continuum: at one end is the true believer, whose actions flow directly from his convictions. At the other end is the cynic, for whom ideology is insignificant as anything but a "smokescreen" for action. Sovietologists who held this view usually referred back to a kind of "golden age" in Soviet history, when the leaders were united around a common worldview which motivated them all in pretty much the same way. At some point, it was argued, cracks began to appear in this monolith, as people lost faith in this or that part of the ideology, or simply lost faith altogether. Instead of a group of true believers, a growing number of cynics emerged who merely used ideology manipulatively. A variant of this view was the argument that a variety of factions eventually appeared, whose members believed different things but did not share a common belief system. They simply used "their" ideology to justify their real, group interests. In either case, the conclusion was that ideology as a coherent body of ideas was no longer of much significance in explaining Soviet political action. In tandem with the process of intellectual disenchantment or fragmentation, ideology became marginalized as a factor in Soviet politics.

Some analysts who subscribed to this view saw the fault line running through the Twentieth Congress, while others located it in the Brezhnev period. Whatever the case, ideology was described by one observer as a "dead language", because it no longer rested on a foundation of genuine faith.[3] The interpretation of perestroika as a final parting with Marxist-Leninist dogma derives from this view. Gorbachev and his allies, runs the argument, resolved to jettison this dead language once and for all. If ideology had already suffered a diminishing significance in the Brezhnev era, it became utterly irrelevant after 1985.[4]

It seems to me that this view is misguided, however, both in its assumptions about the nature of ideology and about how Soviet ideology related to politics. It is more useful to conceptualize ideology as a political language which affects action whether or not its adherents believe it, and thus not as a "belief system" at all. Ideology provides people with a common vocabulary, shared assumptions and arguments, which must be respected in order to be accepted as a speaker of the ideology. This is not to say that ideology cannot influence people's thinking or shape their beliefs, which would be plainly absurd.[5] But the connection between ideology and beliefs is contingent rather than necessary.

Seen in this way, ideology was one of the Soviet system's most important elements throughout the period up to 1985 and in large part explains the relatively sustained stability of the state. It was the fact that the political elite was so united about what could be advocated publicly that made for its great staying power, even in the face of a long-term decline in "true belief" in its ideology. Conversely, one of the main reasons for the rapid demise of the Soviet state is that this language unravelled because of the innovations introduced by the Gorbachev regime, which for their part contributed to the crumbling of one of the main pillars which supported the Soviet political system.

The Dynamics of Soviet Political Language

Having discussed these two views of ideology and related them to Soviet politics prior to 1985, I will say something about the significance of changes in Soviet political language under perestroika. In particular I will focus on the way in which the concept of pluralism was integrated into the official Soviet discourse. To be sure, this was only one of several conceptual innovations in Soviet political language, but it was one of the most important, and the problems which arose in connection with it are of general significance for understanding the whole project of ideological revision undertaken by Gorbachev and his allies.

One way of seeing the acceptance of pluralism is that it revived the regime's political language by giving it a new realism and openness. This was at least what many observers were saying during the first couple of years of perestroika.[6] I would claim instead that this innovation in fact debilitated the official political language and contributed to the regime's destabilization.

This latter view is perhaps more common now than it was three or four years ago. In many ways it became clear that Gorbachev sawed off the branch upon which he was sitting without providing himself with an alternative base of support. It is tempting to conclude that Gorbachev's position was weakened because he surrendered Soviet ideology. I would put the point somewhat differently, and argue that he did not give up the ideology quickly enough, but tried to reform from within a language that was impervious to reform. In accommodating "pluralism" Gorbachev tried to insinuate into official ideological discourse a concept that the discourse could not accommodate, and the failure to make a clear choice between the two led to the ideology's unravelling from within. The choice for Gorbachev and his allies was either to sustain a basically unreformed ideology, and in this way to retain a solid if conservative political constituency, or to a make a decisive break with the old language in search of a new and potentially broader constituency. Rather than choose, he did a bit of both but not enough of either, and thus sacrificed the unity of the regime's old constituency without creating an alternative one.

There are two issues of concern here. The first has to do with the internal dynamics of Soviet political language and the difficulty of introducing into it the vocabulary of pluralism without throwing the whole language overboard. The second has to do with the problems which arose when this language was confronted with the world that it was meant to characterize and order. First, political pluralism in Gorbachev's usage was consistently elaborated in combination with a traditional ideological claim that there remained a single set of legitimate interests and values shared by all of Soviet society. Thus, pluralism was a "synthesis of opinions on the basis of which we get nearer to the truth."[7] Instead of acknowledging a diversity of views as the normal state of affairs, because people have different values, Gorbachev said that we must express different points of view because this is the best way of coming to a better recognition of the socialist values that we all share. Pluralism was to be a dialectical step on the way to unity. If one analyzes this inconsistency as an element of Soviet political language, it appears to be more than just the generic opportunism of a good politician trying to appeal to as many constituencies as possible and to rally everyone around him. Of course Gorbachev was doing that, but there was something else going on at a deeper level, where the strategy reflected a basic incoherence within the reformist discourse. Genuine pluralism had to mean the overthrow of any stipulative assertion of unitary values for society, but Gorbachev refused to part with the language that imposed this assertion on him. His continuing commitment both to the innovation and to the language in which it was expressed left him falling between two stools. He was unable to preserve the ideology because he introduced into it the virus of pluralism, yet he was also unable to draw authority from the emergence of real pluralism because he insisted on forcing it into a conceptual framework that it would not and could not accept.

The second point has to do with what happened when the language of reform met the reality of Soviet politics as it evolved during perestroika. To the foregoing argument some would reply that the inconsistencies in Gorbachev's language did not matter, because objectively Gorbachev made it possible for real pluralism to emerge. He may have continued to talk about how everyone really shared the same values, but in fact he allowed people to express and organize around their divergent beliefs and values.[8] In a certain sense this is true. Gorbachev's ideological innovations indeed made it possible for a real pluralism of values to emerge. But this was the very problem. When one looks beyond official political language to the reality outside of it, Gorbachev's problems multiplied. He helped to create a reality that his language could not comprehend, and the more deeply entrenched real pluralism became, the more it stood as a rebuttal of the ersatz, "socialist pluralism" that remained officially on offer. That he may have belatedly reconciled himself to real pluralism is irrelevant, because it came into being despite his efforts to the contrary. Early on in perestroika he might have been able to draw credit for endorsing real pluralism and agreeing to preside over it; but that moment soon passed, and he could only suffer its consequences.[9]

Ideology as a Political Discourse

Ideology, understood as a discourse, affects political action insofar as an adherent must conform to its conventions.[10] This need not involve believing in the veracity of the conventions. The required attitude is respect, not faith. Ideology provides a medium in which political debate takes place, and its conventions determine the kinds of arguments that can be legitimated. This view of ideology leads to an interpretation of Soviet politics before 1985 and after that is quite different from that advanced by those who understand ideology as a "belief system." In Soviet politics throughout the period up to 1985, the ideological discourse was perhaps the most important resource employed in political debate, a resource with the power to affect the use that could be made of it.

I use the term "conventions" to mean the substance of an ideology: its vocabulary, terms and concepts, figures of speech and patterns of argument, and criteria of coherence and verification. Conventions begin with the basic set of terms used in communication--proletariat, bourgeoisie, class struggle, the Party, and so on. Key terms like these are simultaneously descriptive and evaluative-- they evaluate something in describing it. In the classic Soviet political language, it was impossible to speak of a class struggle between the proletariat and the bourgeoisie without also identifying one's loyalties with the proletariat. Similarly, it was impossible to describe a party policy without implying that it was correct and unimpeachable. To do otherwise would have implied that the speaker had misunderstood the terms being used. This is one kind of convention, having to do with the basic vocabulary of the language. Another, more important kind of convention has to do with the basic propositions that circulated among the elite in political debate. I will not give an exhaustive list of the propositions--indeed, I am not certain such an exercise is possible--but I will mention several which seem to be cornerstones of the traditional discourse. One was the claim that there was a correct, scientific view of the social world, and that Marxism-Leninism was it. Another was the claim that this view was embodied in the Communist Party, which thereby earned the leading role in society's organization and development. Both of these conventions were implicitly echoed by Gorbachev in his assertion of a unitary set of legitimate values for all of society. He basically reiterated the claim to a correct way of viewing the world, and this was provided by official ideology. A third convention was the notion of party-mindedness, which followed from the first two. Democratic centralism was another convention, with its imperative that decisions of higher party bodies were binding on lower ones. Another was the commitment to dynamic order, which encompassed both rapid economic development and a view that this development must be organized by the Party. A final convention was that of the supremacy of state ownership of the means of production and central planning of the economy.

These were for a very long time the building blocks of political debate among the Soviet elite. They provided a structure for communication that had force whether or not anyone believed the propositions to be valid. Regardless of what someone believed, the requirement was to endorse the conventions publicly and shape one's arguments to fit them. This could not be a matter of merely saying one thing and doing another, as the description of ideology as a "smokescreen" implies. The act itself had to conform to its description, if those to whom it was being legitimated were to take it seriously as an act of the described kind. If you want to be a credible practitioner of your ideology, you really must do what you say.[11]

When I use the term "legitimation," I am referring to the Soviet political elite, because in my view ideology was the language of the elite. It was always a commonplace of Soviet studies that the Communist Party "legitimated" its rule to the Soviet people by reference to its ideology. And yet it would be stretching things to say that the Party always kept its word in this relationship. The confusion arises because the word "legitimation" is used in two different and incompatible senses. When one claimed that Soviet ideology was used to legitimate the rule of the Communist Party to the Soviet people, one usually meant that it was an exercise in salesmanship or public relations.[12] But this is a misuse of the concept of legitimation. It assumes, incorrectly, that the Communist Party saw the Soviet people as the source of its legitimacy. According to the classic ideology, the Communist Party derived its right to rule from History, not from the variable opinions of the Soviet people. Of course, the regime wanted to popularize its policies in the interests of stability, but public relations is not legitimation and stability is not legitimacy. When I use the term, I do so in the Weberian sense, and I do not have in mind the relationship between the Party and society at large. Political elites in the classic Soviet system legitimated their actions to each other, not to the Soviet people. Legitimation governed the political elites' internal dialogue amongst themselves. It was in this context that ideology enjoyed a significant power to shape action. Only when political elites legitimated their actions to each other by reference to ideological conventions were they bound to act accordingly, because only the elites were able to constrain each other to act in obedience to the conventions. Insofar as ideology is concerned, for seventy years the Soviet political elite and the Soviet people inhabited different speech communities.

Ideological conventions also shaped the way in which arguments could be made for innovations and corresponding changes in policy. Individual leaders might question the truth of this or that convention, but they could not reject them outright and still expect to be taken seriously by their colleagues as political actors. Innovations had to be made by invoking other conventions that were held fixed: if you wanted to modify the script, you had to rehearse many well-known lines. If, for instance, someone in the leadership wanted to question the practice of central planning, he could not say simply that it was wrong without further elaboration, and expect this argument to have any force. What he might have said was that central planning, while itself correct, was being inefficiently applied. In this case the convention is not really being questioned at all; it is modified but not rejected. A more overtly revisionist move, which we saw more often after 1985, was to attack central planning directly by claiming that the value placed on it was mistaken. But the conventional move was not to attack the practice *tout court*. Rather, one would claim that planning had begun to obstruct another ideological commitment that was taken to be more central, that of economic growth. The argument might be that planning was devised as a means to the rational development of society's economic resources but had begun to inhibit that end. The argument leans on one convention--the commitment to economic growth and prosperity--to modify or reject another--planning; it proposes a better way of seeing the world from a perspective that is recognizably the same.

Other examples of this kind of debate around ideological conventions could be given, but the point should be clear. A member of an ideological group like the Soviet political elite was not able to say just anything, advance any claim or criticism of official policy, and expect to get a hearing. Yet many observers would claim that after 1985 this was no longer the case, and in a superficial sense this may have been true. In contrast to the Brezhnev era, when it was almost impossible in policy debates to attack any of the above-mentioned conventions directly, it is obvious that a dramatic change had occurred. But if one considers the way in which the Gorbachev regime introduced its innovations, the point still applies. The reform was still an internal one, legitimating the new by making it compatible with the old.

For instance, it was possible for Gorbachev to embrace pluralism only by rendering it compatible with some of the old ideology's central conventions. For Gorbachev to have advocated pluralism without qualifications would have signified the outright rejection of the traditional ideology. After all, since the 1920s it had been claimed that there was a unitary set of legitimate values for society, and that these were represented by Communist Party ideology. These values were at one time described as proletarian values, whereas under Gorbachev they were described as "all-human"--but in both cases they were embodied in the Party's ideology. For this reason, it was impossible within the official political language to say squarely that a variety of values exist in society and all are valid. As Gorbachev did not want to break with this language, he did something else. He claimed that pluralism was really a way of getting clear about what society's common values are. Everyone fundamentally wanted the same things, but sometimes it was difficult to see how this translated into policy, so a maximum of openness was necessary to achieve clarity about common ends. In the end, everyone would come to agreement about the way forward. Thus, Gorbachev legitimated this innovation by making it recognizable within the terms of the old ideology. There was a change, and an important one, but it was a change from within the ideology, which allowed the leader to insist that the whole language was not being thrown overboard. Pluralism was offered as an innovation which served an orthodox goal.

At the same time, Gorbachev continuously described ongoing conflicts of opinion as manifestations of groupish self-interest or ambition.[13] This was in fact merely a consequence of his original definition of pluralism. Given the common values and interests shared by everyone, persistent conflicts could not be based on principle--they could only be battles for position and privilege. Once the various views had been exchanged and considered in a spirit of tolerance and openness, agreement would inevitably result among all people of sound mind and good will.[14] Those who continued to behave disagreeably had to have some ulterior motive, some unprincipled scheme in mind. Pluralism thus amounted to a means of consolidating society around a common project. The way Gorbachev described the relationship between pluralism and consolidation is very telling. In a meeting with representatives of the media in the fall of 1988, he said:

> When you regularly follow the papers and journals, you get the impression that certain authors and even organizations have already distributed themselves, divided themselves into certain papers and journals. Today I can tell you exactly which letters this journal will publish and which ones that will. Group passions are appearing. And we must overcome this. Publish everything. There must be a pluralism of opinion. But with such an orientation that the line of perestroika, the interests of socialism are defended and strengthened.[15]

It is characteristic that Gorbachev spoke of group passions rather than values; people were getting over-wrought, letting their emotions blind them to their true interests. In a Western context, it would be strange to propose that journals occupying certain positions on the political spectrum have an obligation to publish more of the other side's views--the reason they exist is to publish their own. Pluralism usually means that people must tolerate a diversity of values because their synthesis is impossible. It has often been noted that the Soviet use of pluralism was an eccentric and instrumental one, as the regime used openness to foster popular support for its reforms, and accepted openness only insofar as it supported these reforms.[16] This was indeed one of the ideological dilemmas of Soviet-style pluralism--a to-and-fro intolerance which tended to discredit the regime in the eyes of its people. The state reserved itself the right to intervene to protect socialist values and therefore limit debate. But this inconsistency in policy was only part of the ideological dilemma, and seemed to become less important with time. Objectively, Gorbachev's version of pluralism contributed to the expression of a great diversity of views, many of them opposed to elements of the state's reforms. In practice, Soviet-style pluralism led to something more and more approaching real pluralism.

But for the reform Communists there remained the problem of making sense of this development. They introduced a formula which legitimated the freer expression of divergent views, yet found themselves unable to endorse their real, that is to say, divisive, effects. Gorbachev helped to create a reality that he could neither accept nor comprehend because of the language he had to use to characterize it. As this reality consolidated itself, Gorbachev's description of it became a lie which discredited him. Conversely, it seems that the regime's failure to limit divisive diversity was just as costly to its authority. This is because its initial assurances that pluralism would unite people were proven false, while the concurrent failure to carry out the implicit threat to intervene in the interest of unity only widened the gap between promises and deeds. The discourse of pluralism was shown to be both false and powerless.

There is another aspect to this problem. Beyond Gorbachev's failure to predict the result of Soviet-style pluralism, he also deepened the divide between language and reality by forcing his own ideological categories onto what did emerge. As noted earlier, he repeatedly complained about "groupishness" and sectional interests as if they were a distortion of pluralism. Popular Fronts were described as narrow extremists who hijacked innocent people behind a project which was against their interest. Much the same was said of opposition movements in Russia. The main charge against Boris Yeltsin, repeated ad infinitum, was that his conflict with Gorbachev reflected an overweening personal ambition. Gorbachev was very slow to recognize publicly that what existed outside the walls of the Kremlin were not groups of extremists consumed by a desire for power, but people with values different from his own--a very natural outcome of the process he set in motion. For several years he consistently cast aspersions on the legitimacy of opposition to official policy by characterizing it as based upon petty motivations. In the end, he alienated everyone: conservatives who were dragged along the path of reform suddenly found that he had made a wrong turn toward revolution, while those who wanted to carry out a real revolution found Gorbachev blocking their way as he searched vainly for the road to reform Communism.

Gorbachev was of course not the only member of the political elite to have advocated pluralism, and the intention here is not to reduce the ideological innovations of the final years of the Soviet period to his role alone.[17] I have concentrated on Gorbachev because his view represents the main trend of Soviet ideological reform-from-above post-1985. It was not an acceptance of pluralism, but pluralism in one ideology, and this notion is nonsensical. Opening society to a diversity of views must either lead to ideological pluralism, or the process of diversification has to be halted and society kept closed. In either case something has to give. It was in this sense unsurprising that, along with the partial crackdown on independence movements and political activism overseen by Gorbachev in the latter period of his tenure, official discussions of political pluralism became rather more defensive and measured. Here again, though, Gorbachev's hesitations and procrastination created the worst kind of halfway house: a fledgling civil society irretrievably alienated from him and determined to resist attempts to undermine it, but still too weakly implanted to overwhelm decisively the defenders of unitarian orthodoxy.

I have focused mainly on the official version of pluralism and its internal contradictions. Taken on its own and considered in a vacuum, the strategy was already incoherent. It combined commitments that were basically incompatible. But once society was brought into the picture, the problems multiplied, because the language of reform was also appropriated quite broadly and spontaneously by popular voices, in order to pursue a dialogue with the state and within civil society itself. Even people hostile to the regime often accepted official descriptions for the expression of their own more radical demands.[18] This was perhaps a sign of the primitiveness of the Soviet public space in the early stage of perestroika, when society lacked even an elementary language with which to formulate popular demands, and therefore readily accepted the terms provided by the regime. With the progress of reform and the maturing of this public space, however, attempts were made to stretch the meaning of new ideological terms beyond the limits originally envisaged for them and thereby to use the regime's own language to push it further than it wanted to go. For instance, the official policy of "self-financing"--originally introduced as a policy of limited enterprise autonomy--was subsequently used to legitimate the economic autonomy demanded by many Soviet republics.[19] They stretched its meaning to work it in their favour. As for the concept of pluralism, Gorbachev's efforts to keep it within ideologically acceptable boundaries failed dramatically, as groups outside the regime exploited the acceptance of pluralism to argue for the legitimacy of a multi-party system.

The regime's reform language was thus a double-edged sword not just because of internal contradictions but also because it was turned against its author by popular voices. The opportunity to manipulate the official vocabulary depended in part on the leadership's inability to decide on the meaning of its own reforms; it lost control of the discourse because in many cases, especially economic policy, it was slow to set the agenda. But the discourse itself was also supposed to be dialogical, that is, society was expected to participate in settling its meaning. As a result, revising ideology in the old-fashioned way, through general secretaries' speeches at Party Congresses and November revolutionary celebrations, mattered less and less. The Soviet political community was no longer a closed club. For a very long time the Soviet language of politics had been a kind of specialized dialect, relevant only to those who participated in public debate. Whatever its other defects, there was a kind of fit between this language and the elite's form of life. For them, the Communist Party really did have the leading role in society, whether or not it was playing this role adequately. One of the most important changes Gorbachev effected was the dissolution of this closed order and the formation of a much broader, popular public space.

This change in the context of political language is very important for understanding the import of changes in it. If one interpreted the Gorbachev innovations as one would have done in the Brezhnev era, one saw only a very impressive set of doctrinal revisions established by official fiat. But viewed against the background disintegration of the institutions of Soviet power and the formation of a new public space taking place concurrently, it was evident that the underpinnings of Soviet ideology were rapidly disappearing; there was no longer a fit between the official discourse and the world it was meant to characterize. The opening of ideology to a community outside the elite only hastened this disintegration and further weakened the discourse. Viewed from this perspective, the innovations seem clearly self-destructive rather than progressive; they were significant not as a liberalization of Soviet ideology but as a catalyst of its collapse and the destabilization of the mechanisms of Soviet power. While ideology had indeed changed rapidly, political life had changed even more dramatically and detached itself from the linguistic and conceptual boundaries within which the regime would have liked to contain it. Thus, the problem was not only that the ideological reforms did not make sense on their own terms. It was also that the regime's political language simply did not fit the reality it was supposed to characterize.

Postscript

The foregoing was originally written in the autumn of 1990, and the issues I have addressed here may seem to some rather passé. Few would deny that perestroika and Mikhail Gorbachev failed in their effort to revitalize the Soviet polity. Yet our understanding of this failure remains limited not only by incomplete information about the recent past but also by deeply ingrained assumptions within "Soviet studies" about the nature of the system and the type of politics that perestroika attempted to transform. Soviet politics was ideological to its very core, and the attempt to transform the polity without a radical break from this ideology was in my view destined to fail, regardless of the degree of tactical skill with which this strategy was carried out.

Indeed, the failed August coup of 1991, which hammered the final nail into the coffin of this system, symbolized perfectly the choice that had been implicit since 1985: on one side, the forces of order with their commitment to the irreversibility of the orthodox "socialist choice," and on the other side the motley defenders of "democracy" (albeit variously understood), for whom socialism had long before lost any meaning. Between these two forces, yet now utterly isolated and politically impotent, stood Gorbachev, still committed to a reformed "socialism" that bore no relationship to the actually existing society over which he presided. It is true, of course, that events since early 1990 had conspired to make this choice--between orthodox Soviet power and no Soviet power--appear all the more stark and Gorbachev's strategy still less feasible. Yet, given the nature of the system founded on this ideology, and given the type of politics it created, in essence the choice had been there all along. It is perhaps a measure of Gorbachev's achievement as a political leader, as much as it is a token of his limitations, that he was able to forestall this choice for so long.

Notes

1. This view is rather widespread in Soviet studies, but one of its most prominent exponents is Jerry Hough. See Jerry Hough, *The Struggle for the Third World: Soviet Debates and American Options* (Washington, DC: The Brookings Institution, 1986), pp. 7, 11, 261, and *passim*. See also Jerry Hough, *Russia and the West: Gorbachev and the Politics of Reform* (New York: Simon & Schuster, 1988). Adam Przeworski has recently made a similar point with respect to all Soviet-type societies. See Adam Przeworski, "The 'East' Becomes the 'South'? The 'Autumn of the People' and the Future of Eastern Europe," *PS - Political Science & Politics* XXIV, no. 1 (March 1991): 20.

2. For a more extended discussion of these two views, see my D. Phil. thesis, "Ideology and the Politics of Soviet Literature under NEP and Perestroika" (Oxford, 1990), esp. chap. 2. For a broad review of the literature on ideology, see Malcolm B. Hamilton, "The Elements of the Concept of Ideology," *Political Studies* 35 (March 1987): 21.

3. Leszek Kolakowski, *Main Currents of Marxism*, Vol. 3: *The Breakdown* (Oxford: Clarendon Press, 1978), p. 529.

4. For an early statement of this view, see R. Daniels, *The Nature of Communism* (New York: Vintage Books, 1963), p. 373. See also Wolfgang Leonhard, *The Kremlin and the West: A Realistic Approach* (New York: W.W. Norton & Co., 1986), pp. 55-59. Some of those who accepted the assumption of growing scepticism among Soviet leaders nonetheless continued to assert a causal influence of ideology on political action; generally they argued that, although there may have been a decline in conscious belief in "Marxism-Leninism," it continued to shape the *unconscious* beliefs of Soviet leaders. The argument in this form was even less compelling to many of its critics, for while it was always difficult to judge what Soviet leaders knowingly believed, it is even less clear how one would go about proving what they believed without knowing it. The claim just hung in mid-air, to be accepted or rejected according to one's prejudices. See Alfred Meyer, *Leninism* (Cambridge: Harvard University Press, 1957), p. 2; Z. Brzezinski, *Ideology and Power in Soviet Politics* (New York: Praeger, 1962), p. 5; Z. Brzezinski and S. Huntington, *Political Power: U.S.A./U.S.S.R.* (New York: The Viking Press, 1963), p. 40; John A. Armstrong, *Ideology, Politics, and Government in the Soviet Union: An Introduction*, 4th ed. (New York: Praeger, 1978), p. 27; Donald D. Barry and Carol Barner-Barry, *Contemporary Soviet Politics: An Introduction*, 3rd ed. (Englewood

Cliffs, NJ: Prentice Hall, 1987), p. 30.

5. Analyses of Soviet ideology very frequently get bogged down in a debate over whether or not the ideology was Marxism-Leninism, or some combination of Marxism-Leninism and Russian nationalism, or something else again. I will not enter into this debate here, because it seems largely sterile. If one views Soviet ideology as the official language of its political elite, then one merely needs to analyze the discourse, look for its patterns, and not worry about adding a label to it.

6. See Archie Brown, "Political Change in the Soviet Union," *World Policy Journal* 3 (Summer 1989): 471-78.

7. M. Gorbachev, "Narashchivat' intellektual'nyi potentsial perestroiki," *Pravda*, Jan. 8, 1989, p. 2. In an early meeting with Soviet writers, Gorbachev called for a "unification on principled foundations," a call he made repeatedly afterward. "Beseda chlenov SP SSSR s M.S. Gorbachevym," *Arkhiv Samizdata* AS5785 (June 19, 1986), p. 5. The principled foundation he had in mind was the "socialist idea," to which Gorbachev continued to pledge allegiance. See, for instance, his speech to Moscow Party members published in *Pravda*, May 14, 1990, p. 1.

8. Several observers drew attention to the evolution in Gorbachev's use of political language, as he progressively expanded the scope of a term like *glasnost* to accommodate more and more innovative forms of expression. See Archie Brown, "Ideology and Political Culture," in *Politics, Society, and Nationality: Inside Gorbachev's Russia*, ed. Seweryn Bialer (Boulder, CO: Westview Press, 1989), pp. 1-40. Yet changes in linguistic usage over time must be interpreted within the practical context of political action. From this perspective, what appeared as "progress" in official terms was revealed as a widening gap between these terms and the political reality they were meant to describe.

9. The decision in the winter of 1990 at the Third Congress of People's Deputies to establish the constitutional basis for a multi-party system may be seen as the marker of an official acceptance of genuine pluralism. Gorbachev's speech to the Central Committee plenum prior to the Congress called on the Party to play its vanguard role without its imposition by "constitutional legitimation." *Pravda*, Feb. 6, 1990, p. 1. Gorbachev later characterized this as a return to the Party's "natural, original role" as conceived by Lenin. *Pravda*, April 28, 1990, pp. 1-2. His conduct in the period leading up to this concession was characteristically ambivalent. In February 1989, speaking to a group of industrial workers, Gorbachev characterized talk of a multi-party system as "rubbish." Central Television, Feb. 15, 1989. As late as December 1989, at the Second Congress of People's Deputies, Gorbachev intervened decisively to defeat a move by radical deputies to have a debate on Article Six of the Soviet constitution included on the agenda.

10. The concept of conventions employed here is drawn from the work of Quentin Skinner. For a selection of Skinner's methodological articles and critical appraisals of his work, see *Meaning and Context: Quentin Skinner and His Critics*, ed. James Tully (Cambridge: Polity Press, 1988). See also David Lewis, *Convention: A Philosophical Study* (Cambridge: Harvard University Press, 1969).

11. Skinner puts the point as follows: "Thus the problem facing an agent who wishes to legitimate what he is doing at the same time as gaining what he wants cannot simply be the instrumental problem of tailoring his normative language in order to fit his projects. It must in part be the problem of tailoring his projects to fit the available normative language." Quentin Skinner, *The Foundations of Modern Political Thought*, 2 vols. (Cambridge: Cambridge University Press, 1978), 1: xii-xiii.

12. "[Ideology] is to convince the citizenry that the Party and its rulers have a legitimate claim to rule them. More broadly, it is to convince the people that the entire system of government is legitimate. Ideology is thus an exercise in salesmanship or public relations. It seeks to persuade the Soviet citizens that theirs is the best of all possible societies." Alfred Meyer, "The Functions of Ideology in the Soviet Political System," *Soviet Studies* (Jan. 1966), 17: 279.

13. This tendency was especially rampant in Gorbachev's discussions of popular fronts and independence movements, which were almost invariably attacked as corrupt and self-serving, and were frequently identified with the interests of the second economy. Hence, "democracy, perestroika arouse stormy changes in all regions of the country, and threaten the interests of the black market. . . . nobody raises the flag of defense of corruption, but one can speculate with the flag of defense of national interests." *Izvestiia*, April 12, 1990, p. 1. For the Soviet president, "all kinds of separatists, chauvinists, and nationalists . . . are hastening to take advantage of the growth in national self-awareness of peoples for their own selfish ends. The intent is obvious: to deal a preventive strike to restructuring, which threatens to thwart their far-reaching schemes." *Pravda*, Feb. 6, 1990, p. 1.

14. Gorbachev tended to use the term "healthy elements" to characterize the parties to this consensus, as in his defense of the proposed new Party Program's capacity to "consolidate all healthy elements" at the Central Committee Plenum in February 1990. See *Pravda*, Feb. 6, 1990, p. 1.

15. M. Gorbachev, "Na perelomnom etape perestroiki," *Pravda*, Sept. 25, 1988, p. 2. Gorbachev also connected the role of the president with the "consolidation of political trends and social movements." See his presidential acceptance speech, *Izvestiia*, March 16, 1990, p. 2.

16. James Scanlan has drawn attention to the Soviet regime's instrumental conception of glasnost, which was meant to assure the success of transformations in the economic sphere. See J. Scanlan, "Reforms and Civil Society in the U.S.S.R.," in *Problems of*

Communism 37 (March-April 1988): 41-46.

17. Prior to his retirement from the Politburo, Alexander Yakovlev offered a re-definition of unity and socialism that was remarkably free of dogma: "What should there be unity about? In our understanding that we want to live freely in a democratic and humane society. Let us argue about the rest." And further: "maybe we should approach the issue in this way--something is socialist which is good for a person, which is useful, gives him wealth, happiness, raises his dignity." A. Yakovlev, "Sotsializm: ot mechti k real'nosti," *Kommunist* 4 (March 1990): 16, 20. The re-definition of socialism and unity in such generic terms would eliminate almost entirely the ideological limits on debate. "Socialism" and "unity" would be wholly reducible to ordinary, everyday language with no necessary relationship to the discourse of Marxism-Leninism. But this more radical revisionist line would create a different dilemma insofar as it continued to proclaim the goal of restoring the prestige and authority of the Communist Party: on what grounds could it claim this authority, once the connection between socialism and the CPSU's definition of it had been broken? Yakovlev's ideological innovation, in resolutely breaking with all vestiges of dogma, defeated its own purpose of revitalizing the Party. See also, for a view close to that of Gorbachev (by a presidential adviser), G. Shakhnazarov, "Obnovlenie ideologii i ideologiia obnovleniia," *Kommunist* 4 (March 1990): 46-59.

18. For instance, Lithuania's Sajudis adopted the name of "Popular Front in Support of Perestroika" on its formation, providing an acceptable umbrella under which its more radical demands could gradually be formulated. Gorbachev recognized this dilemma for the official reformist discourse during his visit to Lithuania in the winter of 1990, when he claimed that speakers at the recent Sajudis Sejm had said "we should say that we support Gorbachev's line, then implement our own." *Pravda*, Jan. 13, 1990, p. 3.

19. See Philip G. Roeder, "Soviet Politics and Ethnic Mobilization," *World Politics* 43, no. 2 (Jan. 1991): 219-20.

Rethinking Islam in the Soviet Union

Mark Saroyan

One did not need to be a Sovietologist to recognize the depth and scope of the transformations that had taken place in the Soviet Union by the end of the 1980s. Mikhail Gorbachev's program of radical socio-economic and political reform touched virtually all spheres of Soviet life and resulted in a climate of near-permanent crisis in a country that once boasted of its social and political stability. Despite a protracted civil war between the Caucasian republics of Armenia and Azerbaijan, assertive independence movements in the Baltic republics and a seemingly unending list of strikes, social movements, demonstrations and periodic violence throughout the country, something was missing from the USSR's increasingly unstable political scene: the emergence of an Islamic opposition to Moscow's rule.

In the 1970s and 1980s, expectations of instability among the USSR's Muslim populations were fueled by journalistic reports and scholarly studies which, having discovered the large and diverse Muslim communities of the Soviet Union, outlined the features of a Muslim "arc of instability" across the USSR's southern tier.[1] The Islamic Revolution in Iran, the Soviet invasion of Afghanistan and the war against the Muslim insurgency there, coupled with a demographic boom among the Soviet Union's Muslim populations, served only to highlight what was viewed as the intrinsic incompatibility of the Soviet state and the Muslim community. In this context, the absence of a massive, militant Muslim insurgency in a Soviet Union of glasnost and perestroika appeared a striking anomaly.[2]

Despite the few voices raised against the conventions of Western thinking about Islam in the Soviet Union, there has been little in the way of a rigorous assessment of this growing field of knowledge.[3] By contrast, a thoughtful sub-literature that explores the theoretical methods and substance of the ever-more extensive discourse on Islam has developed in tandem with the expansion of Muslim studies outside the Soviet field.[4] Given the need for a reexamination of the assumptions and methodologies that have shaped study of the Soviet

This essay was originally written during 1988-1989 and revised with minor alterations in 1990. The author is grateful to Gail Lapidus, Victoria Bonnell, George Breslauer, Michael Cooper and Russ Faeges for their critical comments on these early drafts, and to the ACLS/SSRC Joint Committee on Soviet Studies for financial support during the writing of this essay.

Union's Muslim communities, my purpose here is not to examine Soviet Islam itself but to engage in a critical analysis of Western and Soviet representations of Soviet Islam as they are organized in a scholarly discourse. The fundamental question of this essay is thus not *what* we know about Islam in the Soviet Union, but *how* we know about it.

Students of the Soviet Union have frequently viewed access to information as a problem equal to if not greater than that of theoretical approach. But contemporary policies emanating from Moscow have resulted in a virtual explosion of information about the formerly "blank pages" of Soviet history and politics, thus mitigating the problem of access. In the context of this new wave of data, the excitement over the information itself has frequently resulted in a lack of attention to the manner by which information is received and processed for use in scholarship and analysis. The need to reevaluate the ways in which scholars use theories and paradigms to select, receive and organize data is especially acute.

The problems of information and conceptual approach are closely intertwined, but for reasons of clarity I discuss them separately. In the first instance, a review of the empirical sources for the Western specialist literature on Soviet Islam reveals the intertextuality of this scholarly writing. In other words, the Western literature has developed more in relation to studies of Islam produced in the Soviet Union than it has to the socio-political and religious processes that characterize contemporary Soviet Islam. But there is more than simply a textual kinship between Western and Soviet thinking about Soviet Islam. The conceptual foundations of both Western and Soviet thinking about Islam in the Soviet Union are in fact informed by the same kinds of theoretical assumptions about the nature of religion and social change. I therefore suggest a critique of the way in which the dominant paradigms inform the conventional interpretations of Soviet Islam and the ways in which they are produced and reproduced irrespective of the socio-religious world they seek to explain. Based on this critique of the texts and of the paradigms that inform contemporary scholarship, the third part of this essay presents a preliminary outline of an alternative way of interpreting Soviet Islam independent of the conceptual framework produced by Soviet scholarship.

Reading Between the Texts: Studies of Soviet Islam

Western scholarship on Islam in the Soviet Union originated with the work of historians concerned with the fate of Muslim peoples in the Russian Empire. Although more recently some political scientists have contributed to the formation of this specialized field of knowledge, the production of a scholarly literature on Soviet Islam is dominated mostly by historians who are at times openly hostile to the conceptual methods of the social sciences.[5] Despite the atheoretical, perhaps even anti-theoretical intentions of many observers, historical and other scholarship on Soviet Islam has nonetheless been produced within a framework of conceptual assumptions and has therefore resulted in theoretical outcomes.

The Western literature on Soviet Islam, however, would not exist without specialized studies of Islam produced in the Soviet Union itself. Building on its own traditions of nineteenth-century Russian Orientalism, Soviet scholarly publishing in both central Russia and the republics has been indispensable in the formation of a Western discourse on Soviet Islam. But Soviet scholarship and media sources are not simply a vast source of empirical data for Western scholars. They also provide Western scholars with concepts and a theoretical framework. From the point of view of the sociology of knowledge, then, on many levels Soviet scholarship has effected an intellectual colonization of Western thinking on Soviet Islam.

Whether they are simply re-presenting the evolution of Soviet views of Islam or engaging in secondary research on Soviet Islam itself, virtually all Western students of Soviet Islam depend on the specialized literature produced in the Soviet Union. The significance of these Soviet sources for Western interpretations is widely recognized by Western specialists. "Soviet sources, because of their abundance, can provide a more or less coherent picture of Islam in the Soviet Union," write Alexandre Bennigsen and Enders Wimbush. "But it is obvious," they continue, "that this picture is incomplete, biased and falsified."[6] The nature of that biased and falsified character of Soviet writing on Islam, however, is nowhere clearly specified in the Western specialist literature. Partially as a result of this problem, Western scholarly disputes over both conceptual and empirical issues often revolve around the use and interpretation of Soviet scholarship and press coverage of Soviet Islam.[7]

Western scholars of Soviet Islam employ two interpretive strategies in their use of Soviet texts for empirical data. These can be referred to as direct and indirect extrapolation. The first strategy assumes that Soviet polemical discourse on Soviet Islam can be interpreted as reflecting directly or by implication a "real" situation in Soviet society. In the second, "facts" taken from Soviet sources are reworked into a discourse whose character or intentions has little to do with the context of the original texts in which these "facts" first appeared.

Despite doubts expressed by various authors about the reliability of Soviet data and interpretations, a strategy of direct extrapolation in which Soviet data, organizing concepts and interpretations are reproduced in Western specialist literature is in fact widespread. At times entire articles published by Western specialists are constructed around a single Soviet source or a very limited number of publications.[8] Even in those studies that move beyond a mere paraphrasing of Soviet texts, Western scholars often extract concepts produced in the Soviet literature and employ them to "describe" the Soviet Muslim community. An example of this is the categorization of Muslims based on a continuum of religious thought and practice. In their effort to distinguish among practitioners of Islam between "believers" and "non-believers," Soviet sociologists have developed as many as seven different schemes of categorizing Muslims, ranging from "firm believers" to "hesitant believers" to "committed atheists." These categories have been adopted wholesale into the descriptive Western analysis of Islam. And when disputes arise over the political signifi- cance of Islamic beliefs, these same categories are invariably invoked to substantiate one case against another.[9]

Apart from culling data from Soviet sources and reproducing Soviet sociologi- cal characterizations of Muslims, Western specialists also depend on Soviet sources more broadly in their interpretive strategies. Not only the content of the Soviet literature but the political conditions of its production and transmission influence Western thinking. In substantiating his thesis of "two Islams," Bennigsen draws conclusions not just from the content of Soviet texts but also from the fact of a flurry of Soviet publishing on Islam.

> That Islam has another, unofficial, and more important face in the Soviet Union is suggested by the vociferous anti-religious campaigns directed against Muslim believers, campaigns that would hardly be necessary were Islam as weak as its official face suggests, and by the increasing number of serious monographs on Islam. From these two sources we learn much of what we know about the real situation of Muslims in the USSR: from the first, because of what is attacked, and from the second, because of what is investigated.[10]

Bennigsen's second proposition that the issues investigated in the Soviet literature form the foundations for the Western production of a discourse on Soviet Islam confirms the line of argument presented here. His first proposition is likewise problematic.[11] It assumes that Soviet polemics directed at Muslims, their beliefs or practices can be interpreted as reflective of the actual state of affairs in Soviet Muslim society. Following from this assumption, for example, the intensification of a government ideological campaign against pilgrimages to local shrines is interpreted to mean that there is in fact an upsurge of pilgrim- ages. This practice of directly extrapolating social processes from ideologically- inspired declarations can be an extremely misleading interpretive method, since there is no rigorous way to evaluate exactly what kinds of social processes are actually reflected in Soviet polemics and political campaigns.

Similarly, in their characterizations of Soviet Islam, Western specialists often directly annex interpretations proposed in Soviet texts. In a manner indicative of a pervasive practice, Bennigsen and Broxup note that "according to Soviet sources . . . Sufi organizations are mass organizations numbering hundreds of thousands of adepts" and that "Soviet sources present Sufi brotherhoods as 'dangerous, fanatical, anti-Soviet, anti-Russian reactionary forces.'"[12] Though in principle Bennigsen and others question the reliability of Soviet interpretations, in practice these authors' own analysis follows closely from what they read in the Soviet literature. In line with Soviet views, Bennigsen's extensive publications also portray Sufi orders as carriers of a popular anti-Soviet, anti-Russian Muslim fanaticism.[13] In effect, the authors transform textual manifestations of Soviet ideological anxiety about the religious activities of Soviet Muslims into real, active political threats to the hegemony of the communist party and the stability of the Soviet state.

Indirect elaboration from Soviet texts is another method employed in Western scholarship. Through indirect elaboration, Western writers use information or ideas produced in Soviet texts and transform them into new ideas or information not intended by the original source. An article on pilgrimages in Azerbaijan and Turkmenistan is indicative of the transformations that Soviet data can undergo in Western work. Employing Soviet press accounts that simply identify and describe pilgrimages to holy sites in the two republics, with the stroke of a pen an American author transforms the descriptions of these pilgrimages into organized "Muslim social movements" that become the article's conceptual leitmotif.[14]

In a similar fashion, Bennigsen and Wimbush employ Soviet sources to argue that the Naqshbandi Sufi orders are widespread in Azerbaijan. After criticizing Soviet specialists for not linking ritual practices around the republic's shrines to the Naqshbandi, they point to two proofs of operative Sufi organizations presumably not openly acknowledged or understood by the Soviets. One proof is that Soviet authors often refer to the presence of

> charlatans, self-appointed mullahs, parasites, crooks, vagabond fanatics [that have] invaded the holy places [of Azerbaijan], especially since the fall of Khrushchev. These expressions, as we have seen, generally refer to Sufi adepts.

Their other piece of evidence is the fact that there are references to "obscurantist charlatans [who] are systematically engaged in the transformation of historical monuments into places of pilgrimage." Drawing what they represent as clear conclusions from such references, the authors add: "It is obvious that such a transformation could not be the work of individual 'charlatans' who would be unlikely to defy Soviet power single-handed."[15]

Bennigsen and Wimbush's indirect elaboration from Soviet sources is problematic on a number of counts. First, the authors uncritically assume that denunciation of pilgrims as "parasites," etc., in fact signals that these terms refer to Sufi organizations. Rather than studying the actual practices around the shrines in question, they draw the specious conclusion from Soviet polemics that such pilgrimages must in fact be organized "systematically" and operate on a mass scale. In an instructive manner that reveals their methodology, moreover, they generalize from Soviet scholarship on the North Caucasus, where Sufi practices are in fact widespread, to argue that Sufi orders permeate the Soviet Muslim community more generally. Particularly in the case of Azerbaijan, pilgrimages to shrines and even unofficial religious networks rarely entail any connection with Sufi associations.[16]

Not only are the "factual" products of Soviet research assimilated into Western discourse, but Soviet interpretive schemes have also played an important role in the formation of the conceptual outlook of Western scholarship. The idea of "parallel Islam" became a hallmark of Bennigsen's scholarship on Soviet Islam and served as a fundamental organizational concept for the work of Bennigsen and his associates since the late 1970s. Indeed, it is one of the discursive objects around which the contemporary Western literature on Soviet Islam has come to revolve. The notion "parallel Islam" is connected with the conceptual practice of distinguishing two forms of Islam, "official" and "unofficial," whereby "unofficial," popular Muslim ritual practices are viewed as separate, "parallel" and even hostile to the "official" Soviet Muslim hierarchy that staffs the clerical administrations and mosques.

Although the notion of two Islams--that is, an "official" Islam and an "unofficial" Islam--has an earlier origin, it was only in 1980 that the concept became identified and codified as "parallel Islam."[17] A genealogy of the concept of "parallel Islam" reveals that it originated not with Bennigsen in the West but with his counterpart in the Soviet Union, the dean of Soviet Islamic studies, Lusitsian Klimovich. One of the founding texts that informs Bennigsen and Quelquejay's conception of parallel Islam is an article published in 1966 by Klimovich. In the piece, Klimovich writes:

> In Sunni and Shi'i denominations [of Islam] there are . . . two tendencies. One is the mosque [tendency], now headed in our country by the muftis, the sheikh-ul-islam and the other functionaries of the four official Muslim Religious Boards. The second is the extra-mosque, communitarian, sufi-dervish, or in other words murid [tendency] headed by ishans, pirs, sheikhs and ustazs, whose followers live mostly outside the cities in the kishlaks, auls and villages.[18]

In their first major study of Soviet Islam, *Islam in the Soviet Union*, written before the Klimovich piece was published, Bennigsen and Quelquejay do not as yet emphasize this dichotomous official/non-official scheme. Nonetheless, their limited discussion of the significance of "unofficial" Islam reproduces analysis presented in the Soviet press accounts from which they admittedly derive their views.[19]

It was on the basis of this opposition that Bennigsen and Lemercier-Quelque-jay, and later Bennigsen and Wimbush, consolidated their views of two Islams that have come to permeate Western thinking about Soviet Islam. Following the conceptual framework provided by Klimovich, the authors developed a position that conflates Sufi orders with extra-mosque religious practices and unregistered religious figures into the broad category of an "unofficial" Muslim world separated from an "official" Muslim world composed of mosques and registered clerics. Having obtained a prominent position in Western analysis of Soviet Islam, the concept of two Islams has more recently attracted renewed attention in its intellectual homeland, the Soviet Union.

Glasnost and Soviet Islam: A Hall of Mirrors

Considering the importance of Soviet Islamicist literature in the development of Western thinking about Soviet Islam, it would naturally be interesting to examine the current direction of Soviet scholarship in light of changes in Soviet policies brought about by the Gorbachev leadership after 1985. But, at least within the Soviet academic and journalistic community, the campaign for more public discussion of the problems faced by Soviet society has brought thus far relatively little reevaluation of traditional assumptions about the nature of Islam within Soviet borders.[20] Thus when new interpretations of the Soviet Union's "Islamic question" are offered, they are often accorded a great deal of attention.

One such milestone in changing Soviet views of domestic Islam was a two-part essay on "Islam and Politics," published in 1987 in the weekly paper *Literaturnaia gazeta* and authored by one of the paper's influential international affairs correspondents, Igor Beliaev. Written in a daring and frequently sensationalist tone, Beliaev's article caught the attention of both Soviet and Western readers and has, in fact, become a frequent point of reference for both Soviet and Western analysts of Islam and Muslims in the USSR.

One of the remarkable things about Beliaev's article, at least for some Western observers, was the positive attitude taken toward a number of Western analysts of Soviet Islam who had usually been vilified in the Soviet press.[21] Most prominent among the analysts "rehabilitated" by Beliaev is Alexandre Bennigsen, who, both literally and figuratively, can be considered as representing the dominant paradigm of Western thought on Soviet Islam. After a discussion of Bennigsen's views of the threat to the Soviet state of an operative "Islamic infrastructure" and the organization of underground Sufi brotherhoods, Beliaev asks: "How serious are Bennigsen's arguments? I think it is time to turn serious attention to them."[22]

In addition to Bennigsen's, Beliaev draws on a range of Western work on

Islam in order to remake a research agenda for Soviet specialists of Islam. But it is evident from Beliaev's text that he has not read, perhaps not even seen, the sources to which he refers. Nevertheless, Beliaev manipulates his well-selected library of American, West German, French and British sources in order to enhance his own views of the important issues concerning Islam in the Soviet Union. In this sense, Beliaev draws on these Western texts as talismans, the cultural authority of which he deploys to legitimate his construction of a new agenda for Soviet Muslim studies.

For example, Beliaev refers to the view that Muslim Central Asia could become a Poland within Soviet borders. He was paraphrasing a passage from the two pages devoted to Soviet Muslims toward the end of a 350-page book by Wilhelm Dietl, a West German journalist with little if any experience in the USSR.[23] Similarly, Beliaev asserts that in an edited volume entitled *Shi'ism and Social Protest* published in the United States, "emphasis is placed on Soviet Shi'i Muslims." In fact, only one essay of the eleven that comprise the book examines Shi'i Muslims in the USSR.[24]

As interesting as Beliaev's manipulation of Western talismans, however, is the genealogy of the texts to which he refers. It is ironic that Beliaev's Western texts represent and are at times based almost entirely on research produced by Soviet authors and published in the Soviet Union. In arguing for a new agenda for the study of Islam in his country, Beliaev thus refers to the products of Western scholarship that depend in a very immediate way on the images about Soviet Islam generated by Beliaev and his specialist colleagues!

Thinking Soviet Islam: Reading the Theories

So far my discussion has examined the intertextual references that link Soviet and Western literature on Soviet Islam. In fact, the relation between Soviet and Western discourse on Soviet Islam goes far beyond the surface of these texts. Soviet and Western scholarship share a broader set of assumptions and approaches in their understanding of religion and its place in social change. This is not to deny any distinctiveness to either Soviet or Western studies. Ideological particularities aside, the Soviet literature on Islam is produced by scholars trained in sociology or philosophy, whereas most Western specialists on Soviet Islam are historians and to a lesser extent political scientists. Apart from these purely disciplinary distinctions, Soviet and Western scholars often draw very different conclusions about the character and significance of religious expression in the contemporary Soviet Union.

But even the conflict of interpretations that characterizes current Soviet and Western discussions of Soviet Islam is rooted in a series of largely unexamined assumptions of a social-theoretical order. Thus, despite the controversies concerning Soviet Islam that mark current Western and Soviet discussions of the problem, there are a number of common theoretical notions that unite them. Indeed, it is in the context of these deep structures of significance, which will be worked out in the following pages, that the diverse Soviet and Western studies read often more like a single discourse than two antagonistic, mutually exclusive discourses.

The Classical Tradition on Religion and Social Change

At the foundation of Soviet and Western thinking on Islam lies a nineteenth-century tradition of social thought on the implications of social change for religion. In this view, the emergence of a "modern" industrial society portends the end of religion, often referred to by Soviet writers as religious ideology, as a dominant ideological and institutional force in society. In recent decades, the term secularization, which has come to signify the process by which modern ideologies and institutions replace religion (in both its spiritual and institutional aspects), has been rejected or redefined, but the essential assumptions of this view have been maintained.

The assumption of contemporary modernization theories that the phenomenon of modernity is essentially secular finds it origins in the writings of the founders of modern social science, Karl Marx, Emile Durkheim and Max Weber. These three theorists base their interpretations of religion and social change on the common assumptions of a dichotomized conceptual framework. This two-fold scheme of a religious, traditional society and a secular, modern society, though formulated in different ways by the different authors, reflects a view of social change sometimes referred to as the theory of "the great divide."[25] This type of dichotomous formulation is expressed as feudalism and capitalism in Marx, mechanical and organic division of labor in Durkheim, and traditional and legal-rational (or modern) in Weber.

Marx never wrote systematically on religion, but his writings on problems of ideology and consciousness, along with work on the development of capitalism, have served as the basis for a "Marxist" theory of religion and social change. For Marx, religion can be understood only in relation to the material conditions in which it exists. He held that with the development of capitalist mode of production, workers would move from the "illusory" (i.e., religious) interpretation of their conditions and regain a sense of reason. In this way, workers would recognize that their "real" happiness would be achieved not through religious or other "illusions" but through a rationally-motivated revolutionary transformation of the very social structure generated by the capitalist mode of production.[26] The political structure of capitalism only provides for the freedom from the hegemonic domination of religious ideology, but progress toward socialist revolution would eliminate exploitation, which for Marx served as the material basis of all religious "illusions."[27] Thus, Marx's view that capitalism brings the inevitable decline of religion is joined with a theoretically-based prediction that the evolutionary path from feudalism to capitalism to socialism would completely eliminate religion as a sphere of human intellectual production.

Like Marx, Durkheim saw modernizing, revolutionary changes in the rise of modern capitalism. The development of the social division of labor, the dimension of capitalist development that Durkheim identified as the focus of his work, generates a new form of solidarity referred to as "organic" in the Durkheimian scheme. In his analysis of traditional societies, Durkheim relies on an idealist interpretation of social cohesion by positing that solidarity is maintained through a commonly held set of religious beliefs. In his conception of contemporary society, however, his analysis resembles the materialist interpretation offered by Marx. It is not some set of beliefs or ideas but the material social conditions generated by the division of labor that establishes a basis for social solidarity.[28]

As in Marx's theory, the traditional social role played by religion is replaced in capitalism by the primacy of a more "rational," economic calculation: "In the face of the economic, the administrative, military and religious functions become steadily less important."[29] Durkheim regarded the inevitable decline of religion as part of the process of the emergence of a complex, "organic" social division of labor in society. What is important for Durkheim is the persistent necessity of moral regulation, which in modern society takes on a clearly non-religious, secular character.[30]

For Max Weber, one of the founders of sociology of religion, the rise of modern capitalism also portended an inevitable process of secularization, captured in his use of Schiller's phrase to describe this trend as the "disenchantment of the world."[31] Although Weber generally sought to eschew evolutionary approaches to social change, his description of the fate of religion in modern social change belies a strongly evolutionary character. In Weber as in Marx and Durkheim, religious beliefs as a traditional form of legitimate domination give way to the predominance of economic calculation and rationality in modern capitalism.

For Weber, secularism also appears as an inexorable consequence of modern capitalist development, but the character of Weber's argument differs from that of Marx and Durkheim, for whom secularization occurred as an apparently naturally (unilinear) determined consequence of the social changes attending capitalist development. Instead, Weber's argument on capitalism and secularization is characterized by what Hayden White has termed an "ironic" mode.[32] A prominent point in Weber's thought is the notion that secularization develops from essentially religious origins. Thus, a process of secularization follows out of an essential fundamentalization of religion expressed in Protestant Christianity. In other words, it is out of the fundamentalist return to religion, characteristic of the Protestantism as interpreted by Weber, that the secular nature of modern society ironically emerges.[33]

To a much greater extent than Marx, and to some extent Durkheim, Weber emphasizes not only the intellectual secularization engendered by the modern rational spirit but also the institutional foundations of secularization. Thus, it is the modern bureaucracy, born of the needs of a capitalist market economy, that disestablishes religious considerations in face of an ascendent rational, economic calculation:

> Bureaucracy develops the more perfectly, the more it is 'dehumanized,' the more it completely succeeds in eliminating from official business love, hatred and all purely personal, irrational and emotional elements which escape calculation.[34]

The Classical Tradition Applied:
Soviet and Western Literature on Soviet Islam

Soviet and Western studies of Islam in the USSR often come to different conclusions about "the Muslim question" in Soviet politics, but beneath these disagreements lies a common set of assumptions about religion in contemporary society that have been derived from the classical tradition. The theoretical assumptions of the Soviet literature are more salient than those of Western studies. This is partly explained by the fact that most Soviet scholarship on Islam is produced by sociologists who often deal with explicitly theoretical issues, while many Western specialists of Soviet Islam are historians who, at times, are self-consciously atheoretical in their intentions.[35]

What distinguishes Soviet and Western scholarship on Islam in the Soviet Union is their respective conception of religion and modernization. Briefly stated, the Soviet literature follows from the assumption that modernization has indeed taken place in the USSR, hence what remains of Islam are only its "vestiges." In contrast, the Western specialist literature focuses on the fact of an existing Islam and thus draws the conclusion that the Muslim societies in the USSR have not in fact been modernized.[36]

Unlike Marx and Engels, from whose works they actively draw, Soviet specialists on Islam identify the origins of secularization in the country's Muslim lands not with the establishment of capitalism but with its disestablishment by the revolution of 1917: "The beginning of the process of secularization in the regions of the traditional spread of Islam was set by the Great October Socialist Revolution."[37] Though the emergence of capitalism had contributed to secularizing forces in the European states, Soviet scholars often note, in Russia's Muslim areas capitalism was so weak and tenuous even at the beginning of this century that secularization had not taken hold either.[38]

But socialist construction, like capitalism in Western Europe, was the form that modernization took in the Soviet Union. Socialism as a developmental alternative to capitalism has been particularly stressed in Soviet studies of modernization of the lesser-developed Central Asian republics. In this sense, it is possible to describe Soviet-style socialism as a functional equivalent to capitalism, especially in cases where capitalist development is unsuccessful in overcoming obstacles to its full emergence.[39] For Soviet writers, socialism has been the same inevitable secularizing force as was capitalism for writers of the classical tradition. As described in a collective work produced by leading Soviet specialists: "The process of secularization, which has an objective character, is conditioned by the profound socio-economic, political and cultural transformations that occurred during the years of Soviet power."[40]

It is the grand processes of socialist economic development that are highlighted as the basis for an end to traditional religious forms of ideology and the emergence of a rational, scientific and (modern) outlook among Soviet citizens. In this argument, secularization began in earnest not with the revolution and establishment of Soviet power but with the campaigns for industrialization and collectivization implemented from the end of the 1920s. Mobilization and integration of the Muslim populations into the state system of production, urbanization and social mobility, the implementation of land and water reforms that not only disestablished religious elites but also brought qualitative changes to economic and social relations, all established the material social basis for the decline of religion.[41] Much like the emergent complex division of labor described by Durkheim, these changes, Soviet authors assume, lead naturally to new, secular socialist mentalities. Convinced of their theory that level of religiosity can be directly correlated with level of social and economic development, Soviet authors often point out that religious beliefs tend to be stronger and more tenacious in less urbanized, less developed, that is, less "modern" areas.[42]

But it is not merely changes in the economic and social structures of the country that have promoted secularization. Following from Lenin's voluntarist position that communism can be "taught" to the people,[43] Soviet authors also emphasize changes in the social superstructure that have promoted the spread of secularizing tendencies, including the educational system, scientific-technical progress and, of course, anti-religious agitation and propaganda carried out by communist party organizations.[44]

But Soviet authors have been confronted with a theoretical as well as a practical dilemma. Despite their arguments that socialism has definitively established the hegemony of secular ideas in Soviet society and that the process of secularization is continually moving forward,[45] they have become increasingly cognizant of continuing practices and beliefs associated with the Muslim faith. If secularization is an inevitable result of modernization, and if modernization has been fundamentally achieved in the USSR, then any continuing manifestations of Islam, whether in beliefs or practice, must be, in the Soviet conceptual framework, qualified as the remnants of the previous era. Since the material basis for the reproduction of Islam has essentially been eliminated, what Soviet authors see, conceptually at least, is the objectively baseless maintenance not of Islam as a totality but only of its vestiges. In this context, Soviet specialists at times argue that it is not Islam that they study but only vestiges of Islam.[46]

In explaining the persistence of Islam in Soviet society, numerous authors maintain, bolstering their position with relevant passages from Marx and Engels, that consciousness changes at a much slower pace than social formations. In this view, then, the transformation of consciousness from a religious to secular principles has "lagged" behind changes in the structure of society and the economy. Within the Soviet literature many arguments revolved around the character and persistence of this "lag," but the concept of a "lag," structured by Soviet theory of religion and socialist "modernization," remains an essential foundation assumed by the various participants in the debate.

Similarly, Soviet Islamicists have produced a fairly extensive literature on the nature of these vestiges and the character of the forces that contribute to their reproduction. They have identified the spheres of social life where vestiges are stronger or weaker, and distinguish between the objective, material conditions and the historical and cultural (i.e., superstructural) factors that contribute to the maintenance, even "rejuvenation," of religious vestiges. But a fundamental assumption of all these discussions is the superstructural reproduction, at times revival, of only vestiges of an objectively bygone era.

In contrast to the Soviet image of successful modernization and the remnants of Islam, mainstream Western writing on Soviet Islam represents an inversion of Soviet views. Soviet modes of interpretation are evolutionary and comedic, in that history appears to have a clear, unilinear path from religion to secularism, even if this trajectory is encumbered by the persistence of vestiges along the way.[47] The thrust of Western discourse on Soviet Islam, in contrast, posits that, despite all efforts, modernization has not taken place in the Soviet Union, at least for Soviet Muslims.[48] Thus, in this vein mainstream Western discourse asserts that if Islam has apparently remained intact, then Soviet socialist construction has failed. Emphasizing the "resilience" of Islam to socialist construction, Bennigsen writes that:

> Islam has in no way been contaminated either by Marxism or
> secularism. . . . Islam in the USSR is the same unadulterated,
> pure religion that it had been before 1917. . . .[49]

In the Western view of Islam and socialist modernization, it is not the social or economic aspects of modernization that are denied; rather, emphasis is placed on the failure of the psychological dimension of modernization. Thus, Carrère-d'Encausse argues that traditional society has not been erased by socialist construction but reinforced:

> In the USSR today there is a Moslem society which is united by the bonds of history, culture and tradition. . . . The Homo Islamicus has in effect behind him more than a half-century of cultural revolution intended to create a Homo Sovieticus. . . [But] he demonstrates that the human prototype which socialist society was to shape does not exist. . . . Above all, he demonstrates that while it is relatively easy . . . to change the structures of society, it is extremely difficult to alter minds.[50]

Indeed, the failure of psychosocial modernization in spite of economic and political modernization is a view that pervades Western scholarship of Soviet Islam.[51] For Michael Rywkin, the failure of Muslims to integrate into the larger Soviet society is explained by an amorphous and monolithic "Muslim community spirit."[52] In like manner, Bennigsen writes of an "inborn sense of *umma* [community]" among Soviet Muslims as if it were a genetic and not a social category.[53] In arguing that the Islamic "vestiges" represent the persistence of a deeply religious, traditional society, Western specialists have created a portrait of traditional society protecting itself from Soviet attempts at modernization.

Whether viewed as a totalizing social order or the vestiges of such an order, Soviet and Western specialists agree in their representation of Islam as the force of tradition pitted against the forces of Soviet modernity. For the Western scholars, "tradition" is portrayed as a kind of transhistorical essence that inheres in the society that they describe. In contrast, Soviet scholarship suggests that the inexorable forces of history are successfully transforming society, leaving Islam, as it were, as an expendable encumbrance. Despite the difference in their conclusions, both Soviet and Western scholarship rely on the tradition/modernity dichotomy to construct their arguments.

The Totalitarian Paradigm and Soviet Islam

The notion that "Islam remains the alien body that it was a century ago in Tsarist Russia," as Bennigsen puts it,[54] follows from a view of the Soviet Union, and Soviet society in particular, which is based on the totalitarian model. The view that various forms of community assumed to be unaffected by the totalitarian state are in fact "islands, islands of separateness in the totalitarian sea" directly informs Western scholarship on Soviet Islam.[55] Thus, the same argument is constructed in terms either of the failure of psychological or cultural modernization or, in this case, the resistance of social groupings to the "penetration" of "alien" forms of socio-cultural ideas and organization. The idea that the Soviet Muslim community forms an "island of separateness" in the Soviet Union follows from a view which posits an a priori relation of mutual exclusivity between contemporary Soviet ideology and institutions and "traditional" Muslim ideology and institutions. Just as the totalitarian theorists assumed that both religion and totalitarianism make a total claim on the individual, so do analysts of Soviet Muslims assume that there is an unreconcilable antagonism between Islam and the Soviet state.[56]

The totalitarian paradigm is organized around a sharp conceptual distinction between state and society, and indeed implies the absolute and total opposition of these two categories.[57] In discussions of Islam in the Soviet Union, then, "things Soviet" refer to the party-state, whereas "things Muslim" are described as aspects of society. As with ideal-type analysis in general, the categories of state/society organize a conceptual framework to which empirical data are then assimilated. The intrinsic tendency toward such reification of concepts was recognized by Max Weber, himself a proponent--indeed the modern founder--of ideal-type analysis, who warned against the "danger that the ideal-type and reality will be confused with one another."[58]

Conceptual distinctions nevertheless tend to be transformed into empirical distinctions that dominate representations of actual social processes in both totalitarian and the more specialized study of Soviet Islam. In fact, a whole series of absolute dichotomies such as state/society constitute the conceptual foundations and organizational principles of the totalitarian paradigm.[59] Consequently, studies that are conducted within this paradigm, including those on Soviet Islam, reflect and reproduce these dichotomies.

For the totalitarian theorists, resistance is activity designed to overthrow the totalitarian regime. Thus resistance is qualified as the absolute antithesis to domination and thus precludes within-system resistance or a loyal opposition. Totalitarian domination is considered to be violent and restrictive, whereas resistance in the texts of the totalitarian writers appears to be inherently free and democratic. Totalitarian domination represents the negation of human values, and thus resistance to totalitarianism is constructed definitionally--but not necessarily empirically--as affirming human values.[60]

The role of these conceptual dichotomies is revealed not only in the concept "totalitarian" itself but also in secondary metaphors that shape thinking about social and political processes. For example, the concept of "islands of separateness" is presented to the reader as an image of land in a totalitarian sea. But the mutual exclusivity of the concept goes beyond the transparent metaphorical dichotomy of land and water. One of the means through which the state maintains its power and authority, according to totalitarian theory, is by the use of terror. Hence the state is an unabashedly violent state. By contrast, in the uni-

versities, assuredly one of the "islands of separateness" that by definition falls
into the realm identified as "society," the reader discovers the opposite of the
state's violence--peace. Describing students in the university setting, two
founders of the totalitarian paradigm present the reader with an image of two
separate, indeed opposite, worlds:

> As they enter the island where the quiet of study and inquiry
> reigns, they become separated from the loud battle cries of the
> totalitarian regime.[61]

The island of separateness represents not just land as opposed to the totalitarian
sea, but also represents the "inside" features of peace, truth, harmony,
rationality, resistance and liberation in contrast to the state's war ("battle cries"),
falsehood, conflict, irrationality (the charismatic quality of the totalitarian
regime), conformity and domination. Within such an "island of separateness" as
constructed by the totalitarian authors, any divergent interests in conflict are at
worst definitionally precluded or at best conceptually undervalued.

One can construct a similar list of paired opposites upon which the study of
Soviet Muslims is conventionally based. At times, the dichotomies are quite
openly expressed, as with the notion of official and unofficial or parallel Islam.
And as Enders Wimbush comments, the only choice open to Soviet Muslims is
between the Qur'an and Lenin's works, that is, between Islam or communism.[62] The paired opposites that inform Western writing on Islam in the
Soviet Union include:

state (pro-state)	society (anti-state)
Soviet	Muslim
modern	traditional
artifice	authenticity
nationality	pan-Turkism/pan-Islam
"official Islam"	"parallel Islam"
illegitimacy	legitimate social authority
false ideology	true religion

Muslim Institutions and the Soviet State

The impact of these paired opposites on the conceptualization and practical
empirical analysis of Soviet Islam is especially evident in study of Muslim
institutions in the Soviet Union, particularly the officially recognized Muslim
Religious Boards. Bennigsen and Wimbush's rhetorical question, "On whose
side, therefore, does official Islam stand?" thus more aptly reflects the authors'
conceptual approach than it does the actual choices open to Soviet Muslims. In

a conceptual framework that insists that Islam must be classified either on the side of the state or that of society, conventional Western discourse has opted to identify the institutions of "official Islam" with the Soviet state.

During the Second World War, Muslim Religious Boards were founded, though in some regions similar administrations had been established in the tsarist period. Organized as four regionally-based, independent administrations, these institutions served as regulators of Soviet Muslim religious life. Their functions included the training and appointment of clerics, the operation of mosques, the holding of conferences and seminars and the publication of religious books, periodicals and calendars. Western understanding of these key institutions is limited, in part due to the lack of attention to them by Soviet scholars, but more fundamentally due to the neglect by Western scholars of Soviet institutions other than the communist party.[63]

In considering the activity of the Soviet Union's Muslim administrations, Western specialists speak with one voice. Conventional analysis works from an a priori assumption that the state is monolithic and conflates the Muslim Religious Boards with the Soviet state. From this perspective, while the Muslim administrations operate independently of the state in a formal manner, in reality their activity reflects and promotes the interests of the Soviet state. In this sense, the Muslim Boards could be included in what Louis Althusser has termed "ideological state apparatuses," that is, non-state organizations that serve to reproduce the hegemony of the state not through directly repressive means but through the production and transmission of state-oriented ideology.[64]

Writing on the organization of the Muslim Boards during World War II, one author asserts that:

> the Soviets decided to create a group of Soviet religious intelligentsia[s] that would be the paid workers of the Soviet government and would work as a supportive organ of the communist party.[65]

In a similar vein, Bennigsen and Lemercier-Quelquejay describe the Muslim administrations as "a central Muslim organization which would be loyal and submissive, and through which the Soviet government could exercise complete control over its Muslim subjects."[66] Indeed, virtually all Western commentaries on these religious administrations agree that their role is limited to the two realms of domestic control and foreign policy propaganda.

Numerous analysts labor under the impression that the Muslim Boards have been deployed as an instrument of the state to counterbalance the presumably more threatening "parallel" manifestations of Islam.[67] In the case of Muslim institutions, then, Western discourse again imposes a dual conception based on the mutually exclusive categories of state and society. The legally sanctioned

Muslim Religious Boards are, in Western thinking at least, assimilated to the state, while Sufi organizations along with other "non-official" Muslim practices defined as a "parallel Islam" are identified with a resistant, unassimilable "society."

Attention has also been devoted to the role of the Muslim Religious Boards as propaganda tools in the realization of Soviet foreign policy aims. Arguing that the Boards were created only to serve Soviet foreign policy interests, Baymirza Hayit claims that they serve as "more of a mouthpiece" for Soviet foreign policy than for Soviet Muslims.[68] Echoing this perspective, Bennigsen, too, has emphasized foreign policy concerns as an important function of the administrations.[69]

The view of the Muslim religious administrations as appendages of the Soviet state apparatus is based on a conceptual prejudice. This prejudice is symptomatically expressed by Timur Kocaoglu, who claims that:

> these [Muslim] administrative bodies exist in name only, since
> they have no powers whatsoever to safeguard the interests of
> Islam, i.e., to defend Islam against anti-Islamic attacks in
> public life.[70]

As a result of this orientation, the domestic role of Soviet Muslim institutions has rarely been systematically explored by scholars. Instead, arguments have been proposed that rely more heavily on the conceptual stereotypes than on empirical research. One of the aims of this essay is to suggest the potential value of an in-depth study of the status and activity of these religious institutions, which play a much more complex social and religious role than is usually attributed to them. But accomplishing this task calls for a double reorientation in the study of Soviet Islam: what is needed is not just new subjects for research but also a new theoretical approach to complement such a shift.

Representing Islam: Form and Function in Discursive Practice

The tradition/modernity paradigm, upon which conventional study of Islam is founded, has been extensively debated and criticized, at least in the West.[71] With specific regard to the place of religion in this dichotomous scheme, historians and social theorists have criticized the notion of a "great divide" that artificially opposes an authentically religious pre-industrial feudal society and an inherently secularized modern social order.[72] Similarly, recent theoretical work on secularization also rejects the dichotomies of tradition and modernity and the corresponding categories of "religious" and "secular."[73]

The theoretical reconstructions of modernization theory, however, often affirm the very assumptions they seek to undermine. Thus, whether they suggest the "modernity" of traditions or the traditionalization of modern life, reconstructions of the paradigm suggest a view of tradition and modernity that nonetheless retains the operative value of these categories. In such reconstructions, the idea of mediation, whereby tradition and modernity are synthesized in social practice, seems to dissolve the dichotomy. In fact, mediation only serves to reify social life into a "mix" of these conceptually separate categories.[74]

In bypassing the question of tradition and modernity, the approach suggested here begins from a critique of the literature's confusion of form and function. Both Soviet and Western observers have uncovered what they consider to be indicators of traditional forms, whether in organization, mentalities or practices, and they assume that these reflect similarly traditional functions. The assumption that form defines function, in effect, leads Western and Soviet discourse on Soviet Islam to confuse function with form.[75] For example, Western and Soviet observers agree that Sufi practices that are represented as a so-called "parallel Islam" and which predate Soviet rule should be qualified as traditional, conservative and hence opposed to the modernizing power of Soviet rule since their traditional organizational forms are seen to reflect a wholly traditional outlook and function. While such an argument may appear sound, what is missing from this account is analysis of the discursive practices of the given Muslim movements. Without due attention to the meanings that Muslims attach to these practices, the assumption that these meanings have not changed or do not change--that is, that they remain "traditional"--analytically precludes exploration of the practices and their contemporary meaning.[76]

These comments suggest that Western thinking should move from a discussion of Soviet Islam in the dichotomy of tradition/modernity to one that explores the forms and functions of Islam in Soviet society. By forms, I mean the organization of Muslim practices, including the structures of the clerical administrations and the rites of Islam: the daily and Friday prayers, sermons, the observance of religious holidays and other ritual conduct. While commentary on these "forms" have constituted the bulk of Soviet "concrete sociological investigations" and Western studies of Soviet Islam, what is crucial is the socio-religious functions of these practices. By exploring the function of form, that is, the culturally constructed meanings given to Islamic practices and the resulting meanings that they convey, the analyst is better situated to evaluate the actual role that Islam plays in contemporary Soviet society.

This mode of analysis entails a rejection of monolithic constructions of Islam that originate in ideological or polemical texts outside of the Muslim community and its institutions. In its place I propose an exploration of the actual practices of Muslims and their religious institutions and the diverse meanings that Muslims themselves invest in these practices. Totalizing terms like "Islam," because of their vagueness, often leads to interpretations that may be easy to make but nonetheless fail to capture the actual nuances of social and religious life. In this sense, Islam as a social phenomenon cannot be reduced to the prescriptions of the Qur'an or the written traditions of the prophet Muhammad.[77] Rather, "Islam" must be located in concrete discourses and practices that identify themselves as Muslim. For this reason, the totalizing constructions of Soviet Islam offered in Soviet and Western texts need to be replaced instead with the "texts" of Muslim socio-religious life as the basis for analysis and interpretation.

What I am thus suggesting is a shift from the conventional object of sociological and political analysis--ideological and polemical texts produced by officials of the party and state apparatus--to the indigenous discourses and practices of Soviet Muslim institutions themselves. One of the advantages of this approach is that it allows a point of access to Soviet Islam which is unmediated by ideologically-infused Soviet representations of Muslims and their religion.

Social practice is an aspect of comparative political analysis that should require no introduction. But what is "discourse," and why should it be studied? Simply put, discourse is speaking and writing which through the concepts it generates establishes a mode of thinking about things. I reject the notion that facts simply exist in a discrete and apparently objective fashion. Rather, such "facts" must be considered in connection with the organized system of meanings in which they are produced. This organized system of meaning is what I refer to as a "discourse." As Hayden White points out,

> discourse is intended to constitute the ground whereon to decide *what shall count as a fact* in the matters under consideration and to determine *what mode of comprehension* is best suited to the understanding of the facts thus constituted.[78]

In this way, discourse is both a field of thoughts and a way of understanding those thoughts. It follows, then, that in questioning the social identity and position of Soviet Muslims, it is useful to examine the way in which Muslims define themselves and situate themselves in Soviet society. Although it is important to distinguish between discourse and social consciousness, I nonetheless agree with Hayden White's proposition that discourse can provide one with insights into the actual formation of consciousness. White argues that:

> A discourse is itself a kind of model of the processes of consciousness by which a given area of experience, originally apprehended as simply a field of phenomena demanding understanding, is assimilated by analogy to those areas of experience felt to be *already* understood as to their *essential* natures.[79]

Stated thus, discourse can provide a point of access to the way Muslims think about themselves and constitute themselves as Muslims. While to a certain extent this has been the occupation of previous studies of Soviet Islam, these other studies have largely ignored the indigenous discourse of Soviet Muslims and their institutions and instead have concentrated on analysis of academic or political discourses *about*--but not *by*--Soviet Muslims. By contrast, research that explores the local formation of a Muslim discourse in terms of the distinct forms and functions that it exhibits in social process can avoid an a priori assignation of meaning to religious practice and examine the changing variety of meanings that Soviet Muslims themselves invest in their institutions and practices.

In combination with attention to the patterns of social and religious practice, my emphasis on discourse follows from an implicit assumption about its role in any social formation. Discourse is not some kind of superstructural phenomenon that "floats" above the society in which it is produced. Rather, language and discourse more generally actively inform the social construction of reality and thus partake in the organization of human relations while at the same time reflecting the character of the conditions in which it is produced.[80] Emphasizing the important role of discourse in producing and reproducing social relations, Foucault has written that: "relations of power cannot themselves be established, consolidated nor implemented without the production, accumulation, circulation and functioning of a discourse."[81]

Dominant Conceptions of Power and Soviet Islam

At the base of discussions constructed around the corresponding oppositions of Soviet state and Muslim society, official and parallel Islam, is a distinct view of power. Common to both totalitarian theory and its practical applications in the study of Soviet Islam is a descending conception of power, in which power is considered to be vested wholly in the organs of state and imposed downward on a passive society. Formed in terms of a conceptual dichotomy between state and society, Althusser's analysis of "ideological state apparatuses" belies a similar understanding of power in its state-reductionist orientations.[82]

The conception of power presented here rejects the restricted choice offered by the state/society dichotomy. Rather, I assume that power is dispersed and constituted at different levels within a given social order. In this sense, Foucault's critique of conceptions of bourgeois domination is applicable to totalitarian conceptions of the state. In outlining his method for analyzing power, Foucault writes:

> the important thing is not to attempt some kind of deduction
> of power starting from its centre and aimed at the discovery
> of the extent to which it permeates into the base. . . . One

> must rather conduct an ascending analysis of power, starting,
> that is, from its infinitesimal mechanisms, which each have
> their own history, their own trajectory, their own techniques
> and tactics . . ."[83]

In this sense, the analysis of power need not be a priori assimilated to and identified with the imprecise constructions of "state" or "society." Following the proposition that power is in fact dispersed and not concentrated in the organs of state, power can be analyzed at its points of constitution, as Foucault puts it "outside, below and alongside the State."[84] Working from this position that allows for a "bottom-up" mode of analysis, the constitution of power can be located and assessed in a specific set of institutions and social practices outside the state. The aim of research thus shifts to explore the ways in which what Foucault calls technologies of power are constituted and deployed--in effect concretized--in specifiable institutional settings.[85]

The line of theoretical questioning that I am proposing, then, moves from the restricted one of "on whose side the Muslim Boards stand" to the open one of how power is constituted in Soviet Muslim religious institutions. Here I should underline my use of the term constitution. Unlike much of Foucaultian-oriented research, which emphasizes power as a repressive force, I would highlight power's constitutive dimension in contrast to its repressive function. While I do not reject the connection of power with domination, analysis of the activities of Muslim institutions shows them to be bodies in which power has been constituted in a struggle against both society and the state. Thus, the Muslim clergy can be seen as engaged in a creative process of constructing new forms of identity and religious organization in order to situate and establish itself and its community in a complex set of constantly changing power relations. The repressive means by which the Muslim clergy constitutes itself and its image of the Muslim community are much more relevant to its aspirations for hegemony in Muslim society than to its relations with state authorities.

Methodologically, the novelty of this approach lies in moving away from a mediated analysis of ideological formulations and polemics produced in Soviet scholarly and political discourse. In its place, I propose a sociologically-oriented examination of actual institutions and the discursive practices which operate in, around and through them. The analysis of the forms and functions of these institutionally-based discourses and practices together with an evaluation of the ways in which power is constituted, will allow social and political research to move away from the conceptual constraints imposed by the dyadic mode of thinking inherent in both the tradition/modernity and state/society approach and into the realm of comparative political studies.

Notes

1. See, for example, former Moscow bureau chief Philip Taubman in *The New York Times*, March 6, 1988.

2. In a posthumously published essay, Alexandre Bennigsen qualified the Armenian-Azerbaijani conflict in the Caucasus as the harbinger of an impending crisis throughout the Soviet Muslim lands. "Islam soviétique: le détonateur caucasien," *Arabies*, No. 19-20 (July-August 1988).

3. See Martha Brill Olcott, "Soviet Muslims and World Revolution," *World Politics* 34, no. 4 (July 1982): 487-504; and more recently, Muriel Atkin, *The Subtlest Battle: Islam in Soviet Tajikistan* (Philadelphia: Foreign Policy Research Institute, 1989).

4. This subfield is most immediately concerned with the symbolic relations between Europe and the Islamic Middle East. See, for example, Edward Said, *Orientalism* (New York: Vintage, 1979); Thierry Hentsch, *L'Orient imaginaire* (Paris: Minuit, 1988); Maxime Rodinson, *Europe and the Mystique of Islam* (Seattle: University of Washington Press, 1987).

5. Hans Bräker in his introduction to Alexandre Bennigsen and S. Enders Wimbush, *Muslims of the Soviet Empire: A Guide* (Bloomington: Indiana University Press, 1986), and Bennigsen's letter published in *Problems of Communism* 34 (May-June 1985): 87-91.

6. A. Bennigsen and E. Wimbush, *Mystics and Commissars: Sufism in the Soviet Union* (Berkeley: University of California Press, 1985), p. 162. The appendix B of the book (pp. 157-64) provides a concise outline of Bennigsen and Wimbush's approach to the use of Soviet sources.

7. See, for example, the lengthy exchange of letters between Martha Olcott, Muriel Atkin and Alexandre Bennigsen, in which the problem of Soviet sources and their (mis)use is of central importance. *Problems of Communism* 34 (May-June 1985): 87-91.

8. See, for example, Marie Broxup, "Islam and Atheism in the North Caucasus," *Religion in Communist Lands* 9, no. 1-2 (Spring 1981): 40-49, and her "Recent Developments in Soviet Islam," *Religion in Communist Lands* 11, no. 1 (Spring 1983): 31-35; Jon Soper, "Unofficial Islam: A Muslim Minority in the USSR," *Religion in Communist Lands* 7, no. 4 (Winter 1979): 226-31; David Nissman, "Iran and Soviet Islam: The Azerbaijan and Turkmenistan SSRs" *Central Asian Survey* 2, no. 4 (December 1983): 45-60.

9. For example, Olcott, "Soviet Muslims and World Revolution."

10. A. Bennigsen, "Muslim Conservative Opposition to the Soviet Regime: The Sufi

Brotherhoods in the North Caucasus" in *Soviet Nationality Policies and Practices*, ed. Jeremy R. Azrael (New York: Praeger, 1978), p. 336.

11. It is also pervasive. Consider Bennigsen's statement in *The Islamic Threat to the Soviet State* (New York: St. Martin's, 1983), p. 77: "For the last ten years, anti-religious agitprop in Central Asia and the North Caucasus has been directed against Sufi Islam, a fact which testifies to its power and hold on the population." See also Ro'i's comments that: "The fact that the republican party press has spelt out its anxieties so plainly clearly demonstrates a serious problem. . . . Surely . . . the fact that the Soviets dwelt on the role of the mosques and the Muslim clergy as sources of trouble in Iran is evidence that Moscow has earmarked them as potential sources of danger to itself and has no intention of letting either the official mosque and Establishment Muslim functionaries or the less easily controllable unofficial clergy. . . incite believers against the regime." Yaacov Ro'i, "The Impact of the Islamic Fundamentalist Revival..." in *The USSR and the Muslim World*, ed. Yaacov Ro'i (London: Allen and Unwin, 1984), p. 168.

12. Bennigsen and Broxup, *The Islamic Threat to the Soviet State*, p. 74.

13. This is the view elaborated in Bennigsen and Lemercier-Quelquejay, "L'Islam parallèle en Union soviétique," *Cahiers du monde russe et soviétique* 21, no. 1 (Jan.-March 1980): 49-63, and their "Muslim Religious Conservatism and Dissent in the USSR," *Religion in Communist Lands* 6, no. 3 (Autumn 1978): 153-61. See also Bennigsen and Wimbush, *Mystics and Commissars*.

14. Nissman in fact uses a very limited number of sources, mostly from republican newspapers, in constructing his idea of "Muslim social movements" in these areas. Nissman, "Iran and Soviet Islam."

15. Bennigsen and Wimbush, *Mystics and Commissars*, pp. 126-27.

16. Moreover, the potential for misinterpretation inherent in facile elaboration from more complex Soviet commentaries is exemplified by Bennigsen and Wimbush's reference to the shrine of Kanzasar among the holy sites where they argue that Sufi orders are active. Identified by the authors as a "monument of the thirteenth century," Kanzasar is in fact the former seat of the Albanian Christian Church which has been transformed into an important shrine for the Christian Armenians of the Mountainous Garabagh Autonomous Province. For a description of the monastery and its use by Armenian pilgrims, see Abdulla Ähädov, *"Mügäddäslärä" pärästishin mahiyyäti vä müasir galïglarï haggïnda* (Baku: 1986), p. 34, as well as his "Ganzasar monastry," *Elm vä häïat*, 1985, No. 8: 17-19.

17. For an example of a pre-1980 use of the notion of two Islams, see any of Bennigsen's and Lemercier-Quelquejay's articles from the late 1970s, including: "Muslim Conservative Opposition," in *Soviet Nationality Policies and Practices*, ed. Azrael; "'Official'" Islam in the Soviet Union, *Religion in Communist Lands* 7, no. 3 (Autumn

1979): 148-59; "Muslim Religious Conservatism and Dissent in the USSR. "

18. L. Klimovich, "Bor'ba ortodoksov i modernistov v Islame" *Voprosy nauchnogo ateizma*, 1966, vyp. 2: 65-87. This passage is quoted in Bennigsen and Lemercier-Quelquejay, "L'Islam parallèle en Union soviétique," p. 54. It is noteworthy that their translation of this passage consistently reworks the terms "mosque" and "extra-mosque" by amending respectively to each "official" and "non-official," thus implying a relation to the state not necessarily intended by Klimovich. The same mistranslation is reproduced in Bennigsen's "Muslim Conservative Opposition" in *Soviet Nationality Policies and Practices*, ed. Azrael, pp. 336-37.

19. See A. Bennigsen and C. Lemercier-Quelquejay, *Islam in the Soviet Union* (London: Pall Mall, 1967), especially pp. 180-81.

20. In a recent exception to this trend, Stanislav Prozorov of the Institute of Oriental Studies in St. Petersburg condemned the persistence of Soviet "Islamophobia" as a hindrance to an enhanced understanding of Islam. On his comments, see Paul Goble, "Islamic 'Explosion' Possible in Central Asia," *Report on the USSR* 2, no. 7 (Feb. 16, 1990).

21. Ann Bohr, "Islam in the Soviet Union: Fertile Ground for Foreign Interference?" *Radio Liberty Research Bulletin* 87/88 (Feb. 2, 1988). In fact, Beliaev is hardly alone in his use of Western sources to back up his views. Despite a long history of attacks, inventoried by Michael Rywkin in his article "Alexandre Bennigsen in the Eyes of the Soviet Press," in *Passé turco-tatar, présent soviétique: études offertes à Alexandre Bennigsen* (Paris: Ecole des Hautes Etudes en Sciences Sociales, 1986), Nugman Ashirov cites Bennigsen and Lemercier-Quelquejay in support of his argument that Soviet Muslim society is more secular than religious. See Ashirov's *Evoliutsiia islama v SSSR* (Moscow: Politizdat, 1973), p. 7.

22. *Literaturnaia gazeta*, 1987, No. 21.

23. For the English translation, see Wilhelm Dietl, *Holy War* (New York: Macmillan, 1984).

24. Entitled "Soviet Attitudes Towards Shi'ism and Social Protest," the chapter by Muriel Atkin presents a summary review of the changing Soviet evaluations of Shi'ism within both Soviet and non-Soviet Muslim societies, though the emphasis is placed on Iran and Afghanistan, not the USSR. Atkin's intention is not to comment on what Beliaev presents as the threat of Islam to the USSR but simply to familiarize a Western audience with what the Soviets themselves considered the fundamental issues in studying Islam. *Shi'ism and Social Protest*, eds. Juan R. I. Cole and Nikki R Keddie (New Haven, CT: Yale University Press, 1986).

25. See Nicholas Abercrombie, et al, eds., *The Dominant Ideology Thesis* (London:

Allen and Unwin, 1980), pp. 65-70.

26. Karl Marx, *Critique of Hegel's Theory of Right* (Cambridge: Cambridge University Press, 1978), pp. 131-32.

27. Marx, "On the Jewish Question," in *Early Writings* (New York: Vintage, 1975).

28. Durkheim also introduces the idea that institutional mechanisms, such as the state and corporations or occupational guilds/groups, aid in consolidating social solidarity. *The Division of Labor in Society* (New York: Free Press, 1964).

29. *Ibid.*, p. 3.

30. Anthony Giddens, *Capitalism and Modern Social Theory* (Cambridge: Cambridge University Press, 1971), p. 221. In a similar fashion, Steven Lukes's claim that Durkheim's position on religion was more complex and changed in later years lacks textual support. Lukes's notion follows mostly from his confusing of "religion" and Durkheim's argument as to the functional permanence of collective representations. Steven Lukes, *Emile Durkheim: His Life and Work* (Stanford, CA: Stanford University Press, 1985), pp. 474-76.

31. For a critique of Weber and the Weberian tradition on secularization with reference to Islam, see also Bryan S. Turner, *Weber and Islam: A Critical Study* (London: RKP, 1974), pp. 151-70.

32. Hayden White, *Metahistory: The Historical Imagination in Nineteenth-Century Europe* (Baltimore, MD: The Johns Hopkins University Press, 1973).

33. Max Weber, *The Protestant Ethic and the Spirit of Capitalism* (New York: Scribner's Sons, 1958).

34. Weber, *Economy and Society*, Vol. 2, p. 975.

35. Hans Bräker, for instance, attacks theoretical political science as more obscuring than enlightening about Soviet Islam and Soviet Muslims in his introduction to Bennigsen and Wimbush, *Muslims of the Soviet Empire*, p. vii.

36. In contrast to the specialist literature, traditional generalist work on the USSR assumed that secularization is a natural part of Soviet modernization. See, for example: Alex Inkeles, *Social Change in Soviet Russia* (New York: Simon and Schuster, 1971).

37. *Islam v SSSR* (Moscow: Mysl', 1983), p. 7.

38. T. S. Saidbaev, *Islam i obshchestvo*, 2d ed (Moscow: Nauka, 1984).

39. This has been noted in Soviet as well as Western literature on Soviet social and ecomic development. Trotsky noted that "Russia took the road of proletarian revolution, not because her economy was the first to become ripe for a socialist change, but because she could not develop further on a capitalist basis." *The Revolution Betrayed* (New York: Pathfinder, 1972), p. 5. Trotsky's seminal insight was developed more broadly in the later work of Alexander Gerschenkron and Kenneth Jowitt.

40. *Islam v SSSR*, p. 3.

41. For a description of these changes in greater detail, see: *Islam v SSSR*; V. A. Saprykin, "Sotsialisticheskii gorod i razvitie ateizma," in *Voprosy nauchnogo ateizma*, 1978, No. 22; N. Bairamsakhatov, *Novyi byt i Islam* (Moscow, 1979).

42. See, for example, M.V. Vagabov, *Islam i voprosy ateisticheskogo vospitaniia*, 2d ed (Moscow: Vysshaia shkola, 1982), pp. 109-18; and *Islam v SSSR*, pp. 9ff. Soviet sociology of religion also relied on a type of quantitative analysis reminiscent of Western studies of indicators of modernity (e.g., Inkeles and Smith, *Becoming Modern*) in describing the "transition" from religious to secular world views.

43. V.I. Lenin, "The Tasks of the Youth Leagues," *Selected Works* (Moscow: Progress, 1971), Vol. 3, pp. 470-83.

44. Most Soviet authors emphasize the importance of the material as opposed to the superstructural changes in conditioning secularization. Nevertheless, at times the voluntarist tendency becomes dominant, as with one Azerbaijani author who disproportionately emphasizes the theoretical contributions of Marx, Engels, Lenin and the Azerbaijani communist leader Narimanov in secularizing the Azerbaijani population. See Ä. J. Gurbanov, "Azärbayjanda sekulyarizasiya," in *Islam tarikhdä vä müasir dövrdä* (Baku: Azärbayjan Dövlät Universitetinin näshri, 1981).

45. Ashirov, *Evoliutsiia*, p. 8.

46. Private discussion with Räbiyyät Aslanova, an Azerbaijani scholar of Shi'i Islam.

47. For an insightful use of the term comedic to describe modes of interpretation, see White, *Metahistory*.

48. In his introduction to a volume on religion and modernization in the USSR, Dennis Dunn notes the persistence of religion but asserts that no one has claimed that the continued vitality of religion is due to the failure of the Soviet modernization drive. In fact, the failure to modernize is claimed by Bennigsen and his associates with regard to Soviet Muslims. *Cf. Religion and Modernization in the Soviet Union*, ed. Dennis J Dunn (Boulder, CO: Westview, 1977), p. 2.

49. A. Bennigsen, "Soviet Muslims and the World of Islam," *Problems of Communism*

50 Mark Saroyan

29 (March-April 1980): 39. The essential continuity of the pre-socialist and socialist periods is also asserted by Hans Bräker in his foreword to Bennigsen and Wimbush, *Muslims of the Soviet Empire*, p. ix.

50. Hélène Carrère-d'Encausse, *Decline of an Empire: The Soviet Socialist Republics in Revolt* (New York, NY: Newsweek Books, 1979), pp. 248 and 263-64.

51. This tendency permeates not just the specialized discourse but also more general discussion. Thus, John Armstrong employs the notion of a "cultural impenetrability of [Soviet] Islamic populations" in his "Toward a Framework for Considering Nationalism in East Europe," *Eastern European Politics and Societies* 2, no. 2 (Spring 1988): 280-305.

52. Michael Rywkin, *Moscow's Muslim Challenge: Soviet Central Asia* (Armonk, NY: Sharpe, 1982), p. 115.

53. A. Bennigsen, "Modernization and Conservatism in Soviet Islam," *Religion and Modernization*, ed. Dunn, p. 258. In his assumption of a transhistorical "Moslem unity," Bennigsen also refers to the "Moslem *millet*" of Tsarist Russia, thus drawing a false analogy between a specific Ottoman institution, the *millet* system (along with all its socio-historical implications), and the social structure of the Moslem regions under Tsarist Russian dominion. A. Bennigsen and Ch. Lemercier-Quelquejay, *Les musulmans oubliés: L'Islam en U.R.S.S. aujourd'hui* (Paris: Maspero, 1981), pp. 29 and 35, as well as in other works by the same authors.

54. Bennigsen and Broxup, *The Islamic Threat*, p. 54.

55. Carl J. Friedrich and Zbigniew K. Brzezinski, *Totalitarian Dictatorship and Autocracy*, 2d ed (New York: Praeger, 1961), p. 279.

56. *Ibid.*, p. 302. On the total commitment demanded by each side and the antagonisms that result, see Bennigsen and Lemercier-Quelquejay, *Islam in the Soviet Union*, p. 139.

57. See, for example, the articles included in *Totalitarianism*, ed. Carl J. Friedrich (New York: Grosset and Dunlap, 1964); and *Change in Communist Systems*, ed. Chalmers Johnson (Stanford, CA: Stanford University Press, 1970).

58. Weber similarly commented on the "almost irresistible temptation to do violence to reality in order to prove the real validity of the construct." Max Weber, *The Methodology of the Social Sciences* (Glencoe, IL: The Free Press, 1949), pp. 101-3.

59. In one of the classic texts of totalitarian theory, *Totalitarian Dictatorship and Autocracy*, one can uncover a number of these dichotomous conceptual constructs around which the paradigm is articulated. Some of these parallel dichotomies include: state/society; totalitarianism/democracy; control/freedom; conformity/resistance;

violence/peace; order/disorder; fact/value; bad/good; false/true. These conceptual dichotomies do not simply stand as abstract "ideal types" that help to identify objects of study. They actively organize a social and political analysis characterized by these mutually exclusive, absolutized categories.

60. Friedrich and Brzezinski, *Totalitarian Dictatorship and Autocracy*, pp. 279-89.

61. *Ibid.*, p. 328.

62. S.E. Wimbush, "Soviet Muslims in the 1980s," *Journal Institute of Muslim Minority Affairs*, pp. 152-53.

63. Arguing from what can be best described as structural-functionalist positions, recent work by leading Soviet researchers rejected approaches that consider the activity of Muslim organizations as important. See Talib Saidbaev, *Literaturnaia gazeta*, No. 24 (June 10, 1987): 14, and in his *Islam i obshchestvo* as well as Ashirov, *Evoliutsiia islama*.

64. Louis Althusser, "Ideology and Ideological State Apparatuses" in *Lenin and Philosophy* (New York: Monthly Review Press, 1971).

65. Shams Ud-Din, "Russian Policy Towards Islam and Muslims: An Overview," *Journal Institute of Muslim Minority Affairs* 5, no. 2 (July 1984): 326.

66. Bennigsen and Lemercier-Quelquejay, "'Official' Islam in the Soviet Union."

67. *Ibid.*, pp. 153; 157.

68. Baymirza Hayit, "Western Turkestan: The Russian Dilemma," *Journal Institute of Muslim Minority Affairs* 6, no. 1 (January 1985).

69. Bennigsen, "Soviet Muslims and the World of Islam." For writing informed by similar arguments, see also *Soviet Nationalities in Strategic Perspective*, ed. S.E. Wimbush.

70. Timur Kocaoglu, "Islam in the Soviet Union: Atheistic Propaganda and 'Unofficial' Religious Activities," *Journal Institute of Muslim Minority Affairs* 5, no. 1 (January 1984): 147.

71. See, for example, Reinhard Bendix, "Tradition and Modernity Reconsidered," in *Nation-Building and Citizenship* (Berkeley: University of California Press, 1977).

72. Brian S. Turner, *Religion and Social Theory*; Abercrombie, et al., eds., *The Dominant Ideology Thesis*.

73. David Martin, *Theory of Secularization.*

74. For a useful critique of mediation, see Raymond Williams, *Marxism and Literature* (Oxford: Oxford University Press, 1977), pp. 95-107.

75. My use of the form/function distinction is informed by Abner Cohen's discussion of symbolic form and symbolic function in his *Two-Dimensional Man* (Berkeley: University of California Press, 1974), pp. 3-4; 26-30.

76. For a useful exploration of form and function in Soviet Buryat religious identity and ritual, see Caroline Humphrey, *Karl Marx Collective: Economy, Society and Religion in a Siberian Collective Farm* (Cambridge: Cambridge University Press, 1983).

77. In both Western and Soviet generalist studies of Islam and Muslim movements, "Islam" is often reduced to Qur'anic citations or theological discourse extracted from its social and historical contexts. For an important exception to this trend, see Said Amir Arjomand, *The Shadow of God and the Hidden Imam* (Chicago, IL: University of Chicago Press, 1984), in which the author explores how Shi'i Muslim doctrine's relation to temporal political authority has been constructed and reconstructed in varying historical and political situations.

78. Hayden White, *Tropics of Discourse: Essays in Cultural Criticism* (Baltimore, MD: The Johns Hopkins University Press, 1978), p. 3.

79. *Ibid.*, p. 5.

80. This view has been influenced by Althusser's discussion of the social role of "ideological state apparatuses." See Louis Althusser, "Ideology and Ideological State Apparatuses," in his *Lenin and Philosophy.*

81. Michel Foucault, *Power/Knowledge: Selected Interviews and Other Writings, 1972-77* (Sussex: Harvester, 1980), p. 93.

82. A corollary to this view is its inversion: that power is organized in society and challenges the state from below. Given the dichotomization of the totalitarian conceptual framework, power must be located either in the "state" or in "society."

83. Foucault, *Power/Knowledge*, p. 99.

84. *Ibid.*, p. 60.

85. For a discussion of Foucault's understanding of power with regard to institutions, see Foucault's afterward to Hubert L. Dreyfus and Paul Rabinow, *Michel Foucault: Beyond Structuralism and Hermeneutics*, 2d ed (Chicago, IL: University of Chicago Press, 1983), as well as Dreyfus and Rabinow's own evaluation of this problem, p. 184*ff.*

Bureaucrats vs. Markets?
Rethinking the Bureaucratic Response to Market Reform in Centrally Planned Economies

Joel S. Hellman

Though the growing interest in the application of economic models to politics seems to have bypassed the field of Soviet politics, there is one area in which both the analytical framework and theoretical conclusions have been surprisingly similar--the study of bureaucracy. Just as rational choice theorists have concluded that bureaucrats are one of the most significant threats to the functioning of free markets in capitalist systems, Sovietologists have concluded that state bureaucrats are the greatest obstacle to marketization in centrally planned economies (CPEs). In reaching these conclusions, specialists in Soviet politics have unconsciously or, in some cases, implicitly adopted some fundamental assumptions of the economic approach, though without the rigor and formal methodology of that approach. Soviet bureaucrats[1] are assumed to be more or less rational, self-interested actors responding to incentives in the structure of the centrally planned economy. As such, they are presumed to be driven by the desire to defend and to maximize their self-interests, conventionally defined as some combination of power, privilege, income and status. Marketization is portrayed as a profound threat to these interests. By decreasing reliance on bureaucratic coordination of the economy, marketization makes countless administrative posts superfluous, undermines the power and status associated with economic control, eliminates the privileged access to goods and services linked to administrative positions, and reduces opportunities for extracting bribes and other side payments from economic exchange. As a result, most analysts of the Soviet economic reform process argue that bureaucrats will

I would like to thank the Research Institute on International Change, directed by Seweryn Bialer, and the Center on East-West Trade, Communications and Investment, directed by Jerry Hough, for support for the research in this paper. I also gratefully acknowledge the participants in the Third Annual Social Science Research Council Workshop on Soviet Domestic Politics and Society and especially its directors--Thane Gustafson, Peter Solomon and Susan Solomon--for their helpful comments on earlier versions of this project.

oppose marketization based on a primarily intuitive self-interest analysis of bureaucratic behavior.

This implicit adoption of some of the most elementary assumptions of the ·economic approach suggests that a deeper and more comprehensive examination of this theoretical framework might provide insights into the politics of economic reform in the Soviet Union. In this essay, I will survey economic models of the relationship of bureaucrats to markets and explore the similarities between the underlying logic of these models and the current analysis of the bureaucratic response to reform in the Soviet Union. I also will present some preliminary results of a case study in the Soviet economic reform process--the development of a commercial banking sector--to investigate the commonly held conclusions of rational choice theorists and Sovietologists concerning bureaucratic opposition to marketization. Though the case study raises substantial questions about the validity of these conclusions, I hope however to show how a more explicit and comprehensive use of concepts and methods from rational choice can enhance our analysis of the process of reform in the Soviet Union.

Bureaucrats and Markets in Rational Choice Theory

To explain the perpetual expansion of state intervention in the economy at the cost of declining economic growth, rational choice theorists turned to state bureaucrats as one of the prime culprits. Analysts began to search for the exogenous pressures that push bureaucrats to intervene in economic exchange, as well as the self-interests that lead bureaucrats to increase the scope of their power. The goal of this approach was to find the rational basis of the individual choices that lead ultimately to collectively irrational social outcomes.

Over the years, this research has yielded a comprehensive set of exogenous pressures and bureaucratic self-interests:

Rent-seeking interest groups[2]: Rent-seeking activities can be defined as the efforts of individuals or groups, motivated by self-interest, to escape market competition primarily through the pursuit of special advantages or monopoly rights from governments.[3] Such groups have incentives to pressure politicians and bureaucrats to restrict property rights, legalize monopolies, set quotas, allocate subsidies and fix prices according to their own interests, despite the effects of these policies on the overall performance of the economy. Mancur Olson has argued that the accumulation of these groups over time leads to an ever-increasing range and complexity of government intervention in the economy, creating an "institutional sclerosis" that severely stifles economic growth.[4] In both Olson's work and in the literature on the "rent-seeking society," bureaucrats are portrayed as passive instruments of interest group pressures or, at best, as mediators among competing groups.

In explaining the relationship between interest groups and bureaucrats, the

"Chicago school" of government regulation claims that bureaucrats are routinely "captured" by the very groups they are intended to regulate.[5] The "capture" or producer protection theories suggest that the demand for regulation derives from the regulated groups themselves. Such government interventions as price fixing, entry restrictions, subsidies and licensing serve to limit competition in favor of a single producer or small cartel. In return, bureaucrats are offered a revolving door into the private sector, as well as other perquisites. Like theories of rent-seeking groups, the "capture" theories predict the same results--the size and scope of bureaucratic intervention in the economy will continually expand as these groups multiply.

Budget-maximizing bureaucrats: In contrast to theories that locate the source of growing bureaucratic intervention in the economy as outside the bureaucracy itself, another set of explanations focuses explicitly on the self-interests of the bureaucrats. Here the focus shifts away from the demand for bureaucratic intervention by interest groups and producers to the supply of intervention shaped by the self-interests of politicians and bureaucrats. Anthony Downs provided one of the first investigations of bureaucracy based on the assumption that bureaucrats are rational, self-interested utility maximizers, acting with limited capacities in a context in which information is costly.[6] Downs argued that bureaucrats seek to maximize a broad set of goals: power, money income, prestige, security, convenience, personal loyalty, pride in proficient performance of work and service in the public interest. Downs suggested that most of these interests could be maximized through expanding the size and functions of the bureau, irrespective of the demand for its services.

Based largely on Downs's insights about bureaucrats, William Niskanen proposed the first formal model linking public bureaucracy to government growth.[7] He assumed that almost all the bureaucratic preferences listed by Downs could be satisfied by maximizing the bureau's budget. In this view, bureaucrats are depicted as budget-maximizers in very much the same way as firms are profit-maximizers. Yet bureau budgets are determined not in the competitive market, but in a regularized bargaining game with their sponsors in which the bureaucrats have some distinct advantages. They tend to be monopolist suppliers, who also have exclusive information on the true costs of supply and perfect information on the sponsor's demand for services. Given these advantages, bureaucrats can maximize their budgets beyond socially optimal levels. As a result, bureaucrats continually push to expand the size of their agencies and the scope of their functions despite the demand of interest groups or politicians for their services.[8]

Rent-seeking bureaucrats: Most of the economic analyses of bureaucracy are based on the experiences of democratic systems in which there are strong legal and normative sanctions preventing bureaucrats from using their administrative powers for personal material gain. Consequently, bureaucrats in these systems tend to pursue non-pecuniary goals, such as maximizing the bureau's size, social functions, status, or security. With the increasing integration of findings from cases in the developing world into rational choice theory, there has been a new recognition of the rent-seeking or "predatory" activities of bureaucrats.[9] Bureaucrats have a strong incentive to intervene in the economy to maximize their short-term revenues, especially in the absence of strong sanctions against such behavior. This leads bureaucrats to expand their role in the economy in pursuit of increasingly wider opportunities to extort bribes, tribute and other economic rents, without regard to the effects on their country's economic development. Consequently, bureaucrats become "predators" on their own economies, enriching themselves even as they undermine economic growth.

Political incentives of bureaucrats: The inclusion of the experiences of the developing world into rational choice economy has also highlighted the political incentives that lead bureaucrats to intervene in the market. Robert Bates has argued that state actors strategically distribute price controls, subsidies, supply rations and monopoly rights to bestow favors upon political allies, to penalize political opponents and to build patron-client networks.[10] By intervening in the market, bureaucrats gain a range of tools that can help them maintain effective control over their constituencies. Though the effects on the collective welfare of manipulating these market instruments are detrimental, the short-term political reward for bureaucrats is a network of pacts that smooths the way for policy implementation and substantially eases the burdens of management and control.

The variables summarized above suggest that while rationally pursuing their interests, organized groups and bureaucrats seek a perpetual expansion of state intervention in the economy that leads to the collectively irrational outcome of increased economic inefficiency. The pressures fuelling this expansion have been identified as both exogenous (the demands of rent-seeking interest groups) and endogenous (the budget-maximizing, rent-seeking and political coalition-building interests of bureaucrats). This formidable combination has been one of the pillars of the rational choice critique of the distorting effects of politics on markets. Despite years of scholarly criticism of the detrimental effects of this phenomenon and the rise to prominence of neoliberal political movements in many countries, the pattern of intervention has tenaciously persisted. What accounts for the persistence of this trend? Why have marketization programs that offer significant efficiency gains not been universally adopted or effectively implemented? Rational choice theorists have proposed a set of concepts to explain the intractability of state intervention in the economy in which the self-interests of bureaucrats, as well as institutions, play a central role.

The Sources of Bureaucratic Resistance to Market Reform

In attempting to understand the tenacity of these patterns of individual choices, many rational choice theorists have turned to an analysis of institutions and politics.[11] They have begun to examine how institutions shape the incentives and interests according to which individual choices are made. As political institutions designed to regulate or even transform economic interests and incentives, bureaucracies have been at the center of this neo-institutional approach. Neo-institutionalists have attempted to identify the costs and constraints that lead bureaucrats to oppose decentralizing or market reforms, despite the optimizing gains they might offer.

Political costs: Established institutions reflect, to a large extent, the interests of those in power. Any attempt to alter these institutions sparks costly retaliations from those whose power is threatened. Consequently, institutions, once created, are difficult to change.[12] Though most bureaucracies are originally established to serve the interests of governments, legislators and coalitions of organized groups, the bureaucrats themselves quickly develop a strong stake in the expansion of their bureaus. Marketization entails a fundamental transformation of the structure of bureaucracies and of their role in the economy, reducing the amount of resources under bureaucratic control and decreasing the number, scope and relative importance of the social and economic functions entrusted to them. Clearly, marketization challenges the existing structure of power relations, threatening substantial losses to those bureaucrats whose agencies need to be curtailed or eliminated. In response to this challenge, bureaucrats can be expected to use all the means available to them from the existing institutional structure to oppose and obstruct the changes.

Transaction costs[13]: Neo-institutional theorists analyze institutional reform as a process of contracting among parties to establish new arrangements. This process engenders transaction costs that can be defined as "the costs of deciding, planning, arranging, and negotiating the actions to be taken and the terms of exchange; the costs of changing plans, renegotiating terms, and resolving disputes as changing circumstances may require; and the costs of ensuring that the parties perform as agreed."[14] Whatever gains may come to bureaucrats as a result of market reform must be discounted by the transaction costs arising from the process of institutional change. The shift from bureaucratic coordination to market coordination of economic exchange, or even more so from state-owned to private property, incurs immense transaction costs. It involves an extensive stage of information-gathering to classify and value existing properties and arrangements and to formulate and propose feasible reform programs. The process sparks a long, difficult period of bargaining and compromise among alternative plans as groups and individuals seek to defend and advance their interests through the politics of structural choice. The implementation stage requires massive efforts in transferring and retraining personnel, shifting assets, abolishing existing institutions and building new ones. Finally, the struggle to enforce the new arrangements often entails the establishment of new laws, regulations and governing structures that must be acceptable to a dominant coalition in society and sufficiently powerful to serve as effective enforcement mechanisms. When bureaucrats are charged with developing, implementing, or enforcing marketization and privatization, they bear the brunt of these colossal transaction costs, which frequently outweigh any potential gains to them from institutional reform.

Uncertainty/risk aversion: Recent work on institutions has focused on the minimization of uncertainty as a key factor in the origin of institutions. According to this argument, institutions are designed as ex ante agreements on cooperation among powerful actors to stabilize policy outcomes and reduce transaction costs. They foster repeated and reliable exchanges that diminish the need to gather information on routine trading partners, decrease the costs of enforcement of contracts through building trust, and substantially lower negotiation costs by embedding an agreed upon protocol of exchange. Institutional reform creates uncertainty that threatens a significant increase in transaction costs and, in the most extreme case, an outright loss of control by existing powerholders. Since individuals are assumed to be risk averse, they tend to prefer the certain, albeit lower, incomes from the status quo to the higher, but uncertain, incomes from a reformed institutional order.

Bureaucratic coordination of the economy is an extreme attempt to institutionalize certainty in all economic exchanges. Marketization, on the other hand, requires the institutionalization of a substantial degree of uncertainty. Thus, for bureaucrats, marketization undermines a significant portion of established relationships and routines, thus raising search costs, negotiation costs and information costs, while decreasing their capacity to implement and enforce policy. In short, marketization threatens bureaucrats with a considerable loss of power, prestige and income. As a result, uncertainty leads risk averse bureaucrats to oppose marketization.

Collective action problems: All cases of large-scale institutional change are subject to collective action problems.[15] Even if actions initiating or supporting institutional reform promise significant benefits to all concerned, individual decision-makers have an incentive to "free ride," i.e., to let others pay the costs of collective action to achieve universal, indivisible benefits. As a result, though bureaucrats might have an interest in a marketizing reform that would improve the general standard of living for everyone, themselves included, they would still seek to avoid paying the high costs of change in favor of free-riding. Only if the benefits from marketization could be particularized to the bureaucrats alone, and if sanctions could be applied to minimize free-riding, would it be worthwhile for them to bear the immense costs of collective action.

Neo-institutional theorists have shown that rational bureaucrats not only have strong incentives to expand their role in the economy, but also have an interest in defending this role, even if greater reliance on markets would offer substantial gains to them and to their society as a whole. It is the existing institutional structure that shapes the incentives through which bureaucrats will respond to market reform. Political power considerations, transaction costs, the threat of uncertainty and collective action problems combine to create a formidable set of incentives leading bureaucrats to oppose greater reliance on markets. Clearly, this analysis presents a very pessimistic outlook for the implementation of market reform. Rational, self-interested bureaucrats appear to have every reason to obstruct any significant efforts to marketize or privatize and have the organizational muscle to undermine such efforts. In this analysis, economic liberalization can only be achieved by circumventing the bureaucracy or by breaking its institutional power.

Reform Strategies

If, according to the rational choice and neo-institutional approaches, bureaucrats have such powerful incentives to resist any changes that reduce their capacity to intervene in the economy, how can such changes ever occur? This question did not attract much attention so long as the scope and functions of the state continued to grow in the advanced industrial countries and neoclassical economic programs remained at the fringes of the political spectrum. But as popular movements for political and economic liberalization gained prominence across the globe and privatization became the buzzword of many prominent political leaders, this question achieved new significance. Though rational choice theorists have only just begun to examine this problem, two approaches to undermining the bureaucratic obstacles to marketization already have well-established roots within the rational choice literature.

The first approach, based largely on Mancur Olson's work, suggests that the only way to restore free markets is to uproot the institutional morass created by the rent-seeking demands of entrenched special interest groups. For Olson, such a task is so overwhelming and destabilizing that it can never be undertaken by forces within a given political system. Rather, the catalyst for change must be exogenous. Olson claimed that breaking the bureaucratic stranglehold requires such momentous force that only a catastrophic event--war, foreign occupation, fiscal crisis--can achieve the desired results.[16] Catastrophes tend to result in an overhaul of the existing structure of power, a disruption of standard patterns and routines, and a demand for large-scale reform that can outweigh the interests of the entrenched groups and state actors. Olson referred to post-war Germany and Japan as the only two cases in recent history in which the prevailing patterns of interests and government intervention have been successfully disrupted to restore free markets. Though no one recommends planned catastrophes as a strategy of market reform, the notion that such reform must be exogenous and that it must be focused on physically removing or substantially reducing the bureaucratic apparatus has remained at the center of most marketization strategies. According to these reform scenarios, if the power of the bureaucracy and the entrenched interest groups can be broken, then markets will fill the void left by government coordination of the economy.[17]

The second approach recognizes that market reform can come from inside the state, but only by those "enlightened" forces who manage to rise above the interests and incentives usually associated with their institutional position. Instead of extraordinary events, this approach relies on extraordinary individuals to achieve institutional reform. Wise statesmen or enlightened technocrats are the most likely candidates for this role. Not surprisingly, rational choice theorists often point to economists as the key "institutional entrepreneurs" in the process of marketization.[18] What sets these actors apart from the rest of their colleagues is specialized training in economics or the applied sciences. This training provides the expertise and vision that motivates them to pursue the social gains from market reform, quite apart from their personal interests or institutional incentives. In the analysis of developing countries, the enlightened actors themselves are often exogenous forces.[19] Foreign donors, international bankers and international financial organizations use their leverage to push through market reform as a condition for aid, credit, or debt rescheduling. Without links to the prevailing pattern of interests and incentives in a given country, these international actors can plan and implement reforms that could never gain the necessary support among domestic bureaucrats and interest groups. The enlightened domestic actors in the developing countries are often identified as the products of training or prolonged experience in the West. Their experiences abroad provide them with the motivation to rise above the interests and incentives that lead most of their colleagues to oppose market reform.

By characterizing successful market reform as exogenous or as sparked by actors "above interests," some rational choice analysts have been able to incorporate a theory of change into their approach without challenging their standard portrait of the relationship between bureaucrats and markets. In this view, marketization and privatization are, first and foremost, battles against the entrenched bureaucracy that can succeed only when the imperialistic strivings of the bureaucrats are tamed and the obstructions that they place in the path of reform are forcibly uprooted. To accept an endogenous process of reform, in which bureaucrats themselves initiate and implement marketizing measures, would appear to contradict the whole range of self-interests (political, budget-maximizing, rent-seeking), costs (political, transaction) and constraints (uncertainty, collective action) that have been proposed by the rational choice approach to explain bureaucratic behavior.

The Nature of Soviet Bureaucrats

Though the study of Soviet politics has long been criticized for its isolation from general trends and methods within political science, the efforts of Sovietologists to move away from the predominant totalitarian model led to a widespread conceptual borrowing from political science, especially from Western theories of bureaucracy.[20] In the classic totalitarian model, ideology rather than interests served as the key determinant of behavior.[21] Bureaucrats were characterized not as autonomous actors with their own self-interests, but as pliable servants of the ideologically driven party leadership. Stalin's vicious purges of the Soviet bureaucracy seemed to have obliterated any vestiges of autonomy for bureaucrats. Yet with the decreasing reliance on mass terror in the post-Stalin era and the apparent diffusion of power to vast party and state bureaucracies, Sovietologists began to move away from the totalitarian model and to adopt some generalizations about bureaucracy and organization from the broader comparative politics literature.

In modifying the totalitarian model to fit the new Soviet reality, several scholars suggested that the central focus of a new model should be not ideology, but the dynamics of bureaucracy.[22] Characterizations of the Soviet Union as an "organizational society," "an administered society," or as "USSR, Incorporated" suggested that bureaucrats had become autonomous actors, whose behavior was based on the familiar goals of maximizing their power, privilege and status. In these models, bureaucratic interests replaced ideology as the organizing principle of modern Soviet society. Moreover, these interests were assumed to be common to bureaucrats in all political and economic systems, thus integrating the Soviet Union into the larger framework of comparative politics. As Alfred Meyer argued, "The whole society is a bureaucratic command structure with all the features familiar to students of bureaucracy."[23]

By the 1970s, a strong consensus had developed among specialists that Soviet bureaucrats were self-interested actors responding to the incentives in the structure of the centrally planned system. These interests were identified as career and personal security, material well-being, personal advancement and power. With the erosion of the Communist Party's charismatic ideological mission, Ken Jowitt claimed that the bureaucratic cadres "placed their egoistic interests, their personally selfish and private familial commitments above and even equated them with the party's general interests."[24] The new generation of Soviet bureaucrats, raised after the revolution and the industrialization and collectivization campaigns, was portrayed as grossly materialistic and careerist, more like modern technocrats than ideologically driven cadres.[25] As such, their similarities with their Western counterparts became clearer, since their interests were, as Jerry Hough argued, "perfectly recognizable to anyone familiar with Western bureaucracy."[26] Later studies even adopted an assumption of rationality on the part of Soviet bureaucrats, arguing, as Paul Gregory did, that their behavior was "a predictable response by rational agents to a well-defined incentive system."[27] Once specialists accepted self-interest as the key motivation for Soviet bureaucratic behavior, they began increasingly to integrate notions of the rationality, and therefore utility maximization, into their analyses of that behavior.

The profile of Soviet bureaucrats that has emerged from the writings of Sovietologists since the decline of the totalitarian model has striking similarities to the fundamental assumptions of the rational choice approach. Whether implicitly or explicitly, Soviet bureaucrats have been characterized as rational, self-interested actors seeking to maximize their utility as defined by a set of preferences that are nearly identical with their Western counterparts. The key difference, of course, has been that they operate within a radically different institutional structure that provides a different set of incentives and constraints. Yet in describing the relationship of Soviet bureaucrats to the centrally planned economy, Sovietologists have produced a picture of the incentives to expand bureaucratic intervention and the costs that prevent any reduction of this intervention that bears a surprisingly similar resemblance to the rational choice analysis outlined in the previous section.

Rent-seeking interest groups: With the inclusion of the interest group approach and studies of political participation in the analysis of Soviet politics, a new emphasis was placed on the pressures on state bureaucrats from institutionalized interests, mainly in the economy. In market systems, rent-seeking groups strive to escape market competition to pursue monopoly rents through government intervention. In centrally planned systems, analysts have noticed that interest groups sought to escape the central plan by pressuring bureaucrats for exceptions, modifications and redistributions in the process of plan implementation. Such "covert participation," as it was labelled by Gitelman and DiFranceisco, produced rents for institutions and groups in the form of reduced plan targets, excess labor and material reserves, increased slack time and privileged access to rationed goods and supplies.[28] Jerry Hough's study of local party bureaucrats in the economy argued that the bureaucrats did not resist these rent-seeking pressures in defense of national or party interests, but were themselves "captured" by the very constituents that they were intended to regulate.[29] Because of the pressures of rent-seeking groups and the capture of regulatory bureaucrats by powerful interests, the scope of bureaucratic discretion in the implementation of the plan was increased and, consequently, the extent of bureaucratic involvement in the process of economic exchange grew even beyond the boundaries of the central plan.

Budget-maximizing bureaucrats: Niskanen's model of the budget-maximizing bureaucrat has an implicit parallel in the description of "investment hunger" by specialists on the Soviet economy.[30] The power, privilege and status of the individual bureaucrat in the centrally planned system were a direct function of the size and scope of the functions of his/her organization. Thus, the bureaucrat's personal goals were linked to the maximization of his/her organization's budget, regardless of the demand for its services. As in market systems, this budget was determined in a bargaining game with the organization's sponsors in which the organization had significant advantages regarding information over the costs of production and the maximum production potential. Consequently, bureaucrats had strong incentives to pursue overinvestment in their organizations. Given the soft-budget constraint[31] in centrally planned systems, the incentive to pursue overinvestment reached a significantly higher level than in market systems. Like Niskanen, specialists on the Soviet economy showed that the structure of the centrally planned economy created powerful incentives for bureaucrats to expand their budget allocations, increase the resources under their control and multiply the functions they perform.

Rent-seeking bureaucrats: The introduction of *glasnost* in the Soviet media has led to startling revelations of bureaucratic corruption and profiteering that support some of the most pessimistic accounts of the bureaucracy by Soviet emigre analysts in the pre-reform period.[32] In these accounts, Soviet bureaucrats have been portrayed as predators on their society, extracting bribes and other tributes to the detriment of overall economic growth. Moreover, the bureaucrats have been characterized as imperialist power-grabbers, constantly seeking to expand their opportunities for extracting rents from the economy to supplement their meager incomes and privileges. Consequently, like bureaucrats in developing countries, Soviet bureaucrats appear to have strong incentives to expand their capacity to intervene in the economy in pursuit of their rent-seeking interests.

Political incentives: Intervention in the economy not only offers material gains, but political gains as well. In a shortage economy, such as the Soviet Union's, the distribution of privileged access to scarce goods has generally been acknowledged to be one of the key strategies for building networks of political support. Not only did party and state bureaucrats control a vast network of goods and services to be distributed solely based on political loyalty, but they also had the capacity to intervene in the setting of plan targets, the allocation of capital, the setting of prices and the flow of supplies to reward political allies or punish political enemies. The manipulation of economic targets, the distribution of privileged access to scarce goods and the power of appointment to economic posts as provided by the *nomenklatura* system led bureaucrats at all levels to create interlocking regional, sectoral and organizational fiefdoms based on patron-client relations. For bureaucrats, economic intervention became the basic tool for political management and control.

Implicitly relying on many of the same basic assumptions about bureaucrats as the economic approach, Sovietologists have set out an individually rational basis for bureaucratic intervention beyond the borders of central planning in the Soviet economy. Focusing on the preferences of the individual bureaucrat, they have described a set of endogenous and exogenous incentives that push bureaucrats to expand their role in the economy, despite its effect on overall economic efficiency. Though only a few studies have taken a comprehensive approach to this issue,[33] an overview of the conventional arguments about Soviet bureaucrats reveals a close similarity to the underlying logic and basic direction of the rational choice analysis of the relationship of bureaucrats to the economy in market systems. It should not be surprising that most analysts have assumed that Soviet bureaucrats act just as their capitalist counterparts do when faced with challenges to their capacity to intervene in the economy. As in the rational choice approach, the high costs to bureaucrats of market reform have been the primary basis for assumptions about bureaucratic resistance to economic reform.

Political costs: Clearly, bureaucrats have a "vested interest" in the structure of planned coordination of the economy. It is the very foundation of their power, status and privileges, and these advantages have been considerable. In the absence of a well-developed private sector, the bureaucracy has, after all, been the only path to real power in the Soviet Union. As a result, any challenge to the institutions or power of the bureaucracy is an attack on the existing distribution of power. By reducing radically the role of bureaucrats in coordinating the economy, marketization not only undermines bureaucratic privileges and perquisites, but threatens to dismantle the bureaucrats' institutional positions, to reduce their instruments of political management and to disrupt their patron-client networks. It also creates the potential for an alternative basis of power linked to market performance that could eventually undermine the monopoly position of the bureaucracy in the economic and political spheres. As Seweryn Bialer argued, "In resisting Gorbachev's orders [to reform], the ministerial administrators in Moscow and the high-ranking Party and State officials in the republics and provinces are defending their . . . ways of life."[34]

Uncertainty/risk aversion: Though uncertainty deters change in any type of organization or system, Sovietologists have argued that this factor has been especially potent in the calculus of Soviet bureaucrats. The massive purges of the bureaucracy during the Stalin era constantly threatened bureaucrats with a loss of position and, in many cases, loss of life. The chaos, fear and disorder of that period led bureaucrats to crave stability, personal security and predictability. Thus, Stalinism shaped a bureaucratic culture that is profoundly conservative, especially regarding questions of status and position. Stephen Cohen argues that Soviet bureaucrats oppose reform, not only because it threatens their power and privilege, but also because it undermines much-valued order and stability.[35] Seweryn Bialer concurs: "If there is any single value that dominates the minds and thoughts of the Soviet establishment from the highest to the lowest level, it is the value of order; if there is any single fear that outweighs all others, it is the fear of disorder, chaos, fragmentation, loss of control."[36] With its emphasis on spontaneity and uncertainty, market reform poses a formidable challenge to this bureaucratic culture. Paul Gregory suggests that the excessive risk aversion of Soviet bureaucrats is linked not only to their historical experience, but to the incentives of the command economy.[37] Since bureaucrats faced often severe penalties for non-fulfillment of plans, ranging from significant income reductions to loss of position, risk minimization became their prime consideration. Therefore, on economic as well as cultural grounds, Soviet bureaucrats appear to have a strong interest in and predisposition toward conservatism and resistance to marketization.

Transaction costs: Though analysts of the Soviet economic reform have not explicitly applied the transaction costs approach to the Soviet experience, they have recognized the high costs associated with negotiating, drafting, implementing and enforcing reform measures. Jerry Hough argued early in the process that the key obstacle to reform was not political or cultural resistance, but the sheer complexity and enormity of the task itself. He claimed:

> Even the easiest of reforms--privatization of a substantial part of the services sector--require[s] an almost unimaginable array of decisions about business licenses, the setting of optimal tax rates, rules of business operation, definitions of business expenses for tax purposes, safety standards and nondiscrimination rules, consumer protection measures, the establishment of a reliable supply system, and so forth. . . . Even if Gorbachev had total power, total commitment, and no opposition, it would take years to work out these questions alone.[38]

This process is not only time-consuming, but also extremely costly. In the Soviet Union, these costs are aggravated by the deficit of adequately trained specialists experienced in such matters, the absence of historical examples to serve as a guide to the process, the lack of a well-established institutional framework for political negotiation, and the absence of a developed legal structure to govern the implementation and enforcement of contracts. Bureaucrats bear the brunt of these transaction costs, which serve to discount any potential gains from market reform. Sovietologists have recognized these costs and have characterized them as one of the key sources of bureaucratic resistance to reform.

It is this collection of the formidable costs of market reform, coupled with the powerful incentives pushing bureaucrats to intervene in the economy, that has shaped the predominant view among Sovietologists that bureaucrats are the most significant obstacle to market reform. In addition, bureaucratic resistance appears all the more intractable because it is based not on the vestiges of some outmoded ideological mission, but on the rational response of individual bureaucrats to incentives and constraints in the structure of the centrally planned economy. As Paul Gregory argued, "It would be personally irrational for the potential losers from a successful restructuring to work in [reform's] favor. In view of the past failures of the Soviet economic system to reform itself, it may not be personally rational for the potential winners to favor [reform] either."[39] Given this analysis, most observers have suggested that the political strategy of reform should be focused on undermining or overcoming the resistance of the entrenched bureaucracy through "shock therapy." Once again, the proposed reform strategies bear considerable resemblance to those offered by rational choice theorists.

Anders Åslund has expressed the conventional wisdom in Soviet studies in terms very similar to the standard rational choice critiques of the state: "To break the power of the party and state bureaucracy might be seen as the key problem of reform."[40] Many analysts have suggested that such a task could only be achieved by forces outside the bureaucracy itself. In an argument very similar to Mancur Olson's strategy against institutional sclerosis, Karl Ryavec claimed years before perestroika that only a "general crisis" could achieve such a momentous change in the structure of the Soviet economic system.[41] Others rely on the potential development of a "civil society" in the Soviet Union that could pressure bureaucrats to be more accountable to citizens' preferences, rather than to their own self-interests.[42] David Mandel has even suggested that a revitalized working class would be the only social force with the power to undermine bureaucratic resistance to reform.[43] More recently, political and financial pressures from the international community have been identified as potentially the most effective reform strategy.[44] What links these strategies is the assumption that Soviet bureaucrats will not go against their self-interests and therefore must be neutralized by exogenous forces that have a genuine stake in the advancement of reform.

Another frequently proposed reform strategy with strong similarities to the rational choice approach is the reliance on "enlightened" actors. In the Soviet case, enlightened actors are usually identified as committed reformers who rose up the traditional bureaucratic ranks, but have managed to break free of the interests normally associated with their background and institutional position.[45] These individuals, its is argued, recognize the potential gains from economic reform for society as a whole regardless of the personal incentives they might have to maintain the status quo. Gorbachev was portrayed as the classic enlightened statesman. His role in pushing reform through layers of bureaucratic resistance was the predominant focus of existing studies of the reform process.[46] Considerable attention has also been centered on the group of reform-minded economists who have advised Gorbachev at one time or another.[47] The political fortunes and the high profile reform proposals of these economists have been followed closely by both scholars and the media, as if their progress were a key indicator of the course of reform. The logic behind the "enlightened actor" strategy does not challenge the standard characterization of bureaucratic resistance to reform, because it relies on extraordinary individuals who have managed to rise above the normal interests and constraints that guide the action of the overwhelming majority of their colleagues.

Few Sovietologists would acknowledge any explicit borrowing of concepts from rational choice theory in their own studies. However, their conclusions have supported a range of theories from the rational choice literature. Sovietologists have almost uniformly agreed that Soviet bureaucrats will oppose market reform because it places their current power, status, security and income at risk for potential gains that are heavily discounted by high transaction costs and uncertainty. Like the rational choice theorists, most Sovietologists claim that only exogenous agents or actors "above interests" can force reform through the obstructionist bureaucracy. This has led to a widely noted paradox of reform in centrally planned systems: bureaucrats are being asked to implement a reform that directly contradicts their self-interests.

On the issue of bureaucrats and market reform in Soviet-type economies, an unusual consensus has developed between political scientists and area studies specialists. This consensus also fits comfortably with the popular and political rhetoric about bureaucratic resistance to reform spread by both the "neoconservative" movement in the West and by radical market reformers in the Soviet-type systems. Yet early empirical studies of the reform process in China and Eastern Europe have begun to contradict this consensus and to depict a surprisingly active and innovative role for bureaucrats in the reform process.[48]

The following section will focus on one case study of the reform process--the development of an independent commercial banking network--in order to examine the role that bureaucrats have been playing in obstructing, supporting or promoting institutional and policy change. The analysis will make use of many of the same theoretical concepts introduced by rational choice theorists and implicitly adopted by Sovietologists. Yet the main focus will be on whether the standard assumptions about bureaucrats, in general, and Soviet bureaucrats, in particular, continue to hold in a command economy in transition. The case study is designed to examine how the incentives for bureaucrats are altered by an institutional structure in the very process of fundamental transformation.

The Rise of a Commercial Banking Network

Given the shared assumptions of rational choice theory and Soviet studies about the relationship of bureaucrats to market reform, we should be able to predict the general outlines of a reform scenario in the hypercentralized Soviet banking system.[49] We would expect any decentralizing or marketizing reform to be initiated outside the state monopoly bank, Gosbank, either by a reform-minded central leadership or by a group of banking experts, especially those with some experience with Western banking models. Whatever the specific contours of the reform plan, we might assume that any significant decentralization of Gosbank's powers or demonopolization of its functions would meet with significant opposition from the Gosbank bureaucracy and from many of its clients. Gosbank bureaucrats would surely oppose the reduction of the bank's size and the scope of its monetary functions, since this would entail a loss of jobs, a decrease in the bank's authority and power, a lowering of the status for the bank's top management and personnel, and a loss of control over a range of economic transactions that might have provided substantial rents for the bankers themselves. Besides, the process of reform would incur massive transaction costs related to the formation, implementation and governance of a new banking structure that would significantly increase the workload for Gosbank bureaucrats and would cause serious transitional disruptions in the monetary system as a whole. Whatever new opportunities might be created for Gosbank bureaucrats, the uncertainty and risk involved in building this new banking structure would outweigh any potential gains.

We also might predict that many of Gosbank's clients would oppose reform. Over the years, powerful ministries and large enterprises have developed an advantageous working relationship with their banking regulators in which they had access to an almost unending flow of financial resources at insignificant interest rates in order to facilitate plan fulfillment.[50] These powerful clients, who were able to "capture" their local Gosbank officials to work in their own interests, would surely be skeptical of any greater competition in the banking system that might increase interest rates or interrupt their easy source of credit. As a result, the reformers would be faced with a powerful bloc of opposition to their restructuring of the banking system, which would marshall all its substantial powers to obstruct the implementation of the reform plan. The reformers would make vigorous use of the personnel weapon to bring like-minded officials into the key posts of the banking system and would rely on exogenous pressures such as the legislature or even international financial organizations to push reform through the recalcitrant bureaucracy. Despite the coherence of the original reform plan, its implementation would be fraught with compromises and sabotage from bureaucrats significantly reducing its potential effectiveness.

The first effort at comprehensive reform of the Soviet banking system followed closely the scenario described above. In an attempt to decentralize the banking structure, to make banks more responsive to their clients' needs, and to introduce economic, as opposed to administrative, criteria into the allocation of credit, the monobanking system was reorganized into a "two-tier" banking structure in January 1988.[51] Gosbank lost its commercial banking functions and was transformed into a genuine, regulatory central bank. Commercial banking services were divided among five state-owned "specialized banks" (hereafter, spetsbanks) that were organized along sectoral lines.[52] The reform plan was formulated outside the banking bureaucracy, primarily by economic reformers within the Council of Ministers and the Ministry of Finance.[53] It was widely perceived as an attack on the monopolistic position of Gosbank, which had been criticized as over bureaucratized and unsuited to the new emphasis on decentralized decision-making. Put on the defensive by the reform, Gosbank immediately sought to tailor the implementation of the reform plan to preserve its dominant position in the banking system.[54]

Gosbank retained considerable jurisdiction over the staffing of the new spetsbanks and essentially transferred its branch department staffs en masse to the corresponding spetsbank. Gosbank also secured control over the distribution of resources to the spetsbanks by allocating resource plans and credit lines to the spetsbanks.[55] Gosbank even continued to set interest rates for spetsbank credit and to force the spetsbanks to grant "obligatory objects of credit" based on the central plan.[56] Though the reform plan envisioned Gosbank as a bankers' bank, regulating the spetsbanks through financial instruments like discount loans, required reserve rates and interest rate incentives, Gosbank continued to assert detailed administrative control over the spetsbanks.[57] The upper management staff of the banking system was neither substantially changed nor radically reduced, as the reform plan had targeted.[58] Also, the confusion caused by the division of functions led to a serious deterioration in client services and a sharp increase in complaints by ministries and enterprises without any imposition of a price-rationing standard on capital.[59]

As the individual spetsbanks pushed for greater autonomy, a struggle ensued that polarized the banking community and led to a further deterioration of banking services. The spetsbanks complained to the Council of Ministers of burdensome interference from Gosbank in the allocation of credit and the setting of interest rates that deprived them of flexibility in responding to their clients' needs.[60] Gosbank, in turn, argued that the spetsbanks had created new monopoly fiefdoms which rebuffed its efforts to establish monetary control.[61] The conflict was apparently intense, as evidenced by the report of one specialist: "The Presidium of the Council of Ministers was forced to give a very harsh evaluation of the egoistic positions of the leaders of Gosbank and the spetsbanks. Not one of the other central economic departments has received as much attention at this stage as the banks."[62] In the mean time, the clients complained that their access to credit had been substantially restricted and that increasing delays in the payments system were beginning to affect the production process.[63]

Within less than a year of the creation of the spetsbanks, a broad consensus had developed that the banking reform had been an abysmal failure.[64] Expressing a widely held view, economist Nikolai Petrakov wrote, "We went along the path of breaking the banking system into smaller pieces. All we did was increase the number of armchairs for our bankers."[65] The failure of the spetsbank reform demonstrated many of the bureaucratic incentives and constraints that were predicted above. Forced upon the bankers by reformers outside the banking bureaucracy, the measures were fiercely resisted by Gosbank, which refused to give up its direct control over key aspects of the monetary system and accept a significant reduction in its functions, staff, economic power and political status. By demonopolizing their commercial banking functions, Gosbank bureaucrats were threatened with the loss of the direct links with ministries and enterprises that were the basis for their rent-seeking activities and local clout. Coalitions of producers, mostly in heavy industry, also opposed the reform in the interest of maintaining the rents they received in the form of Gosbank's easy money policies. The spetsbank reform also demonstrated the high transaction costs involved in restructuring the banking system, which wreaked havoc on the settlements network and on the distribution of credit. In sum, the spetsbank reform, though flawed at the outset, was undermined by the obstructive measures of bureaucrats defending their institutional position.

Just as the spetsbanks were put into operation, a second, and ultimately more enduring, wave of banking reform began that has had little in common with the reform scenario derived from the conventional accounts of bureaucratic interests. This has been an endogenous process of reform in which the initiation and implementation of marketizing measures have come from within the economic bureaucracy. Rather than obstructing the reform process, state bankers, ministry officials, party bureaucrats and enterprise managers have been the most active participants in the formation of an independent commercial banking network. Moreover, these bureaucrats have managed to tailor the reform to minimize the political costs, transaction costs and uncertainty while creating new opportunities for rent-seeking and maximizing their political power and status. The very incentives and costs that led bureaucrats to resist reform in the conventional models seem to have motivated their active participation in the process of building a new commercial banking system.

In the beginning of 1988, Gosbank began negotiations with several industrial ministries and cooperatives to establish the first independent commercial and cooperative banks in the Soviet Union. Responding to the disruption caused by the spetsbank reform and eager to gain more control over their finances, the ministries wanted to create small-scale banks that would efficiently serve the credit and payments needs of their constituent enterprises. The cooperatives were forced to create their own banks, since their finances were not included in the central plan, which made them practically ineligible for any credits from the state banking system.[66] For Gosbank, the creation of the new banks was a response to the spetsbank reform. Gosbank officials believed that small commercial banks would be easier to regulate than the large spetsbanks, which faced significant pressures from the "super ministries" designed to rule the different branches of the economy in the July 1987 economic reforms.[67] In addition, Gosbank's own reformers, many of whom were intent on copying Western banking models, believed that a network of independent commercial banks regulated by a genuine central bank came much closer to Western standards than the spetsbank reform. The closed negotiations to create the new banks were held at Gosbank and the final agreement was strictly informal.[68] No Council of Ministers' resolution, central directive, or other law sanctioned these new institutions. The move was only justified ex post facto in the Law on Cooperatives.[69] Rather than following some marketization blueprint from above, Gosbank bureaucrats themselves took the initiative to open entry into a radically new banking system.

By the end of 1989, 224 new commercial and cooperative banks with assets of more than R9 billion had registered with Gosbank.[70] By early 1991, there were more than 700 new banks holding over R39 billion in assets and growing at the rate of up to 15 per day.[71] The overwhelming majority of the commercial banks has been founded not by new market-oriented entrepreneurs, but by the large bureaucratic organizations that have routinely been characterized as forces most hostile to reform--the central industrial ministries and state committees, central and regional party organizations, large state enterprises and associations and the mass social organizations.[72] Approximately 40% of the new banks were founded by ministries or *obedineniia*, such as Aeroflotbank (Ministry of Aviation), Stankinbank (State Supply Committee) and AvtoVAZ-bank (AvtoVAZ automotive works).[73] Political bureaucracies have also been very active in creating commercial banks, such as Finist Bank (Komsomol), Profsoiuzbank (central trade union organ), Mosbiznessbank (Moscow City Soviet) and the powerful bank-holding company Menatep (CPSU).[74] The Leningrad city party organization even set up a commercial bank in the Smolnyi Institute, Lenin's famous headquarters during the revolution.

Having lifted the restrictions on entry into the new banking system, Gosbank never anticipated the flood of requests to create commercial banks and had not adequately prepared for the task of regulating this wave of new banks.[75] The requirements for establishing a new bank were strikingly minimal; any organization or group of organizations that could raise the minimum start-up capital of R500,000 for a cooperative bank, or R5 million for a commercial bank, could apply for a license.[76] By 1990, there were so many requests for licenses that Gosbank's 10 member commercial banking staff hardly had time to verify even the basic capital requirements.[77] In addition, Gosbank set compulsory reserve rates, the capital-to-assets ratio and the maximum allowable risk to a single debtor. Gosbank originally restricted commercial and cooperative banks from engaging in foreign currency transactions and accepting savings deposits from private citizens. Within these skeletal regulations, the new banks had remarkable freedom in shaping their own structure and in establishing their commercial relationships, including the setting of interest rates. Moreover, the fact that new banking laws were approved in December 1990--more than two years into the process of actual commercial banking reform--created a veritable wildcat banking period in the Soviet Union.[78]

Free to structure their own banks and to define a new range of banking activities in the Soviet Union, the bureaucrats tailored the new banks to serve their interests.[79] Organized primarily as limited liability companies, each bank tends to be dominated by a single shareholder, often a ministry or *obedinenie* with their constituent enterprises serving as minority shareholders. The principal shareholder maintains tight control over the bank, providing its premises, appointing its officers (usually from the ranks of the shareholder's own senior management), directing its credit policy and borrowing its resources at highly advantageous terms. The bank's financial activities tend to be concentrated on the economic branch or region defined by the shareholder's sphere of authority. These banks are frequently called "pocket banks" to denote their incestuous relations with their founders and clients. Often, they serve as little more than the finance departments of the ministries, associations and enterprises that created them. Not surprisingly, these new banks have not spearheaded a significant redirection of capital in the Soviet economy. Indeed, they tend to reinforce existing economic ties and relationships that have themselves been threatened by the disintegration accompanying economic reform and the break-up of the union.[80] Created by the established pillars of the old economic order, these new market institutions have been used not to resist economic reform, but to shape the reform to serve the interests of the pre-existing political and economic elites.

Without any pressure from above to establish new commercial banks and in the absence of any banking laws in the formative stages of this process, the commercial banking sector has nevertheless grown at a remarkable pace. The combined capital of the commercial banks rose from R1.8 billion in 1990 to R5.8 billion at the start of 1991. More than R39 billion in deposits, settlement accounts, securities and interbank credits have been invested in the banks, compared with R9.5 billion in 1990. Credit investments by commercial banks in 1991 reached a total of R32.5 billion, up from R9 billion in 1990.[81] The commercial banks' share of the total credit market in the Soviet Union rose from 2% in 1990 to more than 12% in 1991.[82] Their share of the short-term credit markets has been significantly higher. An active market in the secondary trading of inter-enterprise debt ("factoring" in Soviet terms; "commercial paper" in Western parlance) has developed. The banks have created a substantial leasing sector. They have also been actively engaged in illicit currency exchanges between the cash (*nalichnyi*) and non-cash (*beznalichnyi*) monetary circuits and between rubles and foreign currencies.[83] Though the banks may have been created by bureaucrats from the old order, they have proved to be surprisingly innovative and flexible in building a new financial sector to serve as an alternative to the state banking network and as a foundation for a genuine financial market in the Soviet Union.

Despite the rapid growth of the commercial banks, the spetsbanks, or the "elephants" as they have commonly been called by Soviet bankers, were still the powerhouses of the Soviet banking industry. Promstroibank, Agroprombank and Zhilsotsbank maintained a network of more than 5,000 branches with more than R350 billion of credit investments. The Savings Bank, Sberbank, still maintained a complete monopoly over the R350 billion of personal savings in the Soviet Union, as well as a network of more than 10,000 branches in every corner of the country. Vneshekonombank held tight control over all the foreign currency and gold reserves.[84] The spetsbanks maintained close ties with the major enterprises and organizations in the country forged in the central planning process. Also, they had access to central resources in amounts that dwarfed the portfolios of even the largest commercial banks.

But while the commercial banks used their enviable freedom to create new financial instruments and services and to charge market interest rates for them, the spetsbanks were still burdened with detailed administrative direction of their activities linked to the central plan. A large portion of their credit resources was automatically allocated to "obligatory objects of credit" that were earmarked for planned investment projects, regardless of their potential profitability. Interest rates continued to be fixed at a range of 0-3% annually, reflecting not the cost of capital, but charges for the administration of credit. Promstroibank and Agroprombank were saddled with a mountain of unpaid loans and a credit portfolio of long-term investments at negative real interest rates for largely obsolete projects. Sberbank's resources were directed straight into the central budget. Spetsbank directors constantly complained of their inability to respond flexibly to the financial needs of their clients, especially considering increasing scope of the commercial banks' activities.[85]

In an effort to increase the efficiency of the spetsbanks, as well as to restore monetary discipline in the Soviet financial system, the Council of Ministers approved a series of measures that struck a further blow to the spetsbanks' ability to compete with the commercial banks.[86] First, the spetsbanks' credit resources were cut by up to 25% across the board. This led the spetsbanks to cut back significantly on short-term credits to finance the current accounts of enterprises, in turn leaving enterprises scrambling for loans to pay off their suppliers and workers. These enterprises were forced to turn to the new commercial banks, despite interest rates that were substantially higher than at the spetsbanks. Second, the Council of Ministers granted enterprises the right to choose their own bank instead of the standard policy of assigning each enterprise to an individual spetsbank branch.[87] Though this measure was intended to introduce competition among the different spetsbanks, it gave many enterprises the opportunity to open accounts in commercial banks while still maintaining a relationship with their spetsbank branch. Third, the spetsbanks were placed on *khozraschet* (cost accounting), which put pressure on the spetsbank managers to be concerned with profitability. With fixed negative real interest rates, substantial administrative interference in the allocation of credit and a crushing backlog of non-performing loans, the spetsbank managers were placed in an impossible position. As the more flexible commercial banks continued to make real inroads into the spetsbank's domain and the pressure from above to become profitable increased, many spetsbank bureaucrats chose an unexpected path of rebellion against their central administrations.

Complaining that they could not function profitably under continued restrictions from the center, several regional branches of Agroprombank and Zhilsotsbank independently split from the spetsbank network, attracted their own shareholders and registered themselves as commercial banks.[88] Though this process began originally on the initiative of the local spetsbank managers, it later was taken over by the newly independent RSFSR Central Bank, which was eager to decentralize control over the banking system.[89] By the end of 1990, the defections had decimated the centralized structures of Agroprombank and Zhilsotsbank.[90] In the RSFSR alone, 578 new commercial banks with more than 1400 branches had been created from the two spetsbanks. Though the central board of Promstroibank threatened strict measures to prevent this process, 187 new commercial banks encompassing 522 former branch offices managed to break away.[91] The structures of Sberbank and Vneshekonombank were not affected. Like the rise of the commercial banks, the demonopolization and commercialization of the spetsbanks was initiated and implemented by middle-level bureaucrats responding not to some centrally devised reform program, but to their own pressures and opportunities.

Though it is still too early to make any generalizations about these new commercialized spetsbanks, some trends are already apparent. The former spetsbanks have clearly attempted to turn their accumulated power, privileges and connections from the old order into a superior position in the new banking market. The largest of these banks still possess an access to credit resources, a network of branches, an established client base and a foundation of basic equipment and technology that no other commercial bank can match. Commercialization has simply allowed these banks to charge market rates for their capital and services, as well as to offer a significantly wider range of services. Pre-existing long-term credits have been renegotiated or subsidized by the state. Economic criteria have been introduced, to some extent, in evaluating new credit investments. Some former spetsbanks have already begun to dominate the commercial banking system. In Moscow, Mosbiznessbank was established on the basis of all the Zhilsotsbank branches in the Moscow oblast with an extraordinary starting capital of R800 million and more than 300 shareholders.

Lenpromstroibank, created from the Leningrad oblast Promstroibank network, has already become the leading commercial bank in its region. More recently, the central administrations of the individual spetsbanks have announced plans for commercialization, which should dwarf any existing commercial bank.[92]

In contrast to conventional images of the reform process, in which enlightened reformers at the center struggle to ram their program through the recalcitrant bureaucracy, the development of a new commercial banking network followed a reverse path. The de facto institutional changes in the banking system since early 1988, forged by the initiative of middle-level bureaucrats, were rammed through the economic reformers in Gorbachev's administration and in the Supreme Soviet during the course of negotiations over new banking laws. In the end, almost all the "spontaneous" institutional developments in the banking system were written into the all-union and republican banking laws. This was hardly coincidental as the new commercial bankers and commercialized spetsbankers played a decisive role in the drafting of the new laws.

The first drafts of the all-union banking laws were written by Gosbank staffers with the participation of the representatives from the spetsbanks, Council of Ministers and academic specialists.[93] Circulated in early 1989, the laws preserved the basic structure of the Soviet banking system, while legalizing the development of commercial banks and placing them under a strict regulatory regime controlled by Gosbank. In response to the early drafts as well as to attempts by the Gorbachev administration to reign in their activities, the commercial bankers formed three lobbying groups to represent their interests in the negotiations over the banking laws.[94] By the time the Commission on Planning, Budget and Finance of the USSR Supreme Soviet sat down to draft the new laws in August 1990, the commercial bankers had established a major role for themselves as expert advisers and as an influential interest group in the process.[95] The most influential bankers' lobby, the Moscow Banking Union, sent a permanent delegation to the Supreme Soviet to participate in drafting the laws. Menatep, the powerful bankholding company, submitted its own model drafts of the laws. Many commercial bankers spoke before the Commission and submitted written commentaries on the draft laws at various stages. The newly independent RSFSR Central Bank was especially active in the process, not only as an advocate for a radical decentralization of Gosbank, but also on behalf of the commercial banks and of the commercialization of the spetsbanks.

The final drafts of the banking laws bore little resemblance to the original drafts submitted by Gosbank and approved by Leonid Abalkin's reform team in the Council of Ministers.[96] Instead, it established a federal reserve system, hastened the commercialization of the spetsbanks and anointed the commercial banks as the basic providers of banking services throughout the country giving them a wide latitude to conduct their operations. The final drafts closely followed the commercial bankers' interests except in two areas. First, to prevent new commercial banks from becoming "pocket banks," the Supreme Soviet legislators forbade a single shareholder from owning more than 35% of the bank's capital. Second, the legislators also gave Gosbank certain emergency powers to inflict strict monetary discipline on the banking system in case of hyperinflation or some other monetary crisis. Yet both these provisions were excluded from the RSFSR banking laws, in the drafting of which the commercial bankers played an even larger role than at the all-union level.[97] The confusion created by the subsequent "war of laws" between the center and the republics (especially the RSFSR) gave most commercial banks the opportunity to ignore both sets of laws. In the final analysis, the new banking laws at the all-union and republican levels did not create a new banking system from above, but rather codified and slightly modified the endogenous institutional developments that had occurred over the previous three years.

Bureaucratic Incentives Reconsidered

The case of Soviet banking reform has defied predictions about the bureaucratic response to reform and, consequently, about the nature of the reform process. The development of a commercial banking network and the demonopolization of the state banking structure have not been the product of a struggle between radical market reformers with a grand design for a modern banking system and recalcitrant bureaucrats fighting to defend their positions against fundamental institutional change. Rather, the banking reform has been driven by middle-level bureaucrats with a stake in the old structure and a strategy for preserving their power and privilege in the new structure, whatever that might turn out to be.

What interests have motivated this surprising bureaucratic role in the reform process? Have the conventional accounts of bureaucratic interests in both rational choice and Soviet studies misinterpreted these interests or have they simply misapplied them in the current context? What were the differences between the first and second waves of banking reforms that might explain the radically different bureaucratic responses? The case of Soviet banking reform suggests that while the conventional account of bureaucratic interests remains valid, changes in the structure of the command economy created a new set of incentives for bureaucrats to play a very different role in the reform process.

Two key differences in the structure of the Soviet economy can be identified that distinguish the context of the first and second waves of banking reform. First, in approving the proposals for the establishment of commercial and cooperative banks, Gosbank removed the administrative restrictions on entry into the banking system. Whereas the spetsbank reform restructured the banking system by imposing a concrete set of new institutions that were exogenously devised, Gosbank's decision to allow any organization to create its own commercial bank opened up the possibility for the endogenous formation of new banks. As a result, the commercial banking reform did not confront bureaucrats with the choice of accepting or rejecting a pre-packaged set of new institutions, but presented them with the opportunity to structure their own financial institutions "from scratch" according to their own interests. Second, by not fixing interest rates for commercial banks at the early stages of the reform, Gosbank also removed the administrative restrictions on pricing. New commercial banks were free to attract resources, allocate credit and provide services at "market" rates. Moreover, the sharp cutback in lending by the spetsbanks and the increased financial demands linked to rising supply prices and wage bills led to a significant change in the relative price of capital. By lifting the restrictions on pricing, Gosbank opened up the opportunity for commercial banks to take advantage of the increased demand for capital.

The lifting of the administrative restrictions on entry and on price in the new banking system confronted state bureaucrats with a new economic structure and, consequently, a new set of opportunities that simply did not exist before 1988. The banking case suggests that many of the same interests that led bureaucrats to obstruct reform efforts in the framework of the command economy led many bureaucrats to "cross over" to new non-state institutions when restrictions on entry and price were removed. As a result, these very same interests can explain why bureaucrats become the key actors driving the process of institutional change in the reform process.

Rent-seeking interests: The rising price of capital, the deregulation of interest rates, the continued distortion of the financial system and the initial monopoly positions of many "pocket banks" in their economic sectors or regions created opportunities for both bankers and their shareholders to earn extremely high profits linked to monopoly rents.[98] Ministries, enterprises and other powerful organizations continued to borrow money from the state banking sector at 0-5% interest rates which they reinvested in their own commercial banks that were lending at rates from 15 to 200%. Desperate for capital to meet rising supply and labor costs and protected against bankruptcy or closure, enterprises were willing to pay almost any interest rate for short-term credit. In addition, as enterprises were granted greater power over their retained earnings, they were immediately attracted to the higher rates of return at the commercial banks, which often outpaced the spetsbanks by a wide margin. Commercial banks offered their founders an attractive alternative path to invest their earnings and high rents linked to early commercial banking monopolies. For the bureaucrats who crossed over to positions in the commercial banks, the lack of administrative restrictions on wage levels led to salaries that were reported to be 5-6 times higher than average state sector wages.[99] In terms of material gain, the commercial banks offered bureaucrats the chance to legalize the extraction of rents from the economy (through market interest rates, fees, etc.) and to create a new set of legal and illicit profit-making opportunities (hard currency deals, currency speculation, etc.) that dwarfed their earnings and kickbacks from the old command system.

Budget-maximizing interests: While we have seen that bureaucrats have a strong incentive to maximize their budget and expand their organization, budget-financing in the Soviet Union was accompanied by extreme restrictions on how the money could be spent. Under the command system, every organization's resources were strictly divided into separate funds that were not interchangeable. All payment and other disbursements were required to be justified by the annual plan and settled through Gosbank's notoriously slow and inefficient settlements network. All financial flows were closely monitored by agents from Gosbank or the Ministry of Finance. Though, in principle, the creation of a commercial bank shifted a significant range of functions away from the founding organization, it also granted the organization partial refuge from the tight financial monitoring and control linked to the budget and the plan. Money held in commercial banks could be channelled to any use, regardless of plan restrictions or guidelines for special funds, and any income earned from these assets could be retained. In addition, commercial banks expanded the range of financial instruments and services available to bureaucrats for fulfilling centrally planned, as well as their own, targets. Though the commercial banks are not under the direct control over their founding bureaus, the emergence of the pocket bank structure has allowed the founders to exert significant pressure on their banks' activities. As a result, bureaucrats in the founding organization did not give up a significant degree of control in shifting their budgetary resources to an independent commercial bank, while they gained a much greater degree of autonomy and flexibility over their financial resources.

Political incentives: As we have seen, radical economic reform poses ominous threats to the power, status, privileges and even the position of bureaucrats. Since 1985, Soviet bureaucrats have lived under the constant threat of radical institutional restructuring from above, of the sheer disintegration of existing institutions as a result of economic degeneration and republican rivalries, and of a popular reaction against established bureaucratic privileges. Rather than simply defend their positions against a possible onslaught, the creators of the commercial banks have chosen to create a "safe haven" in the new political and economic structure. Relying on the power and capacity of their institutional positions in the old order, they have established new institutions that can preserve, if not extend, that power in a reformed political economy. The creation of commercial banks has been dominated by a massive transfer of resources from the institutions that appear to be most threatened by reform--economic ministries, the CPSU and local party organs, Komsomol, the trade unions and even organizations like the Soviet Peace Committee.[100] There are widespread rumors about "money-laundering" and efforts to hide assets in commercial banks. Once invested in commercial banks, these resources are protected from arbitrary actions from above or below (such as money confiscation, freezing of accounts, etc.).[101] Commercial banks have served not only to protect assets, but to create many new positions with high incomes and status to which ex-bureaucrats can cross over in the new economic structure. In this way, bureaucrats have been able to turn their existing political prerogatives into economic power that might serve as the basis of power in the reformed system. Paradoxically, many bureaucrats have recognized that the best strategy to defend their power and privilege against the reformist onslaught has been not to obstruct reform, but to embrace it and mold the new institutions according to their own interests.

For bureaucrats, the creation of commercial banks has offered significant gains. These gains must be weighed against the costs of reform, which we have already described as overwhelming. Yet the reform of the banking system suggests that bureaucrats are in a unique position to minimize these costs.

Transaction costs: By creating new commercial banks within the framework of existing institutions, the transaction costs associated with the process have been substantially minimized. New banks obtain their premises and personnel from their founders. Their activities tend to be concentrated on financing well-established exchanges and relationships that have been threatened by the cuts in lending from the state banks or by the general dislocation caused by the broader economic reform process.[102] As a result, the banks are undertaking a familiar set of functions with a list of clients that they already know well. This minimizes the need for new contracting and negotiating, reduces the costs of information-gathering, and simplifies implementation and enforcement, since these are based on the existing governance structures maintained by each bank's founders. Pocket banks have been created not simply to secure the founder's control over the bank's activities, but to take advantage of the relationships developed within the old order to reduce the transaction costs of establishing new institutions.

Uncertainty/risk aversion: Similarly, by building the new banks as parallel structures to existing institutions, the bureaucrats have reduced the uncertainty and risk of the endeavor by translating their accumulated power, connections and resources into market advantages. Consequently, each new commercial bank begins with a "ready-made" market. It can rely automatically on a stable capital base and a network of well-known and trusted clients seeking financing for existing exchange relationships, often guaranteed by ministries or other established state organs. Rather than striking into the unknown where the risk of failure is high, the new banks have started by simply commercializing those transactions and relationships that were once dictated by the central plan. As a result, the bank's risk of failure is usually only as high as its founder's risk, since their business is so closely intertwined. In many cases, the bank's position may even be more solid than that of its founders, especially when it has been created as a safe haven for bureaucrats from threatened institutions. The bank also can become a hedge against the uncertainty facing existing institutions.

Collective action problem: Whereas large-scale institutional reform directed from above faces a significant "free rider" problem, the endogenous creation of commercial banks does not encounter this obstacle. The establishment of a single commercial bank does not require participation on a wide scale, rather it is the decision of a small group of managers who can start the bank with a skeletal staff. Though the costs of creating the bank are concentrated in a few hands, so too are the monopoly rents earned by the bank. As this process can be repeated on a small scale in almost every branch of the economy and in every region, the rapid formation of a commercial banking network (a "public good") can be achieved without requiring coordinated collective action.

The removal of administrative restrictions on entry and on price has transformed the path of institutional restructuring from a threat to an opportunity for bureaucrats. In the case of banking, reform has offered them substantial economic rents, increased autonomy and control over their own finances and the solution to some pressing problems in their existing organizations. By forming new institutions that feed off the accumulated advantages of the old order, bureaucrats have found a way to minimize costs and risks, both in political and economic terms, in an environment of extreme uncertainty. The radical decentralization of the Soviet banking system and the shift of a whole range of financial functions to an independent banking sector have not been construed as a challenge to bureaucratic interests, but as an expression of bureaucratic interests in an economy already on the path of fundamental transformation (or disintegration).

Of course, institutions created to serve such bureaucratic interests should hardly be expected to behave like ideal market institutions. At this stage, Soviet commercial banks bear little resemblance to their counterparts throughout the world. As we have seen, they tend to be structured as pocket banks tightly controlled by their founders and designed to attend to the latter's short-term financial concerns. The banks have been used paradoxically to prop up the relationships and behavioral patterns of the old command system as they have been put under pressure by other elements of the economic reform and by the rapid disintegration of central economic control. Consequently, cooperatives and joint ventures have been starved for capital while loans continue to be poured into powerful, but hopelessly inefficient, state enterprises.[103] Commercial credit has come to serve as a replacement for the limitless capital flows that were guaranteed to enterprises and investment projects in the centrally planned system. Paradoxically, these new reformed banks have undermined the efforts of the central authorities to reassert monetary discipline in an economy quickly slipping toward hyperinflation.[104] One might argue that because the restructuring of the banking system has been shaped by the bureaucrats of the old order, the new banks will serve their interests at the cost of the broader goals of economic reform. In this view, the new banks may have been so distorted by bureaucratic interests that they undermine economic reform by increasing inflation, preventing the center's effort to impose a hard-budget constraint on enterprises, and extracting excessive and unproductive rents from an economy whose productivity level is already plummeting.

Though the founders of the new commercial banks never intended to create true entrepreneurial institutions or to perfect the Soviet financial system as a whole, the very establishment of the new institutions has forged a new set of incentives, pressures and constraints that have begun to push banks away from the distortions linked to bureaucratic interests. There are already strong signs that this process is currently underway. The sheer number of commercial banks has fostered a significant degree of competition in the banking market that has forced the pocket banks to reconsider some of their original policies. Regional and branch banking monopolies have been challenged and, consequently, interest rates have begun to stabilize at relatively uniform levels across the country.[105] Pocket banks have begun to give up the policy of granting credit to their founders at advantageous rates as it seriously hinders their competitiveness. They have also begun to resist administrative intervention by their founders in the allocation of their credit resources, which has led to several well-publicized disputes between the bankers and their founders.[106] Most of the commercial banks have begun to expand their client base and open new branches reaching beyond the borders of the economic branch or region defined by their founders' interests.[107]

In fact, there are clear indications that the interests of the new bankers are beginning to diverge from those of their founders, forcing the former to push for greater independence from the latter. Many of the largest commercial banks have made a concerted effort to expand the number of their shareholders. This move both increases the bank's own capital, but also serves to dilute the voting power of the founders on the bank's board. A wave of commercial banks has even begun to offer shares to the public on the rudimentary financial exchanges.[108] With thousands of small shareholders and assets reaching R2-4 billion, these banks have been able to establish themselves as powerful, independent institutions, no longer catering to the interests of a dominant founder. Moreover, the banks have concentrated on building a corps of personnel with specialized training in standardized banking practices. Countless visits by Western bankers and training seminars offered by Western banks in the Soviet Union and abroad, as well as the opening of several new "business schools," have contributed to a growing professionalization of banking cadres. The competition for Western investment and hard currency has also pushed Soviet bankers to mimic their Western counterparts in order to show their adherence to international standards and norms and thus their preparedness to handle hard currency transactions. The Soviet bankers have even begun to organize themselves into independent trade associations and lobbying organizations to defend their common interests.[109] These developments contribute to an increasing distance between the interests and concerns of the commercial bankers and those of the organizations that created them.

Though these developments in the Soviet banking industry are still in their infancy, they suggest that a bureaucratically driven institutional reform does not necessarily undermine the movement toward competitive markets. Whatever the original goals that led bureaucrats to establish commercial banks and to commercialize the spetsbanks, the reforms shifted the institutional basis of power and resources, which subsequently redirected the course of change to points well beyond the original intentions. In taking the initiative to establish commercial banks, Gosbank did not intend to create a network of independent banks that would extend beyond its own regulatory reach. In forming commercial banks within their existing organizations, bureaucrats did not intend to build autonomous institutions that would perform universal financial services for a broad range of clients. Yet it has been the state bureaucrats, so long considered the greatest opponents of reform, that have built the foundation for the establishment of an independent, competitive banking system.

Conclusions

The restructuring of the Soviet banking system suggests that the process of economic reform has been developing in an unexpected direction. Not the mortal enemies of reform as most observers predicted, bureaucrats have taken advantage of the reform process to commercialize their political power and to establish a new basis for that power and privilege in the developing market structure. This opens up the possibility that market reform in other sectors need not be achieved through some exogenous shock therapy imposed on obstructionist bureaucrats, but can proceed endogenously with the active participation of those very power-holders whose position in the old order would appear to be most threatened by reform. There are already strong indications that this bureaucratic role in the reform process can be generalized to other sectors and to other command economies in transition as well. The example of other former socialist countries is instructive. In Hungary, a process of "spontaneous privatization" has occurred in which enterprise managers and the political nomenklatura bought out enterprises before the establishment of the State Property Agency in a last ditch effort to "salvage their power."[110] In Poland, Jadwiga Stanizskis claims that the growing number of "nomenklatura companies" has created a system of "political capitalism" in which economic power is simply a transfiguration of political power relations from the old command system.[111] Finally, in China, the extent of bureaucratic involvement in the new market institutions was so pervasive that it became one of the key issues of the

Tiananmen Square demonstrations.[112]

The Soviet banking case suggests that the basic framework and concepts of rational choice theory can still explain the bureaucratic response to reform when they are properly applied to the changing structure of incentives linked to the command economy in transition. The very interests that lead bureaucrats to expand their intervention in the economy and to oppose further marketizing reforms in a stable market economy with a well-established private sector appear to lead to just the opposite response in a command economy in the process of building a private sector. As the two successive waves of banking reform demonstrate, the thresholds that spur bureaucrats to cross over into new market institutions are an elimination or substantial reduction of restrictions on entry into the private sector and on pricing, which are controlled at the very top of the political and economic hierarchy. As a result, the bureaucratic "reform from the middle" is still dependent, to a certain degree, on "reform from above," though not in the form of detailed institutional design, but in the form of loosening the centralized administrative restrictions on economic exchange.

The analysis of a single case, like the Soviet banking reform, can only be suggestive of the broader politics of economic reform in the former centrally planned economies. By focusing on the underlying incentives and interests that motivate individuals to pursue or obstruct institutional reform, we can begin to construct a generalizable model of the reform process to compare similar cases and to contrast marketization in different political and economic systems. This will provide us with a better understanding of how the structure of the command administrative system shapes the origins and development of market institutions. It also will explain why these new institutions--like banks, stock exchanges, cooperatives, etc.--look very different from their Western counterparts. Created not by revolutionary entrepreneurs, but by bureaucrats of the existing structure seeking to preserve their power and privileges in a radically different system, the new institutions will perform a very delicate balancing act defending the interests of their founders while responding to the competitive pressures of the developing market. An understanding of this interplay of individual interests reacting to a rapidly changing political and economic structure could certainly contribute to the recent surge of research and theoretical inquiry in political science on the nature of institutional change and the origins of competitive markets.

Notes

1. Clearly, it is difficult to define a state bureaucrat in the Soviet Union since everything, in theory, is owned and administered by the state. The tendency within the literature, and one which I share, is to limit the definition of state bureaucrats to the middle level of state officials charged with contributing to, implementing and overseeing policies formed

by higher state organs in a specific sphere of the economy and society. This group has traditionally been referred to as the "nomenklatura." They should be distinguished from central policy-makers at the top, who have some interest in or responsibility for the overall performance of the society.

2. For a review of the interest group literature, see William C. Mitchell and Michael C. Munger, "Economic Models of Interest Groups: An Introductory Survey," *American Journal of Political Science* 35, no. 2 (May 1991).

3. See David C. Collander, "Introduction," in *Neoclassical Political Economy: The Analysis of Rent-Seeking and DUP Activities*, ed. David C. Collander (Cambridge, MA: Ballinger, 1984); Anne O. Kreuger, "The Political Economy of the Rent-Seeking Society," *American Economic Review* 64, no. 3 (June 1974); and *Toward a Theory of the Rent-Seeking Society*, eds. James Buchanan, Robert Tollison and Gordon Tullock (College Station: Texas A & M University Press, 1980).

4. Mancur Olson, *The Rise and Decline of Nations* (New Haven: Yale University Press, 1980).

5. George J. Stigler, "The Theory of Economic Regulation," in Stigler, *The Citizen and the State* (Chicago: University of Chicago Press, 1971), and Sam Peltzman, "Toward a More General Theory of Regulation," *Journal of Law and Economics* (1976).

6. Anthony Downs, *Inside Bureaucracy* (Boston: Little Brown, 1967).

7. William A. Niskanen, Jr., *Bureaucracy and Representative Government* (Chicago: Aldine, Atherton, 1971).

8. For a summary of Niskanen's model, a discussion of its influence and a review of the critiques and amendments to the model, see Gary J. Miller and Terry M. Moe, "Bureaucrats, Legislators and the Size of Government," *American Political Science Review* 77, no. 2 (1983): 297-322; John A. C. Conybeare, "Bureaucracy, Monopoly, and Competition: A Critical Analysis of the Budget-Maximizing Model of Bureaucracy," *American Journal of Political Science* 78, no. 3 (August 1984): 497-502; and Norman Frohlich and Joe A. Oppenheimer, *Modern Political Economy* (Englewood Cliffs, NJ: Prentice Hall, 1978), pp. 80-81.

9. See Deepak Lal, "The Political Economy of the Predatory State," World Bank Discussion Paper DRD 105 (1984), and John A.C. Conybeare, "The Rent-Seeking State and Revenue Diversification," *World Politics* 35, no. 1 (Oct. 1982): 25-42.

10. Robert H. Bates, *Markets and States in Tropical Africa* (Berkeley: University of California Press, 1981) and Bates, "Macropolitical Economy in the Field of Development," in *Perspectives on Positive Political Economy*, eds. James E. Alt and Kenneth A. Shepsle (Cambridge: Cambridge University Press, 1990).

11. For a summary, see Thrainn Eggertsson, *Economic Behavior and Institutions* (Cambridge: Cambridge University Press, 1990); Terry M. Moe, "The New Economics of Organization," *American Journal of Political Science* 28, no. 4 (1984): 739-77; and James E. Alt and Kenneth A. Shepsle, "Introduction," in *Perspectives on Positive Political Economy*, eds. Alt and Shepsle.

12. Douglass C. North, *Institutions, Institutional Change and Economic Performance* (Cambridge: Cambridge University Press, 1990).

13. The basic work on the transaction costs approach is Oliver E. Williamson, *The Economic Institutions of Capitalism* (New York: The Free Press, 1985).

14. Paul Milgrom and John Roberts, "Bargaining Costs, Influence Costs, and the Organization of Economic Activity," in *Perspectives on Positive Political Economy*, eds. Alt and Shepsle, p. 60.

15. Mancur Olson, *The Logic of Collective Action* (Cambridge: Harvard University Press, 1965).

16. Olson, *The Rise and Decline*.

17. For a summary of this approach and an interesting critique, see Merilee Grindle, "The New Political Economy: Positive Economics and Negative Politics," Paper presented at the Conference on the New Political Economy, Lake Paipa, Colombia (July 1989).

18. For example, Kenneth J. Koford and David C. Collander, "Taming the Rent-Seeker," in *Neoclassical Political Economy*, ed. Collander, p. 206

19. For example, the so-called "Chicago boys" in Chile.

20. For a good account of these developments, see Jerry F. Hough, "The Bureaucratic Model and the Nature of the Soviet System," in Jerry F. Hough, *The Soviet Union and Social Science Theory* (Cambridge: Harvard University Press, 1977).

21. See Carl Friedrich and Zbigniew Brzezinski, *Totalitarian Dictatorship and Autocracy* (Cambridge: Harvard University Press, 1956), and Juan Linz's definition of totalitarianism in *The Handbook of Political Science*, ed. Fred Greenstein (Reading, MA: Addison Wesley, 1975).

22. Barrington Moore, *Terror and Progress in the USSR* (Cambridge: Harvard University Press, 1954); Allen Kassof, "The Administered Society: Totalitarianism without Terror," *World Politics* 16, no. 4 (July 1964): 558-75; and T.H. Rigby, "Traditional, Market and Organizational Societies and the USSR," *World Politics* 16, no. 4 (July 1964): 539-57.

23. Alfred Meyer, "USSR Incorporated," *Slavic Review* 20 (Oct. 1961): 320.

24. Ken Jowitt, "Gorbachev: Bolshevik or Menshevik?" in *Developments in Soviet Politics*, eds. Stephen White, Alex Pravda and Zvi Gitelman (Durham, NC: Duke University Press, 1990), p. 275.

25. See Bialer's description in *Stalin's Successors* (Cambridge: Cambridge University Press, 1980), pp. 104-107.

26. Jerry F. Hough, *Russia and the West* (New York: Simon & Schuster, 1988), p. 87.

27. Paul R. Gregory, *Restructuring the Soviet Economic Bureaucracy* (Cambridge: Cambridge University Press, 1990), p. 5. See also Karl W. Ryavec, *Implementation of Soviet Economic Reforms* (New York: Praeger, 1975), p. 292.

28. Wayne DiFranceisco and Zvi Gitelman, "Soviet Political Culture and 'Covert Participation' in Policy Implementation," *American Political Science Review* 78, no. 1 (1984): 603-21. A recent challenge to this approach has come from Donna Bahry and Brian D. Silver, "Soviet Citizen Participation on the Eve of Democratization," *American Political Science Review* 84, no. 3 (Sept. 1990): 821-47.

29. Jerry F. Hough, *The Soviet Prefects* (Cambridge: Harvard University Press, 1969), pp. 175-76.

30. See Alec Nove, *The Soviet Economic System*, 2d ed. (London: George Allen & Unwin, 1977), chap. 6.

31. For most Soviet firms and other economic organizations, profit is not the principal success indicator, the costs of investment are minimal, bank credit is simple and cheap and risk is virtually nil given that firms never face bankruptcy. As a result, the rational manager or bureaucrat has virtually no constraints on his desire to expand, except those defined by Gosplan, the central planning organ. Janos Kornai, *The Economics of Shortage* (Amsterdam: North Holland Publishing Co., 1980).

32. See, for example, Mikhail Voslenskii, *Nomenklatura* (New York: Doubleday, 1984); Konstantin Simis, *USSR: Secrets of a Corrupt Society* (London: Dent, 1982); and I. Zemtsov, *The Private Life of the Soviet Elite* (New York: Crane Russak, 1985).

33. See studies by Ryavec and Gregory mentioned above.

34. Seweryn Bialer, "Gorbachev's Program of Change: Sources, Significance, Prospects," in *Gorbachev's Russia and American Foreign Policy*, eds. Seweryn Bialer and Michael Mandelbaum (Boulder, CO: Westview Press, 1988), p. 279.

35. Stephen Cohen, "The Friends and Foes of Change: Reformism and Conservatism in the Soviet Union," in *The Soviet Union Since Stalin*, eds. Stephen Cohen, Alexander Rabinowitch and Robert Sharlet (Bloomington: Indiana University Press, 1980).

36. Bialer, *Stalin's Successors*, p. 145.

37. Gregory, *Restructuring the Soviet Economic Bureaucracy*, p. 47.

38. Jerry F. Hough, *Opening up the Soviet Economy* (Washington, DC: The Brookings Institution, 1988), p. 46.

39. Gregory, *Restructuring the Soviet Economic Bureaucracy*, p. 167.

40. Anders Åslund, *Gorbachev's Struggle for Economic Reform* (Ithaca: Cornell University Press, 1989), p. 12.

41. Ryavec, *Implementation of Soviet Economic Reforms*, p. 92.

42. See the article by Gail Lapidus, "Gorbachev and the Reform of the Soviet System," *Daedalus* 116, no. 2 (Spring 1987).

43. David Mandel, "The Social Basis of Perestroika," in *Developments in Soviet Politics*, eds. White, Pravda and Gitelman.

44. Thus, recent reform plans have suggested linking aid from the World Bank and the IMF to progress in marketizing the economy.

45. The role of enlightened officials has a strong referent in Russian history. The "Great Reforms" of Alexander II, which included among other things freeing the serfs, have been credited to enlightened officials around the tsar who were strongly influenced by the example of Western Europe. See the work of Walter Yaney. Stephen Cohen refers to this tradition with reference to modern-day reformers in "The Friends and Foes," p. 25.

46. It is interesting that one of the most (if not the only) significant controversies to develop within the study of current Soviet politics was a debate over Gorbachev's leadership qualities and whether he had been working from a master reform plan or reacting to events and crises as they developed. See the recent exchange by George Breslauer, Jerry Hough, Peter Reddaway and Archie Brown in successive issues of *Soviet Economy* (1989-1990), Vols. 5-7.

47. See especially Åslund, *Gorbachev's Struggle*.

48. See the essays in *Remaking the Economic Institutions of Socialism: China and Eastern Europe*, eds. David Stark and Victor Nee (Palo Alto: Stanford University Press, 1989); the essays by Dorothy J. Solinger, Connie Squires Meaney and Jean C. Oi in *Reform and Reaction in Post-Mao China*, ed. Richard Baum (New York: Routledge, 1991); and Jadwiga Staniszkis, "'Political Capitalism' in Poland," *East European Politics and Society* 5, no. 1 (Winter 1991).

49. The Soviet banking system prior to January 1988 could be described as a monobanking system. The State Bank, Gosbank, served as both the central bank of issue and the main commercial bank for nearly all Soviet enterprises. Though foreign trade, capital investment and private savings were handled by separate banks, they were all in fact subsidiaries of Gosbank. Thus, Gosbank performed its functions without competition and enterprises were assigned to specific Gosbank branches. Gosbank functioned not as a bank in the common sense of the term, but as an administrative agency of the central government charged with issuing currency, granting enterprise credit and monitoring the fulfillment of financial plans all as predetermined by the central plan. For a description, see George Garvy, *Money, Financial Flows, and Credit in the Soviet Union* (Washington, DC: National Bureau of Economic Research, 1977) and O. Kuschpeta, *The Banking and Credit System of the USSR* (Leiden: Martinus Nijhoff, 1978). For a basic Soviet text on the banking system, see V.S. Zakharov, *Bankovskaia sistema i ee rol' v upravlenii ekonomikoi* (Moscow, 1984).

50. For a description, see Gregory Grossman, "Gold and Sword: Money in the Soviet Command Economy," in *Industrialization in Two Systems*, ed. Henry Rosovsky (New York: John Wiley and Sons, 1966) and Gregory Grossman, "Monetary and Financial Aspects of Gorbachev's Reform," in *Financial Reform in Socialist Economies*, eds. Christine Kessides, *et al.* (Washington, DC: The World Bank, 1989), pp. 28-33. For a Soviet account, see L. Braginskii and P. Subbotin, "Sovmestnoe zasedanie biuro otdeleniia ekonomiki AN SSSR i Pravleniia Gosbanka SSSR," *Voprosy ekonomiki*, 1987, No. 8.

51. See the resolution, "O sovershenstvovanii bankov v strane i usilenii ikh vozdeistviia na povyshenie effecktivnosti ekonomiki," in *O korennoi perestroike upravleniia ekonomikoi* (Moscow, 1987).

52. The five spetsbanks were called the Bank for Industry and Construction (Promstroibank), the Agro-Industrial Bank (Agroprombank), the Bank for Housing and Social Development (Zhilsotsbank), the Bank of Foreign Economic Affairs (Vneshekonombank), and the Savings Bank (Sberbank). For a detailed description of these banks, see I.V. Levchuk, *Banki v usloviiakh samofinansirovaniia khoziaistva* (Moscow, 1990).

53. The drafting process of the spetsbank reform was described in interviews conducted by the author with two participants: A.A. Khandruev, director of the Finance and Banking Research Institute under Gosbank, and Dr. Oleg Lavrushin, chairman of the Department of Money and Credit Circulation, Moscow Finance Institute. See also Ed A. Hewett, *Reforming the Soviet Economy* (Washington, DC: The Brookings Institution, 1988), pp. 322-25.

54. N.V. Garetovskii, "Perestroika bankovskoi sistemy," *Ekonomicheskaia gazeta*, No. 50 (Dec. 1987).

55. For evidence of this, see: "Bankovskaia sistema: kakoi ei byt'?," *Den'gi i kredit*, 1989, No. 12; "Sovershenna li bankovskaia sistema?," *Ekonomicheskaia gazeta*, No. 4

(1989); and "Zhilsotsbank i prepriiatie (vstrecha v otdelenii banka)," *Den'gi i kredit*, 1988, No. 9.

56. For examples of spetsbank complaints about this practice, see E.E. Kharkovets and A.P. Khimicheva, "Novyi kreditnyi mekhanizm," *Den'gi i kredit*, 1988, No. 10, and "Iz pochti redaktsii," *Den'gi i kredit*, 1988, No. 9.

57. S. Amirbaev, "Kak ustranit' aritmiiu?," *Kazakhstanskaia pravda*, Oct. 2, 1988; V. Tkachenko, "Kak ptitsa feniks," *Ekonomicheskaia gazeta*, No. 31 (July 1988); and N.P. Nikitenko, "O kreditovanii kooperativnoi i individual'noi trudovoi deiatel'nosti," *Den'gi i kredit*, 1988, No. 10.

58. For a description, see N.V. Garetovskii, "Vedomstvennost' v bankovskoi sisteme?" *Ekonomicheskaia gazeta*, No. 37 (Sept. 1989).

59. Anecdotal evidence of the serious decline in services was obtained by the author in an interview survey of 50 Soviet enterprise managers participating in a management training program at the Fuqua School of Business, Duke University. Additional evidence was provided in an interview with Iuliia Babicheva, Head of the Banking Policy Division, Finance and Banking Research Institute. There was also a wave of complaints in the press. Among them: A. Ivanenko, *et al.*, "Bank: chto meshaet stat' partnerom?" *Ekonomicheskaia gazeta*, No. 50 (Dec. 1988); R. Trotsko, "Izderzhki reorganizatsii," *Sovetskaia litva*, June 7, 1988; and "Voprosy koordinatsii bankovskoi raboty (vstrecha 'za kruglym stolom')," *Den'gi i kredit*, 1988, No. 5.

60. Amirbaev, "Kak ustranit' aritmiiu?"; Aleksandr Levikov, "Bankiry v LG," *Literaturnaia gazeta*, No. 21 (May 25, 1988); N.P. Nikitenko, "O kreditovanii kooperativnoi i individual'noi trudovoi deiatel'nosti," *Den'gi i kredit*, 1988, No. 10; and V. Tkachenko, "Kak ptitsa feniks," *Ekonomicheskaia gazeta*, No. 31 (July 1988).

61. N.V. Garetovskii, "Vedomstvennost' v bankovskoi sisteme?," *Ekonomicheskaia gazeta*, No. 37 (Sept. 1989), and N.V. Garetovskii, "Govoriat delegaty XIX vsesoiuznoi konferentsii KPSS," *Voprosy ekonomiki*, 1988, No. 9.

62. S. Assekritov, "Banki: vzgliad v zavtra," *Ekonomicheskaia gazeta*, No. 9 (Feb. 1989).

63. L. Iatsenko and E. Godlevskaia, "Reorganizatsiia razdula shtat," *Ekonomicheskaia gazeta*, No. 46 (Nov. 1988), and "Sovershenna li bankovskaia sistema?," *Ekonomicheskaia gazeta*, No. 4 (1989).

64. See a review article in *EKO*, 1989, No. 2, and M.M. Titarev, "Perestroika bankovskoi sistemy," *Den'gi i kredit*, 1989, No. 7.

65. *Rabochaia tribuna*, Feb. 2, 1990.

90   *Joel S. Hellman*

66. See the description of the motivations for creating Vostok Bank, one of the largest Soviet banks founded by a group of cooperatives, in Rafis F. Kadyrov, *Zapiski bankira ili trudnyi put' k rynochnoi ekonomike* (Ufa, 1990). A similar account was given by Aleksandr Smolenskii, Chairman of the cooperative bank Stolichnyi Bank, in an interview with the author.

67. For the views of Gosbank officials, see "Bankovskaia sistema: kakoi ei byt'?" *Den'gi i kredit*, 1989, No. 12, and "Sovershenna li bankovskaia sistema?," *Ekonomicheskaia gazeta*, No. 4 (1989).

68. A detailed description of the negotiations was provided to the author by a participant, A.A. Khandruev.

69. "O Kooperative v SSSR," *Ekonomicheskaia gazeta*, No. 24 (1988).

70. For the first list of the commercial and cooperative banks registered with Gosbank, see *Den'gi i kredit*, 1990, Nos. 3 and 4. The latest list of commercial banks in the Russian republic is *Kommercheskie banki Rossii: Spravochnik* (Moscow 1991). For the assets, see *Banki v SSSR* (Moscow, 1990), p. 151.

71. These figures have been included in the quarterly reports on commercial banks published by the Finance and Banking Research Institute under Gosbank USSR. See *Obzor deiatel'nosti kommercheskikh bankov* (hereafter, *Obzor*), Nos. 1-4 (Moscow: Gosbank, 1990). Unfortunately, these figures are highly unreliable since they are reported to Gosbank by the commercial banks themselves without any independent verification by Gosbank or an external auditor. Given tax incentives and the large portion of off-balance sheet activities undertaken by commercial banks, one would expect these reported figures to be lower than the actual figures. Yet they are still the most comprehensive and most reliable statistics on commercial banks currently compiled.

72. Though reliable data categorizing the founders of the commercial banks are not yet available, a survey is currently underway by the Finance and Banking Research Institute.

73. See the breakdown of commercial and cooperative banks provided in "Kommercheskie banki: igra bez pravil," *Delovye liudi*, No. 3 (July-Aug. 1990).

74. Interviews with Aleksei Golubovich, Director of Planning, Menatep; Aleksandr Shcherbakov, Chairman of the Board, Finist Bank; Valery Matveichuk, Officer, Konversbank. See also the frequent profiles of commercial banks in the weekly newspaper, *Kommersant*.

75. "Kommercheskie Banki: igra bez pravila," *Delovye liudi*, No. 3 (July-Aug. 1990).

76. The original Gosbank directives forming and regulating the commercial and cooperative banks have been reprinted in *Kommercheskie i kooperativnye banki SSSR: Spravochnik* (Moscow: Razvitie, 1990).

77. Interview with Anatolii Tsemianskii, Head of the Commercial Banking Department, Gosbank USSR.

78. Ronald MacKinnon used this term to describe Soviet commercial banks in *The Order of Economic Liberalization* (Baltimore: Johns Hopkins University Press, 1991), p. 144.

79. The following account is based on interviews with representatives of 20 commercial banks in Moscow, Leningrad and Minsk, as well as an especially useful set of interviews with three commercial bank "regulators" from the Commercial Banking Department, Gosbank USSR. For a typical Soviet analysis of the nature of commercial banking and the influence of the principal shareholders, see Sergei Rodionov, "Na kogo rabotaet kommercheskii bank?" *Ekonomika i zhizn'*, No. 20 (May 1990).

80. Thus, commercial banks give predominantly short-term loans (under 3 months) to provide working capital to state enterprises, as opposed to long-term investments. In the last quarter of 1990, 85% of the aggregate credit portfolio of the commercial banks was invested in short-term credits. Of the total credit investments, 74% were granted to state enterprises with only 13% going to cooperatives and joint ventures. Resources from state enterprises also make up over half of the liabilities of commercial banks with the remainder coming from interbank credits (28%) and cooperatives (4%). See the *Obzor*, No. 4.

81. See the *Obzor*.

82. See "Pravila bankovskoi igry," *Ekonomika i zhizn'*, No. 16 (1990).

83. These off-balance sheet and illegal activities are impossible to measure with any accuracy. Evidence of these widespread practices comes from numerous interviews with commercial bankers and frequent reports in the business press, esp. *Kommersant*.

84. For a full description of the spetsbanks, see *Banki v SSSR* (Moscow 1990).

85. Interviews with Iurii L'vov, Chairman of the former Leningrad Branch of Zhilsotsbank (now Lenbank), and Leonid Shveidel, Head of the Planning Department of the former Leningrad branch of Promstroibank (now Lenpromstroibank). See also L. Zaitseva, "Nostal'giia po komandnym metodam," *Ekonomicheskaia gazeta*, No. 52 (Dec. 1989).

86. Postanovlenie No. 280: "O perevode gosudarstvennykh spetsializirovannykh bankov SSSR na polnyi khozraschet i samofinansirovanie." March 31, 1989. (Joint decree by the CPSU Central Committee and the USSR Council of Ministers.)

87. This was included in Postanovlenie No. 280.

88. The process is described in two internal memos prepared by Sergei Rodionov, Head of the Commercial Banking Department of the RSFSR Central Bank: "O khode perevoda

bankov respubliki na kommercheskie printsipy raboty" (Dec. 7, 1990) and "Memorandum" (March 15, 1991).

89. A July 13, 1990, resolution of the RSFSR Congress of Peoples' Deputies declared that all banks on Russian territory were the property of the Russian republic. The resolution gave a legal justification for the splintering of Russian republican spetsbank branches from all-union subordination. See text in *Rossiiskaia gazeta*, July 14, 1990.

90. All of the following statistics on the commercialization of the spetsbanks were provided by the Commercial Banking Department of the RSFSR Central Bank. The statistics pertain only to the situation in the Russian republic where the process has advanced the furthest. No information has been published as yet on the commercialization process in other republics.

91. See the rather threatening article by Iakob Dubenetskii, Chairman of Promstroibank, "Polozhenie v bankovskoi sisteme vyzyvaet trevogu," *Bizness i banki*, No. 9 (Oct. 1990).

92. "Reorganizatsiia Promstroibanka: novoe plat'e so starymi dyrami," *Kommersant*, No. 43 (Nov. 4-11, 1991); Maksim Aksimov, "Reorganizatsiia Promstroibanka: naslednik oboshelsia bez ukazki," *Kommersant*, No. 46 (Nov. 28-Dec. 2, 1991); and Marina Shpagina, "Sberbank SSSR umer, no legche drugikh," *Kommersant*, No. 42 (Oct. 28-Nov. 4, 1991).

93. See the first drafts of the laws in *Den'gi i kredit*, 1990, Nos. 3 and 5.

94. Interview with Sergei Egorov, Head of the Moscow Banking Union.

95. Participants in the drafting process and their contributions were detailed in a set of internal memos provided to the author by the Commission on Planning, Budget, and Finance of the USSR Supreme Soviet. A full description was also provided in interviews with: Aleksandr Orlov, Deputy Chairman of the Commission; his assistant, Evgenii Fedorovich; Sergei Egorov; and Aleksandr Asatiani, a permanent representative to the drafting commission from the commercial bank Mosinkombank.

96. For a text of the law, see *Biznes i Banki*, No. 3 (Feb. 1991).

97. For a text of the law, see *Biznes i Banki*, No. 4 (Feb. 1991).

98. "V pravlenii Gosbanki SSSR," *Den'gi i kredit*, 1990, No. 4.

99. Interview with Iulia Babicheva, Head of the Commercial Banking Department, Finance and Banking Research Institute.

100. Though documentation of this transfer of resources is inherently difficult, there is much anecdotal evidence. A survey currently underway by the Finance and Banking Research Institute will identify the starting capital invested in commercial banks by such

organizations. Investigations into this transfer are only just beginning. For the first investigation of the Communist Party's role in this process, see "KPSS i ee depozity: pochti vse bylo po pravilam," *Kommersant*, No. 44 (Nov. 11-18, 1991).

101. This became especially pertinent given the arbitrary and confiscatory money reforms implemented by the former Prime Minister, Valentin Pavlov.

102. This information comes from a random collection of commercial bank balance sheets collected in an informal mail survey by the author of 150 commercial banks.

103. See the quarterly *Obzor* for the declining proportion of credits to cooperatives and joint ventures.

104. For the view of the International Monetary Fund on this question, see its report, *The Economy of the Former USSR in 1991* (Washington, DC: International Monetary Fund, 1992).

105. See the monthly interest rate reports in the monthly supplement to *Kommersant*.

106. One of the largest commercial banks, Kredobank, has been engaged in a protracted battle with its founder, the powerful BUTEK concern, over the former's refusal to grant the latter credit on advantageous terms. There were several stories on this dispute in *Kommersant* throughout 1991.

107. The wide expansion of the network of branches of individual commercial banks is documented in *Kommercheskie banki Rossii: Spravochnik* (Moscow, 1991).

108. The bankholding company Menatep and Mosinkombank have already offered fixed dividend preferred and common stock to the public. Yet these shares have little in common with the understanding of shares in the West. There is no real secondary market for stocks as yet.

109. "Sozdana Rossiiskaia liga bankov," *Kommersant*, No. 44 (Nov. 11-18, 1991).

110. David Stark, "Privatization in Hungary: From Plan to Market or From Plan to Clan?" *East European Politics and Societies* 4, no. 3 (1990).

111. Staniszkis, "'Political Capitalism' in Poland."

112. On the Chinese case, see the essays referred to in note 48.

Intellectuals and Anti-Nuclear Protest in the USSR

Jane I. Dawson

Introduction

The sharp erosion of state control over public discussion and collective activities which occurred as a result of perestroika represented a dramatic shift in the state-society relationship in the Soviet Union. The absence of an autonomous public realm between state and household has long been acknowledged as a defining and critical feature of communist systems. Thus, the emergence in the Soviet Union of autonomous public activities in the late 1980s marked a critical juncture in Soviet socio-political development. While most observers agreed on the novelty of this explosion of popular activities in the USSR, there had been little consensus among scholars in conceptualizing this radical change in Soviet state-society relations, and determining its implications for future political development. The concept of civil society, which evolved within the context of Western socio-political development, has frequently been suggested as a tool for understanding the current redefinition of state-society relations in the Soviet Union and Eastern Europe.

While a number of variants on the theme of civil society may be discerned in the Western literature,[1] the variant most relevant to changes in Soviet state-society relations was that which focused on the role of autonomous groups in facilitating and protecting the institutions of democracy. This political under-standing of civil society has occasionally been distinguished from its economic and cultural counterparts by the term "public."[2] Broadly defined, a public may be viewed as "an autonomous source of critical evaluation for regime policies."[3] By considering the ability of intellectual elites to provide "an autonomous source of critical evaluation" on Soviet nuclear power policy, in this paper I will test whether current popular activities indicate the emergence of a public and consider the prospects for the consolidation of a stable public realm in the future.

I would like to thank George Breslauer, John Holdren, Jerry Hough, Ken Jowitt, Gail Lapidus and Susan Solomon for useful comments on this and earlier drafts. I am also grateful to the Carnegie Foundation, the Social Science Research Council and the MacArthur Foundation for financial support. An earlier version of this essay appeared as "The Soviet Scientific-Technical Intelligentsia: An Emerging Public?" in *Analyzing the Gorbachev Era* (Berkeley: Berkeley-Stanford Publication, 1989).

Theoretical Background: The Significance of a Public

The absence of a public realm in communist societies has long been a feature of the dominant models of Sovietology. Beginning with the totalitarian model, which envisioned an all-powerful state penetrating all aspects of social life and dominating over a terrorized and atomized society, the lack of opportunities for autonomous collective activities has been recognized as a defining feature of communist systems. Despite limited liberalization in the post-Stalin period, mainstream Sovietologists continued to emphasize the state's ability to prevent the emergence of an autonomous public as a central feature of these regimes. Thus, Rigby's "mono-organizational society," Kassof's "totalitarianism without terror," and Meyer's "USSR, Inc." all maintained the fundamental state-society relationship that marked the earlier totalitarian approach.[4] Even the most liberal interpretations of Soviet state-society relations, which borrowed heavily from Western interest group and pluralist approaches, generally accepted the distinction between Western and communist interest groups, acknowledging that autonomous organization and attempts to mobilize public opinion outside official channels were highly circumscribed in communist systems.[5]

Despite their agreement on the absence of a public realm in Soviet-type systems, Sovietologists differed in their assessment of the possibility for a public realm to emerge and eventually play an influential role in Soviet socio-political development. For those scholars who adhered to a modernization interpretation of communist development, the social changes wrought through industrialization and economic development in communist societies were bound to affect the system of governance and bring about the transformation to a more rational, participatory system of rule. Within this context, Gorbachev's reforms were interpreted as a natural result of the modernization process and a logical response to the demands of an increasingly articulate and sophisticated society for a redefinition of the skewed Soviet state-society relationship. This point of view was well expressed in a number of recent articles by Lapidus, Ruble, Lewin and Starr, as well as in Lowenthal's earlier theoretical treatment of development in Communist societies.[6]

An alternative interpretation focuses on the distinctive and defining features of Leninist regimes which shape the developmental path and obstruct the formation of a viable public realm in these societies. According to Jowitt, the existence of an autonomous public realm was antithetical to the core principles of Leninism, and thus the emergence of independent activities would be strenuously resisted by the regime. Their appearance would be likely to precipitate a backlash or crisis within the system. While modernization theorists were optimistic about the potential for a public realm to emerge and play a significant role in Soviet political development, Jowitt's approach led to a much more pessimistic assessment of current socio-political changes in the USSR.

Richard Lowenthal's landmark article, "Development vs. Utopia in Communist Policy," formed the theoretical basis for the modernization interpretation of the dramatic transformation currently taking place in the Soviet Union. Building on the insights of Apter, deSchweinitz and Gerschenkron,[7] Lowenthal contended that communist ideology was particularly well suited to bringing about "politically forced development"[8] in countries where economic development had failed to arise spontaneously. In such cases, Lowenthal hypothesized that,

> (m)ost likely to succeed would appear to be political systems
> that combine strong governmental powers, severely limiting
> the representation of independent interests and the expression
> of independent opinions, with a modernizing ideology that
> legitimates these powers by invoking the urgency of material
> and national progress and the will of the people.[9]

Thus, initially, a totalitarian system would emerge to allow the state to assume control of the modernization process. During this early developmental stage, autonomous activity by social sectors outside the Communist Party would be rigorously suppressed and a public sector notably absent.

Tension between the objectives of economic development and the creation of a Marxist "utopia," however, prevented the totalitarian system from maintaining itself indefinitely. While Marxist ideology emphasized social egalitarianism and the continued leadership of the Communist Party, the process of modernization unleashed forces which are antithetical to both objectives and these forces eventually acquired a momentum of their own. As the economy developed, the continued intervention of the totalitarian state into established social and economic procedures became more and more disruptive to economic growth. Social forces supporting the new economic rationality expanded and confronted the state with increasing demands for a greater role in shaping policy. As independent economic and political interests began to play an increasing role in the policy-making process, an autonomous public sector gradually emerged.

Lowenthal predicted that the opposing tendencies of social participation and monopoly control by the Communist Party would lead to a series of crises in the political legitimation of the party. As the economy developed, the party was expected to become less able to employ coercion to wrench society away from its natural path of development, and Lowenthal envisioned a "long-term trend towards the victory of modernization over utopianism."[10] In this later stage of development the relationship between state and society would be reversed, because "the political system has to respond to the pressures generated by an increasingly advanced society."[11]

According to a number of Sovietologists, including Lapidus, Lewin, Ruble and Starr, the social transformation predicted in Lowenthal's theoretical study was currently well under way in the Soviet Union. The social and demographic changes which have taken place over the past seven decades led to the transformation of "the passive and inarticulate peasant society of the Stalin era into an urban industrial society with an increasingly articulate and assertive middle class."[12] The social transformation from illiterate peasant masses to a sophisticated urban society radically altered social attitudes and behaviors, and created an increased demand for avenues of participation by articulate social groups outside the leadership. Over the past several decades, this demand had been met by an expansion in the opportunities available for social input into the policy-making process. According to Lapidus,

> The image of "revolution from above," with all its connotations of state domination of a passive society, no longer corresponds to a reality in which social forces have achieved a degree of autonomy, and indeed actively impinge on the political system in unprecedented ways.[13]

Thus, as Lowenthal predicted, the totalitarian system of the early developmental period was giving way to a more participatory system in which the interests of the population were feeding back onto the state. Looking at the Gorbachev period, scholars adhering to this perspective often pointed to glasnost and the proliferation of informal groups as key indicators of the emergence of an "embryonic civil society."[14]

While modernization theorists were optimistic that an autonomous public sector would eventually solidify in the Soviet Union, Jowitt's model of the Leninist developmental path led us to more sobering conclusions. Rather than envisioning the Soviet party-state simply as a vehicle for modernization, Jowitt postulated that Leninism represented a distinctive and novel form of social organization. Leninist regimes might be identified by certain genetic features, which are maintained continuously throughout the developmental process. While the genetic features of a Leninist regime remained constant, however, the organizational profile of the regime changed as the party moved successively from one organizational task to the next. Thus Jowitt shifts our attention to how the Leninist regime consolidated its position and responded to challenges from an ever more sophisticated society.

Like the modernization theorists, Jowitt recognized rapid economic and social development as a central objective of Leninist regimes. Marxist-Leninist ideology was viewed as a revolutionary ideology, which was implicitly linked to the development of society's economic and social bases. The pursuit of economic and social development mandated an empirical and scientific approach to policy-making, consistent with Weberian notions of modernity. Jowitt argued, however, that along with this modern orientation, Leninist regimes incorporated elements of charismatic and traditional authority.

As a charismatic entity, the Leninist party was able to elicit absolute loyalty and sacrifice from its members. Party doctrine took on an aura of divine truth, unassailable by loyal cadres and the rest of society. Thus, the existence of an autonomous public realm was antithetical to the genetic and defining features of Leninism.

The Leninist organization was identified not by its charismatic or modern orientations alone, but rather by the capacity of charismatic leadership to reconcile contradictory elements of tradition, charisma, and modernity, which was predicted to lead to the bizarre juxtaposition of conflicting practices, such as:

> command and obedience with debate and discussion; belief in inexorable laws of historical change with empirical investiga-tion of social development; heroic action with a persistent concern for scientific and sober operation of an economy and society. . . .[15]

While all three elements were present within Leninist organizations, Jowitt contended that the Leninist party was predominantly modern and charismatic, and "its traditional features [were] more structural than substantive in nature."[16]

While the precarious balance of charisma, modernity and tradition gave Leninist regimes their genetic features which persisted over time, the organiz-ational profile of Leninist regimes was expected to change and develop. Once the party had achieved a military and political breakthrough, it would move on to consolidating its gains and creating the nucleus of a new political community in the midst of an unreconstructed society. Throughout the developmental process, the charismatic identity of the party would be maintained and reinforced through the identification of heroic tasks for the party cadres.

Thereafter, the party was expected to shift from consolidation to inclusion. Recognizing that modernization had transformed a society of "mute masses" into increasingly sophisticated "articulate audiences," the party would now have to respond to the demands of these articulate audiences to be treated as full members of society. Thus, the task of inclusion was to incorporate articulate audiences into the political process while simultaneously preventing the emergence of autonomous publics which would threaten the charismatic identity of the Leninist regime.

This final stage of inclusion was expected to be particularly difficult for Leninist organizations. The task of inclusion was in fact inconsistent with the maintenance of the party's charismatic identity. In the midst of a relatively benign and articulate society, the party would likely be unable to find a task of heroic proportions to maintain the integrity of the cadres. In the absence of a suitable combat task, charisma would be likely to degenerate toward its traditional analogue thus leading to corruption and the erosion of organizational integrity. During this slide toward neotraditionalism, party cadres would confuse their particular interests with the general interest of the party and rampant corruption would invade the Leninist organization.

In the face of the contradictory pressures of inclusion, Jowitt postulated that party elites would undertake periodic anti-corruption campaigns to reassert the authority of the party in society and curb its neotraditional decline. Thus the last stage of Leninist development would be characterized by oscillation between neotraditional decay and strenuous attempts to rejuvenate the party. While defacto publics might emerge during periods of decline, Jowitt's developmental theory predicted that the regime would periodically react to reassert the party's authority, suppressing these incipient publics and preventing their institutionalization within the system.

Thus the modernization and Leninist developmental path approaches led us to two very different conclusions. From the modernization perspective, movement in the direction of the emergence of a genuine public sector was already observable, while from the perspective of the Leninist developmental path, regime toleration of defacto public activities was at best temporary and was unlikely to lead to institutionalization of a public realm.

Methodology: Operationalizing the Concept of a Public

Definitions

In analyzing Western European development, numerous scholars have noted the emergence of a new sector in society which made obsolete the simple division into rulers and ruled, and transformed society into a trinity of state, civil society, and household. Scholars have differed in their characterization of this new realm and its impact on socio-political, economic and cultural development. Hegel, Marx and Polanyi pointed to the autonomy of economic activity as the defining feature of this new realm; Durkheim focused attention on professional "corporations" striving toward the creation of new meanings to guide society; Tocqueville, Paine, and Poggi highlighted the role of autonomous associations, referred to here as "publics," in protecting democracy and preventing state despotism.[17] Because of the confluence of informal group emergence and the initiation of a policy of "democratization" in the USSR in the late 1980s, it is this latter theoretical strand which appears most relevant to understanding these developments in Soviet state-society relations.

Drawing on the Tocquevillian approach to group activities, Jowitt stressed the importance of autonomy as the critical and defining feature of a public realm. While an articulate audience was envisioned as

a diverse set of social groups in contemporary Leninist
regimes [which] are politically knowledgeable and oriented
[but] restricted in their political behavior to those roles and
actions prescribed by the regime itself,[18]

a public was defined as "citizens who voluntarily organize themselves around
major political issues"[19] outside the auspices of the state. A public was a
distinct, political domain separate from the official apparatus, which acted as an
"autonomous source of critical evaluation for regime policies."[20] Unlike an
audience, which acts as a docile tool of the state, a public acts independently and
irrespective of the policies and preferences of the state.

It is important to note that the concept of a public implied a certain persistent
pattern of behavior. While fleeting instances of autonomous behavior may be
observable within a communist society, this behavior cannot amount to a
significant change in the state-society relationship unless it is sustained over an
extended period of time and generates a new pattern in the interactions of state
and society. Thus, the role of a public must somehow achieve an institutionalized status which permits its continued functioning.

In this paper, I examine the activities of Soviet intellectual elites, and
particularly the scientific-technical intelligentsia, in promoting their views on the
issue of nuclear safety and consider whether this social stratum showed signs of
moving beyond an articulate audience to becoming a genuine public.

Agenda Building

While the relative autonomy of a social sector may appear difficult to test
empirically, one clear indicator of autonomy from the state lies in the ability of
a group to coalesce around a particular issue and openly present their views on
the issue to society. Thus, the more successful a group is in publicizing and
prompting public discussion of an issue which runs contrary to the policies of
the state, the more solid the proof that the emergence of an autonomous sector
is being tolerated by the state. In this paper, I use the ability of a social sector
to publicize a platform in opposition to state policy as the primary indicator of
the emergence of a public.[21]

A useful framework for analyzing the ability of a group to publicize an issue
has been provided by Cobb, Ross and Ross.[22] According to the authors, agenda
building represents the first stage in the decision making process, followed by
the actual decision making stage and finally implementation. Agenda building
refers to the process through which an issue is initiated and moved onto the
leadership's formal agenda.

The formal agenda is defined as "the list of items which decision makers have
formally accepted for serious consideration,"[23] while the public agenda includes

all issues which (1) are the subject of widespread attention or
at least awareness; (2) require action, in the view of a sizeable
proportion of the public; and (3) are the appropriate concern
of some governmental unit, in the perception of community
members.[24]

The goal of agenda building theory is to determine how issues are moved onto
the public and formal agendas, and what patterns of movement between the two
agendas appear to predominate in a given system. Cobb proposes three alternative models to describe the agenda building process in differing political
systems: the "outside initiative" model, "mobilizational" model, and "inside
initiative" model. The outside initiative model is expected to predominate in
highly participatory, "egalitarian"[25] systems, while the mobilizational and inside
initiative models imply an extremely limited role for groups operating outside
official decision making channels.

The outside initiative model focuses on the creation of an issue by groups
outside the leadership and its movement from the public to the formal agenda.
Utilization of this technique of agenda building is largely consistent with our
definition of a public. In this model, individuals and groups outside the formal
decision making apparatus are able to introduce an issue before the public eye
and eventually to force the issue onto the formal agenda. The first stage of this
process consists merely of the articulation of a grievance. This is followed by
the specification stage, during which the grievance is converted into a set of
specific demands. The third stage involves the expansion of the issue to extend
public support to groups outside the initiating group. Strategies of expansion
vary depending on the characteristics of the issue and may include appealing to
certain specific sectors of the "attentive public," or attempting to appeal to the
entire "general public."[26] The final stage in the agenda building process is the
actual movement of the issue from the public agenda onto the formal agenda.[27]
It is important to recognize, however, that movement onto the formal agenda is
not directly relevant to the definition of a public and is thus not considered in
this study.

In contrast to the emphasis on the participation of outside groups and their role
in propelling an issue onto the formal agenda found in the outside initiative
model, the mobilizational model envisions the movement of an issue in the
opposite direction. In this model, the issue is initiated by the decision makers
themselves and thus starts out on the formal agenda. Thorough implementation
of the resulting policy, however, requires the active participation of certain
sectors of society, and thus, late in the decision making process, the decision
makers finally move the issue from the formal to the public agenda in order to
mobilize support for the final decision.

Similarly, the inside initiative model typifies systems with a minimum of participation from outside groups. In this model, government leaders or elites with direct access to the leadership initiate an issue and move it quickly onto the formal agenda, without its prior appearance on the public agenda. Furthermore, the government intentionally blocks the movement of the issue onto the public agenda, and implementation proceeds without the issue ever appearing in front of the public eye. Although outside elites may participate in the decision-making process, their participation is limited to inside channels and thus does not qualify as indicative of a public role.

While the authors postulate that all three models of the agenda building process may appear in any given system, one model is expected to predominate. Thus, in democratically-oriented, participatory societies, the outside initiative model of agenda building is expected to be dominant, while the inside initiative and mobilizational models are expected to appear less frequently. According to our definition of a public, autonomous public activity is expected to be highly correlated with the appearance of the outside initiative model of agenda building. John Lowenhardt has utilized this agenda building framework in his study of the ability of specialist elites to establish a public agenda during the Khrushchev and Brezhnev eras.[28] Lowenhardt's generalized conclusions will serve as a baseline for judging the possible changes in the agenda building capability of specialists under Gorbachev.

Lowenhardt utilizes the movement of an issue through the various levels of the press as the primary indicator of its position on the public agenda. In his model, the appearance of an issue in the Soviet press is an indication that the issue has made it past the "gatekeepers" and onto the public agenda. The expansion of this issue to larger segments of the population can thus be traced by looking at the movement of the issue from the low circulation specialized or local press into the high circulation mass media. In this paper, I also rely on the appearance of an issue in the press or media as an indicator of its presence on the public agenda.

On the basis of ten case studies, Lowenhardt concluded that specialists had been very successful in utilizing the inside initiative model to propel an issue onto the formal agenda. Their ability to employ the outside initiative model of agenda building, however, was found to possess two very serious limitations. First, Lowenhardt discovered that specialists' ability to publicize an issue was directly dependent on whether that issue fell within the specialists' area of expertise. Second, according to Lowenhardt's findings, specialists were unable to initiate public discussion on an issue which was of more than peripheral interest to the leadership. On issues of central concern to the leadership, specialists failed to publicize points of view which did not conform to regime preferences. It is these two restrictions on the agenda building capabilities of intellectual elites that I intend to test in this paper.

The issue of nuclear power is an unusual one because it is of interest to the scientific-technical intelligentsia, to the cultural elite, and to the central leadership. An examination of this issue also provides an opportunity to test whether the limitations on the public activities of scientific specialists and intellectual elites began to diminish under Gorbachev and thus to assess the extent to which the "outside initiative" model of agenda building can be considered to have been operative in recent years.

Case Study: Nuclear Power in the Post-Chernobyl Era

Background

At the 27ᵗʰ CPSU Congress in February of 1986, an ambitious program for the rapid expansion of the nuclear power sector was confirmed as a key element of the 12ᵗʰ Five-Year Plan (1986-90). During the 12ᵗʰ Five-Year Plan period nuclear capacity was expected to increase from 28,358 MW to 69,300 MW--an almost threefold expansion.[29] This projected growth in the nuclear power sector during the 12ᵗʰ Five-Year Plan, however, was not a departure from previous energy policy, but rather a continuation of a deliberate policy initiated in the late 1970s, aimed at shifting the balance of energy sources utilized domestically in the direction of nuclear power. This shift away from conventional energy sources toward nuclear power generation arose out of the economic conditions of the late 1970s; diminishing cost effectiveness in extracting and transporting conventional fuels, such as coal and oil, as well as rising world oil prices which increased the opportunity costs of utilizing oil domestically, led Soviet planners to see nuclear power as a logical alternative for domestic power generation. By 1985, forty-one nuclear reactors were in operation, and nuclear power accounted for 11% of the total power capacity of the Soviet Union.[30] It is within this context of an immense redistribution of the energy balance that the disaster at the Chernobyl Atomic Energy Station (AES) must be viewed.

The disaster at Chernobyl confronted the Soviet leadership with a costly dilemma. Would it be wiser to forge ahead with the planned expansion of the nuclear power industry, despite potential risks of public opposition or, even worse, another disaster, or to cut losses immediately and shift the entire long-term energy program in a new direction? The question was by no means a simple one: another disaster in the nuclear power industry could entirely discredit the viability of nuclear power generation and seriously damage the political standing of the current leadership. Furthermore, substantial popular opposition could conceivably retard construction, hinder the formation of an effective work force, and, in a worst case scenario, result in the abandonment of projects at a further point in development, involving an even higher loss in investment. The opposing alternative, however, would entail an immediate loss in billions of rubles already invested in projects now under construction and a

6-10 year lag period for switching to alternative energy sources, which could leave the Soviet Union with a significant energy shortage in the short-run.

Attitudes toward Nuclear Power and Safety Prior to Chernobyl

Prior to the Chernobyl disaster, the Soviet leadership had succeeded in creating an aura of absolute and unquestionable reliability and safety around the nuclear power industry. As one observer noted, an "official myth of (the) absolute safety" of the nuclear power industry was spread with incredible "zeal" throughout Soviet society over the two decades preceding Chernobyl.[31] In fact, the propagation of this official myth appears to have been so successful that even leading political and scientific figures fell under its sway.[32] Recent interviews with Soviet energy specialists confirm the absence of significant opposition to nuclear power among the scientific community prior to April of 1986.

Evidence of the complacency of leading political and scientific figures on this issue abounds. Such complacency was clearly demonstrated in 1984 when then President of the USSR Academy of Sciences, A. Aleksandrov, actively campaigned for a program to construct nuclear power and heating stations (ATETs) in close proximity to densely populated areas.[33] This proposal was in fact adopted and plans for the construction of at least six of these ATETs were incorporated into the 12th Five-Year Plan.[34] The overall disregard for the hazards implicit in nuclear power production in the early 1980s impressed foreign observers.[35]

Although individual concerns about low quality construction and lax safety regulations at specific nuclear power plants can be found in the central press prior to the Chernobyl disaster, no overt calls to reconsider the safety of nuclear power in general are in evidence. While authoritative assurances about the safety of nuclear power are plentiful, generalized concerns about its hazards were clearly taboo in the central media.

The Official Response to Chernobyl

While the extensive information published in the Soviet media describing the day-to-day conditions in the Chernobyl crisis zone following the accident convinced many in the West of the vitality and scope of the newly professed policy of glasnost, the total absence of attention given to general questions of nuclear safety in the media following the disaster may be said to demonstrate the exact opposite. An in-depth media search of the centrally published high circulation press in the months following the disaster yields an almost unbroken silence on general concerns about nuclear safety and the future of nuclear energy in the Soviet Union--quite striking when one remembers that this is a country which has just suffered the most catastrophic nuclear accident in history.

Instead of open discussion of the advantages and disadvantages of nuclear energy, the official response to the disaster from both political and scientific figures seemed to be intended to shift attention away from the question of the safety of nuclear power stations, and toward the international implications of nuclear disasters in general. Rather than discussing the issue of safety, the entire disaster was immediately transformed into a propaganda tool supporting Gorbachev's calls for nuclear disarmament. Over and over again, both political and scientific figures reiterated the "lessons of Chernobyl":

> The tocsin of Chernobyl sounds as a warning of the threat hanging over our planet. The Soviet programme for the complete abolition of nuclear weapons put forward on January 15, 1986, makes it possible to eliminate this threat altogether.[36]

Another approach to the crisis widely utilized in the Soviet press immediately following the accident was to deflect attention from Soviet performance by attacking the West for its hostile "propaganda" usage of the disaster to "whip up hysteria and panic"[37] and to generate a "hate campaign"[38] against the Soviet Union. This shift from defensive to offensive tactics also entailed extensive coverage of previous nuclear accidents purported to have taken place in the West, in order to demonstrate that Soviet nuclear facilities were in no way inferior to those in the West.[39] This tactic, as we shall see, however, appears to have had the unintended consequence of fueling fears about nuclear energy rather than settling them.

In fact, the blanket of secrecy surrounding the safety issue seems to have been so air-tight that any public concerns over the safety of rapidly expanding the nuclear power sector in the Soviet Union were completely and successfully blocked from appearing in any of the high circulation central press during the year and a half following the disaster. While numerous references were made to improvements in safety regulations for the nuclear power industry following the disaster, the Soviet leadership was also quick to assure the public that the disaster was caused by human error rather than technical deficiency,[40] and thus the nuclear program would continue at its planned pace.[41] Even the plan for building ATETs heating and power stations in close proximity to highly populated areas was reaffirmed on numerous occasions throughout 1986 and 1987.[42]

1988: An Abrupt Reversal

Suddenly, almost without warning, the nuclear issue was catapulted into the arena of public discussion in the first several months of 1988. *Moscow News* abruptly adopted the issue as a question for public debate and published the two dichotomous views on the prospects for nuclear energy side-by-side in its second issue of 1988, thus stimulating a debate which would be continued in the pages of *Moscow News* for the next several months.[43]

In the first three months of 1988, *Moscow News* published a total of eight views on the question of nuclear power in the USSR. Five contributors expressed reservations about the future of nuclear power in the Soviet Union, while only three defended the current energy strategy. While the defenders of the nuclear power program relied heavily on the contention that nuclear energy was the "only" solution to current energy problems in the Soviet Union, the arguments presented against the nuclear energy strategy displayed much greater variety and on the whole appear more persuasive than those of their opponents. Several economists argued that the shortfall in energy supplies caused by curtailing the nuclear energy program could feasibly be met through conservation and efficient utilization of conventional energy sources. Academician Sakharov lent his authority to the opposition by proposing the immediate suspension of all nuclear construction projects, and the adoption of a plan to build nuclear reactors underground. All of the opponents of the current nuclear power strategy stressed the hazards of first-generation nuclear power production, and based their arguments on the assumption that this safety hazard was beyond the limits of toleration.

While *Moscow News* was responsible for the first widely publicized debate over the future of nuclear power in the USSR, the debate was further fueled by the unexpected death of Academician Legasov in April of 1988. Valerii Legasov had led the clean-up operation at Chernobyl, and his suicide on the day following the second anniversary of the Chernobyl disaster seemed to confirm the worst suspicions of the opponents of nuclear power. In his memoirs, published in *Pravda*, Legasov condemned the incompetence, complacency, shoddy workmanship, and poor management which he believed were characteristic of the entire nuclear power sector.[44] The magnitude and scope of the shortcomings found in all aspects of nuclear power production led Legasov to the despondent conclusion that the obstacles to correcting the situation in the nuclear power sector were in all likelihood insurmountable.[45]

Following the death of Legasov, Belorussian writer Ales Adamovich quickly stepped forward to publicize Legasov's concerns and to call for a review of the Soviet Union's planned energy program.[46] Citing an interview just prior to Legasov's suicide, Adamovich quotes him as saying, "Another Chernobyl could happen at any station of that type. In any sequence."[47] In his blunt and extensive article in *Novyi mir*, Adamovich highlights the safety concerns of Legasov and other members of the scientific community, and blames departmental and personal factors in the nuclear power sector for impeding the correction of these problems. Adamovich calls upon concerned citizens to act, saying, "Our salvation requires drastic intervention by the public to stop this departmental madness . . ."[48] According to Adamovich,

> The atomic program must be reviewed. All who are not involved in departmental interests and scientists' games completely and categorically agree: atomic power construction is impermissible in the European part of our country. Those stations that pose a threat of catastrophe must be halted, closed and dismantled.[49]

Even more striking was the concurrent flood of announcements on the immediate suspension or cancellation of the construction of a sizable number of nuclear power plants currently in the planning or construction stages. On January 21, 1988, *Pravda* announced that the construction of an atomic energy station in the Krasnodar territory had been halted, and noted that a decision to cancel the project resulted from scientific concerns over the seismicity dangers in the region.[50] This announcement was quickly followed by a caustic article in *Komsomol'skaia pravda* attributing the decision to halt the project to the force of public opinion, and heavily deriding the ignorance of the public and the senseless loss of 25 billion rubles already invested in the project.[51] This article appears to be the first concrete confirmation in the central press that the nuclear energy program had run into strong public opposition. In fact, the author informs us that,

> The case of the Krasnodar Atomic Power Station . . . is not unique. . . . People are now writing to the Ministry of Atomic Energy from the Ukraine, from Belorussia, from all over the country. Two dozen operating atomic power stations and almost all of those under construction are being bitterly questioned by local residents. It's a chain reaction.[52]

Since the Chernobyl disaster, approximately forty reactors which were either in operation, under construction, or in the late planning stages have been either closed, cancelled, or suspended.[53] These include reactors in Archangelsk, Azerbaijan, Armenia, Bashkir, Chernobyl, Chigirin, Crimea, Gorky, Ivanova, Karelia, Khmelnitsky, Kiev, Krasnodar, Kursk, Minsk, Odessa, Rostov, Rovno, Smolensk, South Ukraine, Tataria, and Voronezh.[54] Even more important, after the first hints of widespread opposition to nuclear power in early 1988, references to a growing and increasingly influential popular movement became ever more common in the central press and the existence of strong anti-nuclear sentiment in the Soviet population could no longer be questioned. Thus, despite the government's success in limiting discussion of the nuclear power issue in the central press during the first several years following the Chernobyl disaster, large and vocal popular movements have apparently succeeded in coalescing in the various localities targeted for nuclear expansion.

In retrospect, it appears clear that 1988 marked a turning point in public discussions on the nuclear power issue. Whereas prior to 1988, open discussions of the problems associated with nuclear power and the popular movement opposing its continuation were cle..'ly restricted from appearing in the high circulation central press, the issue began to receive cautious attention in 1988 and finally flooded the media in 1989 and the early months of 1990. During 1989, discussion of the nuclear power issue became relatively common in the central press.[55] While support for the continuation of the nuclear power program appeared to continue to dominate the media, it no longer held a position of virtual monopoly.[56]

In order to understand and analyze the growth of the popular movement against nuclear power, it is necessary to delve beyond the minimal evidence available at the national level and examine the dynamics of this growing movement at the local level. Because Ukraine was the setting for the Chernobyl disaster and because it is expected to carry such a disproportionately large percentage of the nuclear burden,[57] the anti-nuclear movement in this locale has been particularly strong and vocal.

Nuclear Power and Ukraine

The drive to promote public discussion and eventually propel the question of the further expansion of the nuclear power sector onto the leadership's formal agenda was led by two sectors of the Ukrainian intelligentsia--the writers and the physical scientists. While each sector waged its own campaign during the first phase of the agenda building process, by late 1987 it became apparent that these two groups had tacitly decided to make profitable use of their complementary capabilities and work together to publicize their concerns about nuclear safety.

While certain members of the Ukrainian writers' community had voiced their opposition to nuclear power in Ukraine prior to the Chernobyl disaster, the disaster itself acted as a trigger event which mobilized writers with anti-nuclear sentiments to come forward and attempt to publicize their concerns. Immediately following the Chernobyl disaster, speeches by key figures in the writers' community stressing the dangers and unreliability of the "peaceful atom" began to appear with some frequency in the literary journal, *Literaturnaia Ukraina*. In August of 1987, a collective letter signed by seven leading writers protesting the construction of a new AES at Chigirin was published in *Literaturnaia Ukraina*. During the following months a clear attempt was made to expand the issue beyond an isolated and specific construction project to the more general issue of the expansion of nuclear power in Ukraine. In October of 1987, a leading

Ukrainian writer, O. Honchar, demanded bluntly, "who will say that each of these atomic power stations, built or planned, does not conceal another potential Chernobyl?"[58] It is interesting to note that, while Honchar's speech was eventually published in *Literaturnaia gazeta*, the above sentence was deleted from the text.[59]

While the writers' community was pressing ahead to publicize their concerns about nuclear safety, the scientific community appeared to be slowly building up steam to enter the fray. In March of 1987, a key scientific forum was held in Kiev which seemed to mark a turning point for scientific involvement in this issue. More than sixty scientists from various branches of both academic and industrial science were convened in Kiev to discuss whether construction of the partially completed fifth and sixth reactors at Chernobyl should continue or be cancelled. The discussion that followed was reported at length in *Literaturnaia gazeta*,[60] and appears to have been both frank and highly useful. At the end of the meeting a vote was taken as to whether to recommend continuation of construction, and it was reported that only two scientists voted in favor of the recommendation. The advice of the scientific community appears to have had some impact on the leadership, as the announcement of the decision to cancel construction of reactors five and six appeared simultaneously with the article describing this meeting in *Literaturnaia gazeta*.

It is highly likely that this scientific forum provided the opportunity for scientists with doubts about the wisdom of the Soviet nuclear energy program to meet other like-minded scientists and take their first step towards active participation in this issue. While individual scientists may have voiced isolated concerns about nuclear safety prior to this time, this appears to be the first occasion in which scientists banded together to advocate curtailment of the program for the rapid expansion of nuclear power plants.

During the remainder of 1987 other meetings of scientists and engineers were apparently held to discuss the nuclear power situation in Ukraine. A particularly important scientific meeting was held on August 25, 1987, to consider the planned expansion of the existing nuclear facilities at Rovno, Khmelnitsky, and South Ukraine. At this meeting, scientists agreed that the maximum capacity of an individual nuclear facility should not exceed 4000 MW, and thus recommended to the Ministry of Atomic Energy that the expansion projects at the Rovno, Khmelnitsky, and South Ukraine AES's be halted. During the fall of 1987, however, the Ministry of Atomic Energy reconfirmed its intention to continue all three expansions, and was even able to bring at least one of the new reactors on line by the end of the year.[61]

While no reports of these meetings appeared in the Ukrainian press at the time, details of the August 25 meeting (as well as other meetings) and its results appeared in a joint letter of thirteen leading scientists which was published in *Literaturnaia Ukraina* in January of 1988. The thirteen scientists strongly opposed the expansion of the three above-mentioned Ukrainian AES's, and complained that the USSR Ministry of Atomic Energy had completely disregarded the recommendations of the August 25 session. The Ministry's disregard for the scientists' advice and the apparent inability of the scientists to get their scientific view published in the press during the entire fall of 1987 led the thirteen to complain that "the problems connected with the development of atomic energy still remain a forbidden subject for public analysis and discussion in the press."[62]

By late 1987, it became apparent that writers and scientists were beginning to recognize the potential benefit of forming a coalition to publicize their concerns. In December of 1987, *Literaturnaia Ukraina* and the Ukrainian Communist Party newspaper *Radianska Ukraina* organized a conference entitled, "Scientific-Technological Progress and Morality," which brought together both writers and scientists to discuss ethical dilemmas associated with high technologies. At this conference, writers demonstrated a new strategy of utilizing scientific data to justify their stand on nuclear energy. Poet Ivan Drach noted that scientists had already calculated the maximum nuclear capacity sustainable on the remaining appropriate sites in Ukraine and had concluded that this maximum would be reached when the reactors currently under construction were finished, thus making any further expansion of nuclear power in Ukraine inadvisable. Thus, Drach continued, "all of us, as one community, should support the position of our leading scientists."[63]

This coalition between the scientific and literary communities would appear to have been highly advantageous for the promotion of the nuclear issue due to the complementarity between the skills of the two sectors. Such an alliance possessed both the media skills needed to gain public attention for their cause, and the scientific authority to combat claims that the anti-nuclear movement was fueled by ignorance and "technical illiteracy."[64] The attacks on the public opposition to nuclear power which appeared in *Komsomol'skaia pravda* and *Moscow News* focused heavily on the argument that only ignorance breeds fear. While the issue should be discussed "broadly and democratically," *Komsomol'-skaia pravda* advised that the debate should be carried out "accurately and in a well argued way."[65] Thus the real weapon of the scientific community was the possession of authoritative knowledge based on scientific facts, which could easily demolish the simplistic attack on the anti-nuclear lobby employed in *Komsomol'skaia pravda* and *Moscow News*.[66]

Following the authoritative letter of the thirteen scientists in January of 1988, the question of nuclear safety continued to hold its place in the Ukrainian public eye. On March 17, 1988, *Literaturnaia Ukraina* printed two more collective letters from members of the scientific community protesting the expansion of nuclear power in Ukraine. At least fifteen mathematicians, over half of whom were full or corresponding members of the Ukrainian Academy of Sciences, wrote to protest the lack of attention paid to Ukrainian specialist recommendations in the Soviet leadership's decision to continue the planned expansion of nuclear power in Ukraine. The second collective letter came from a group of cyberneticians complaining that only one side of the nuclear issue was being covered in the media, and that the central leadership was insensitive to the concerns of the Ukrainian scientific-technical community. The same issue of *Literaturnaia Ukraina* also noted that collective letters on this issue had been received from teachers at M.V. Lysenko Lvov State Conservatory and residents of Truskavets in the Lvov Oblast.

Despite the increased involvement of the Ukrainian scientific community in the publicized nuclear power debate, it is important to note that significant barriers to the open presentation of anti-nuclear views persisted in Ukraine well into 1988. While the debate appeared to be expanding, it was still largely carried out in the Ukrainian literary press and other lower circulation publications, and was apparently barred from the high circulation mass media in Ukraine. In 1988, the high circulation Ukrainian press continued to be used solely as a vehicle to publicize authoritative assurances on the wisdom of the nuclear power program, rather than as a forum for open discussion.[67] Further evidence of the inability of scientific opponents of nuclear power to present their views openly to the public may be found in a series of television programs focusing on the nuclear power issue which were aired in Ukraine during the spring of 1988. While Ukrainian scientists opposing nuclear power were nominally featured in at least one of the programs, the televised version was edited in such a way as to delete all coherent explanations of their concerns and even make the anti-nuclear scientists appear foolish and naive.[68]

While 1988 represented a turning point in public discussion on the nuclear power issue at the all-union level, 1989 was clearly the watershed year for Ukraine. During 1988, pressure for Ukrainian authorities to permit the restructuring of state-society relations already well underway in other parts of the Soviet Union intensified, and a change in climate for social activities began to be observed. While the introduction of glasnost, freedom of association, and official toleration of mass demonstrations in Ukraine lagged far behind Moscow, Leningrad, and the Baltic republics, due to the continued conservative party leadership in Ukraine, numerous participants in informal activities have noted that opportunities for independent activities began to expand significantly in 1988. Thus in 1988 early attempts to form informal groups, hold demonstrations, and publish oppositional views, while frequently met with hostility by Ukrainian authorities, were nonetheless observable. In 1989, however, independent collective activities finally emerged full-blown on the Ukrainian socio-political stage.

During 1988-89, the opposition to nuclear power in Ukraine underwent a tremendous transformation in character, shifting from intellectual discussions to a powerful mass-based movement. Signs of mass opposition to nuclear power in Ukraine began to be evident in 1988. On July 14, *Sotsialisticheskaia industriia* noted that over 20,000 local residents had signed a petition opposing the Crimean AES, then under construction. While providing few details, reports on AES cancellations in Ukraine also frequently noted the role of popular protest in these decisions. Interviews with Ukrainian environmental activists reveal that 1988 was marked by the emergence of small, informal environmental groups in numerous locales across Ukraine. One of the most important of these groups was Zeleniy svit.

In December of 1987, members of the Writers' Union and the Union of Cinematographers came together to form the environmental club, Zelenyi svit (Green World). Initial membership has been estimated at 10-30, and the club consisted almost exclusively of Kiev intellectuals (primarily writers and cinematographers). While remaining divided during much of 1988 on the question of whether Zelenyi svit should attempt to appeal to a mass audience, the members of the club quickly agreed that Zelenyi svit should be an all-republic organization. Thus, a conference of writers was held in Kiev in March of 1988 with the specific goal of bringing together ecologists from different regions of Ukraine and creating an all-Ukraine organization. While not limited to the nuclear power question, opposition to nuclear power in Ukraine constituted a key component of Zelenyi svit's acknowledged mission.

In 1989, opportunities to hold mass demonstrations, organize collectivities, and publish oppositional viewpoints expanded tremendously.[69] During this period, Zelenyi svit took the plunge from a narrow network of intellectual elites to form a broad umbrella organization sheltering a wide variety of environmental groups located across the entire Ukraine. In the spring of 1989, buoyed up by the successful election of Zelenyi svit member Yuri Shcherbak to the Congress of Peoples Deputies, a preliminary conference was held in Kiev to establish Zelenyi svit as an umbrella for the entire Ukrainian environmental movement. The founding congress of Zelenyi svit was finally held in Kiev in October, at which time a secretariat and council were selected to administer the all-republic organization. The council was to be composed of one representative of each of the member groups of Zelenyi svit, and ideally would meet monthly to coordinate activities and deal with technical questions. Council membership was initially approximately 100.

The almost exponential growth of a mass environmental and anti-nuclear power movement in Ukraine can be discerned in the number of people signing anti-nuclear petitions during 1989. Whereas 1988 saw petitions of tens of thousands of signatures, the petitions circulated in 1989 often included hundreds of thousands of signatures. Environmental groups proliferated quickly during 1989, and the Zelenyi svit secretariat estimated the number of groups under its umbrella at 200-300, in 1991. Journalist and Zelenyi svit secretariat member,

Andrei Glazovoi, contends that a referendum on the continuation of nuclear power in Ukraine would currently be likely to yield at least 90% of the population in opposition. The magnitude of the mass movement can also be discerned in its extraordinary level of success in achieving its anti-nuclear objectives during 1989 and early 1990.[70]

Yet intellectuals have continued to play a key role in mobilizing public opinion against nuclear power in Ukraine. Zelenyi svit continues to be directed by a secretariat of core activists composed almost exclusively of Kiev intellectuals. While physical scientists were slow to join the environmental movement in Ukraine, they now play a key role in Zelenyi svit. At least fifty percent of the Zelenyi svit secretariat is in fact drawn from the scientific community. Although scientists involved in areas closely linked to nuclear issues are still under-represented in Zelenyi svit, it has been estimated that at least fifty percent of the remaining scientists of the Ukrainian Academy of Sciences support Zelenyi svit.[71] Despite Zelenyi svit's shift towards a mass audience during 1989, scientific and intellectual activities have continued in parallel with mass activities. Thus, Zelenyi svit continues to sponsor scientific seminars and working groups of intellectuals to formulate scientifically-literate environmental programs for Ukraine.

During 1989, access to the press expanded significantly and scientific arguments against nuclear power in Ukraine became more common. In addition, however, new voices joined the printed debate, often bringing very little scientific knowledge and precision to the discussion. As glasnost expanded and nuclear power and the consequences of the Chernobyl disaster became accepted topics of public discussion, sensationalism also began to creep into the Ukrainian media. The horror stories of the radioactive contamination, some well-substantiated and others not, began to become almost common fare of the Ukrainian press and undoubtedly played a major role in the subsequent exponential growth of popular opposition to nuclear power. Officials representing the nuclear power industry have even privately complained that they are now being barred from much of the local press in Ukraine and Belorussia, and that the bias has shifted in the opposite direction.[72]

The impact of intellectually-generated demands and mass popular protest on environmental and nuclear power decision-making in Ukraine was substantial. In addition to numerous cancellations of nuclear reactors, Zelenyi svit had a clear impact on Ukrainian politics. In February of 1990, Zelenyi svit scored a remarkable (and largely unexpected) success when the Ukrainian Supreme Soviet accepted some of Zelenyi svit's most radical demands and proposals at a special environmental session. A month later, local elections brought environmentalists into the official political structure, with 6-10 Zelenyi svit members entering the Ukrainian Supreme Soviet, approximately 20 in the Kiev Soviet, and reports of even higher success rates in a number of areas outside Kiev. As Glazovoi has noted, however, the strength of the anti-nuclear power movement should not be gauged by Zelenyi svit's level of success in the 1989 elections since virtually all candidates from across the political spectrum jumped on the anti-nuclear power bandwagon. In the aftermath of the local elections, movement success became even more marked as local city and oblast soviets took authority into their own hands and voted to cancel unpopular nuclear expansion projects.

Zelenyi svit succeeded in mobilizing the masses and achieving concrete concessions from local, republic, and all-union decision-makers. Its intellectual elites drafted environmental proposals which were accepted almost without change by the Ukrainian Supreme Soviet, and environmentalism had clearly taken a solid place on the official Ukrainian agenda. In July of 1991, the Ukrainian Supreme Soviet moved to declare the entire Ukraine an "environmental disaster area," and to mandate a costly program to remedy the environmental crisis confronting the republic.[73] Having succeeded so well in its objectives, the question remains as to what role this movement may play in the future.

Implications of the Nuclear Power Case Study

The outside initiative model of agenda building, which implies extensive ability of independent actors to establish a public agenda, clearly fails to provide a useful interpretative framework for understanding the Soviet nuclear power debate in 1986-87. During the first eighteen months following the Chernobyl disaster, access to the media by intellectuals opposing official policy preferences was clearly severely restricted, thus indicating low official tolerance for the emergence of a public realm in the USSR.

In theory, there was little significant change during 1986-87 from the Brezhnev era baseline, despite the official introduction of the policy of glasnost. But events of 1988-89 dramatically reversed these findings. Although some complaints were still heard of restricted access to the media (especially television and radio), the nuclear power issue received wide coverage in the press during 1988-89 and claims that nuclear power advocates held an absolute monopoly on discussion of this issue were no longer valid. In fact, both sides of the debate now appeared in both the central and republican presses, and it would require an extensive content analysis study to determine which side was receiving more press coverage.

Because this topic has been fiercely debated since early 1988 and is still unresolved, it is unlikely that a mobilizational model of agenda building provides an accurate interpretation of the new glasnost in the debate in 1988-89. Such an interpretation would indicate the adoption of a high-level policy decision to curtail nuclear power production in the Soviet Union prior to the publication of anti-nuclear power views in early 1988. The continued construction of numerous reactors and official confirmation of plans to go forward with the Soviet Union's ambitious nuclear power program during the period 1989-90, however, make such an interpretation of the expansion of discussion unlikely.

I would contend that the dramatic expansion of the nuclear power debate during 1989-90 was indicative of an increased ability of intellectual elites to utilize the outside initiative model of agenda building. Cultural and scientific elites succeeded in creating a public agenda on an issue of critical and controversial importance to the Soviet regime. Yet not all the initiative came from the outside. Discussions with Soviet journalists have revealed that the expansion in the nuclear power debate might largely be attributed to a decision by the leadership to extend glasnost into the realm of nuclear power.[74] Early in 1988, tight censorship restrictions on the nuclear power debate were finally lifted, thus permitting both sides of the argument to be heard. The leadership's decision to permit open discussion of viewpoints contrary to official policy on an issue of critical importance to the regime is indicative of an expanding tolerance for the creation of a genuine public realm in the Soviet Union.

While a review of the central press indicates a shift toward an outside initiative model of agenda building, it is useful to move to the republic and local level to understand the complex strategy of agenda building used by various sectors of society in creating a public agenda on nuclear power. The three stages of issue initiation, specification, and expansion, postulated by Cobb, Ross, and Ross, can be clearly discerned in the Ukrainian movement. Initially it was the writers' community--not the scientific-technical elite--that took the lead in initiating the discussion of the nuclear safety issue following the Chernobyl disaster. Throughout the two year period following the disaster, the writers continued to play a key role in publicizing this issue. While the initial demands of the writers in 1986 were generally limited to the suspension of a particular construction project (the Chigirin AES), during 1987 the writers expanded their demands to encompass all ongoing construction of nuclear power installations in Ukraine. This expansion in the specification of demands may represent a tentative attempt to appeal to anti-nuclear sentiments within a larger Ukrainian "general public,"[75] rather than residents of the Chigirin area only.

During the expansion stage of the outside initiative model of agenda building, the initial identification group may also attempt to appeal to other articulate groups in society. It is in this way that a single opinion group may be transformed into a policy coalition. In the Ukrainian case, it appears likely that the writers' community recognized the presence of anti-nuclear sentiments among the scientific community (perhaps following the media coverage of the March 1987 scientific conference in Kiev), and attempted to take advantage of the authoritative weight of scientific opinion by expanding the issue into the scientific realm. Thus, the conference on "Scientific-Technological Progress and Morality," which was sponsored in part by the literary journal, *Literaturnaia*

Ukraina, marked a critical turning point in the writers' strategy for expanding the public discussion to new articulate sectors of society. While this policy coalition of writers and scientists appears to have been a "marriage of conveni- ence," the complementarity of the two groups provided an unusual potential for effective action on the agenda building front.[76]

During 1988 and 1989, however, a much more dramatic expansion of the nuclear power issue was undertaken in an effort to move beyond intellectual elites and appeal to a mass audience. Rather than simply appealing to serious local concerns over nuclear safety, anti-nuclear proponents attempted to reframe the issue in terms of Ukrainian national rights via the center so as to appeal to nationalist sentiments within the population. The letters published in *Literatur- naia Ukraina* in 1988 and 1989 demonstrated a growing tendency to represent the nuclear debate as a case in which the Soviet leadership had been insensitive to Ukrainian concerns and was unfairly thrusting the burden of nuclear power onto the Ukrainian people.[77] This again represented an attempt to move beyond discrete articulate audiences, and to appeal to a larger mass audience. The convergence of nationalist sentiment with mass popular opposition to nuclear power provided the explosive components for a powerful movement which the Soviet leadership had little success in defusing.

Conclusions: An Emerging Public in the USSR?

The results of this study indicate that the ability of intellectual elites to create a public agenda on controversial issues of high-priority to the regime increased substantially under Gorbachev. While restrictions and inequalities in access to the press and the right to organize collectivities outside the state undoubtedly persisted throughout the 1980s, there were indications that these obstacles to the creation and maintenance of autonomous publics were diminishing. In addition, the promulgation of new laws governing freedom of the press and association[78] represented a significant step toward the institutionalization of a public realm in the USSR. Thus, this case study may cautiously be interpreted as supporting the modernization interpretation of Soviet socio-political development in the Gorbachev period. Conversely, the obvious increase in regime tolerance for autonomous activities was indicative of a significant erosion of the genetic features of Leninism postulated in Jowitt's development model.

The emergence of a public realm in the USSR, however, represents only a small part of the story that unfolded in the late 1980s. While public activities did, in fact, increase substantially under Gorbachev, their emergence was accompanied by a dramatic erosion in state authority during the same period. Rather than simply pushing the old regime to incorporate larger sectors of society into the political process and struggling for the further democratization of the system, these new social forces challenged state authority and demanded not just reform, but revolution. By the beginning of the 1990s, the Soviet state was under seige at all levels and the system appeared on the verge of complete collapse. While modernization theorists had expected the gradual consolidation of an independent public realm in the USSR, they had not anticipated that the expansion in public activities might bring about the disintegration of the system. Furthermore, modernization theorists had not considered the possibility that these newly freed social forces might, in fact, push for a system of government based on principles other than democratic ones.

The emergence of elite and mass movements based on preexisting national identities was, in fact, not anticipated by either of the two leading theoretical schools. Most analysts had accepted claims that seventy years of Soviet rule had succeeded in supplanting preexisting national identities with a sense of citizenship in the Soviet nation. During the late 1980s, however, it became clear that these national identities were far from dead and, in fact, represented a powerful force for mobilizing society. Further research has revealed that even the anti-nuclear movements in most republics of the USSR incorporated a strong nationalist element, and, in some cases, might even be viewed as surrogates for hidden nationalist aspirations.[79] The strength of these preexisting national identities was largely overlooked in both the modernization and Leninist developmental path interpretations of communist development.

The survival of preexisting national identities in the USSR, despite the government's rigorous attempts to suppress them, provides a challenge to those analysts attempting to unravel the mystery of communist (and particularly Soviet) development. By assuming that these identities had long ago lost their potency, Sovietologists overlooked a key piece of the puzzle and were unprepared for the events of 1990-91. The reemergence of nationalism in the USSR demands a thorough reassessment of our previous understanding of the nature of communist development, as well as the nature of national identities and their susceptibility to government manipulation.

Notes

1. For an excellent review of this literature, see J. Keane (ed.), *Civil Society and the State* (London: Verso, 1988).

2. G. Poggi, *The Development of the Modern State* (Stanford, CA: Stanford University Press, 1978); K. Jowitt, "Inclusion and Mobilization in European Leninist Regimes," *World Politics* 28, no. 1 (Oct. 1975): 69-96.

3. K. Jowitt, lecture, University of California, Berkeley, 1987.

4. T. Rigby, "Organizational, Traditional, and Market Societies," *World Politics* 16, no.

4 (July 1964): 539-57; A. Kassof, "The Administered Society: Totalitarianism without Terror," *World Politics* 16, no. 4 (July 1964): 558-75; A. Meyer, "USSR Incorporated," *Slavic Review* 20 (1961).

5. See, for example, *Interest Groups in Soviet Politics*, eds. H.G. Skilling and F. Griffiths (Princeton: Princeton University Press, 1971); J. Hough, *The Soviet Union and Social Science Theory* (Cambridge: Harvard University Press, 1977). For a concise statement on the differences between Soviet and Western interest group politics, see: A. Janos, "Interest Groups and the Structure of Power: Critique and Comparisons," *Studies inComparative Communism* 12, no. 1 (Spring 1979): 6-20.

6. G. Lapidus, "Gorbachev and the Reform of the Soviet System," *Daedalus* 116, no. 2 (Spring 1987); B. Ruble, "The Soviet Union's Quiet Revolution," in *Can Gorbachev's Reforms Succeed?*, ed. G. Breslauer (Berkeley, CA: Berkeley-Stanford Publications, 1990); M. Lewin, *The Gorbachev Phenomenon* (Berkeley: University of California Press, 1988); F. Starr, "Soviet Union: A Civil Society," *Foreign Policy* 70 (Spring 1988); R. Lowenthal, "Development vs. Utopia in Communist Policy," in *Change in Communist Systems*, ed. C. Johnson (Stanford, CA: Stanford University Press, 1970).

7. D. Apter, *The Politics of Modernization* (Chicago: University of Chicago Press, 1965); K. deSchweinitz, *Industrialization and Democracy* (New York: Free Press, 1964); A. Gerschenkron, *Economic Backwardness in Historical Perspective* (Cambridge: Harvard University Press, 1962).

8. Lowenthal, "Development vs. Utopia," p. 34.

9. *Ibid.*, p. 38.

10. *Ibid.*, p. 54.

11. *Ibid.*, p. 112.

12. Lapidus, "Gorbachev and the Reform of the Soviet System," p. 6.

13. *Ibid.*, pp. 7-8.

14. *Ibid.*, p. 4.

15. K. Jowitt, *The Leninist Response to National Dependency* (Berkeley, CA: Institute for International Studies, 1978), p. 36.

16. *Ibid.*, p. 48.

17. See, for example, E. Durkheim, *The Division of Labor in Society* (Glencoe, IL: The Free Press, 1964); K. Polanyi, *The Great Transformation* (Boston: Beacon Press, 1957);

Karl Marx and Friedrich Engels, "Preface to a Contribution to the Critique of Political Economy," *Basic Writings on Politics and Philosophy*, ed. L. Feuer (London, 1969); T. Paine, *Rights of Man* (New York, 1967); A. de Tocqueville, *Democracy in America* (New York: Modern Library, 1981); G. Poggi, *The Development of the Modern State* (Stanford, CA: Stanford University Press, 1978).

18. Jowitt, "Inclusion and Mobilization in European Leninist Regimes," p. 71.

19. *Ibid.*, p. 71.

20. Kenneth Jowitt, lecture, University of California, Berkeley, Fall 1987.

21. It should be noted, however, that this ability to publicize an issue is being employed here as an indicator of a public, and is not necessarily a defining feature of a public.

22. R. Cobb, J. Ross and M. Ross, "Agenda Building as a Comparative Political Process," *American Political Science Review* 50, no. 1 (March 1976): 126-38.

23. *Ibid.*, p. 126.

24. *Ibid.*, p. 127.

25. Cobb's use of the term "egalitarian" appears to refer to democratic or pluralistic societies, but its exact meaning is never specified.

26. Cobb's distinction between an "attentive public" and a "general public" focuses on the political literacy and sophistication of the former relative to the latter.

27. Note that movement onto the formal agenda does not necessarily imply a favorable outcome in the final decision by the leadership itself.

28. John Lowenhardt, *Decision Making in Soviet Politics* (New York: St. Martin's Press, 1981). Lowenhardt examined ten case studies previously researched by a number of Western scholars and attempted to determine the conditions under which specialist groups in the Soviet Union had been able to utilize the outside initiative model of agenda building.

29. Judith Thornton, "Soviet Electric Power After Chernobyl: Economic Consequences and Options," *Soviet Economy* 2, no. 2 (April-June 1986): 139.

30. *Ibid.*, p. 139.

31. Sergei Voronitsyn, "The Chernobyl Disaster and the Myth of the Safety of Nuclear Power Stations," *Radio Liberty* (202/86), p. 1.

32. Lapidus notes that "Widespread complacency in scientific and political circles concerning the safety of nuclear power further contributed to an environment in which belief in the possibility of nuclear accidents was minimized; distinguished Soviet physicists would later acknowledge that they never thought such an event was possible." Gail Lapidus, "KAL 007 and Chernobyl: The Soviet Management of Crises," *Survival* (May-June 1987): 216.

33. Gubarev, "S legkim parom" (With a Little Steam), *Pravda*, Jan. 30, 1984. In this article, Gubarev quotes Aleksandrov as recommending that ATETs be constructed in "several hundred" population centers throughout the Soviet Union.

34. For a list of reactors under construction in 1986, see Thornton, "Soviet Electric Power After Chernobyl," pp. 133-37.

35. Robert Campbell noted that "the combination of large size, desire to use by-product heat, and commitment to large-scale use of the breeder, combine to produce, what would seem to an outsider, an extraordinary safety hazard in the form of extremely large plants using novel technology, located in close proximity to large population concentrations. The factors that inhibit this line of development in the United States do not seem to operate in the Soviet case. Robert Campbell, *Basic Data on Soviet Energy Branches* (Santa Monica, CA: Rand N1332DOE, 1979), cited in Thornton, "Soviet Electric Power After Chernobyl," p. 145.

36. Editorial, "The Lessons of Chernobyl," *New Times*, 1987, No. 18: 2.

37. Yuri Zhukov, "Nevol'noe samorazoblachenie" (Unintentional Self-exposure), *Pravda*, May 6, 1986, p. 4.

38. G. Arbatov, "Bumerang" (Boomerang), *Pravda*, May 9, 1986, p. 4.

39. For example, see "Avarii na atomnykh stantsiiakh" (Accidents at Atomic Stations), *Izvestiia*, May 5, 1986 p. 4. The author claims that in the US (in 1979 alone!), more than 2,310 nuclear accidents took place.

40. "Report of Special Politburo Meeting on Chernobyl," issued July 20, 1986, reprinted in *Soviet Economy* 2, no. 2 (April-June 1986): 180-85.

41. The commitment to continue the planned expansion of nuclear power was reiterated frequently by Andranik Petrosyants, Chairman of the USSR State Committee for the Utilization of Nuclear Energy. See, for example, TASS, April 25, 1987, reprinted in *Foreign Broadcast Information Service*, *(FBIS)*, Soviet Union, April 28, 1987.

42. See, for example, TASS, March 11, 1988, reported in *Radio Liberty* (108/88).

43. This debate appeared in *Moscow News*, 1988, Nos. 2, 7, 9 and 11. Several months

later, *Moscow News* also printed an interview with anti-nuclear writer Ales Adamovich (1988, No. 29) and a set of responses to this interview from *Moscow News* readers (1988, No. 36).

44. Valerii Legasov, "Moi dolg rasskazat' ob etom..." (It Is My Duty to Tell About This...), *Pravda*, May 20, 1988, p. 3.

45. Legasov noted that "After being at Chernobyl I drew the unequivocal conclusion that the Chernobyl accident was the apotheosis, the summit of all the incorrect running of the economy which had been going on in our country for many decades." *Ibid.*, translated by *FBIS*, May 20, 1988, p. 57.

46. Ales Adamovich, "Chestnoe slovo, bol'she ne vzorvetsia, ili mnenie nespetsialista" (My Word of Honor, No More Explosions, Or the Opinion of a Nonspecialist), *Novyi mir*, 1988, No. 9: 164-79; Ales Adamovich, "My Word of Honour, No More Explosions," *Moscow News*, 1988, No. 29: 10.

47. Adamovich, "Chestnoe slovo," p. 164.

48. *Ibid.*, p. 166.

49. *Ibid.*, p. 171.

50. K. Aksenov, "Tishina nad Perepravnoi" (All Quiet Over Perepravnaia), *Pravda*, Jan. 21, 1988, p. 6.

51. V. Umnov, "Tsepnaia reaktsiia" (Chain Reaction), *Komsomol'skaia pravda*, Jan. 27, 1988, p. 2.

52. *Ibid.*, translated by *Current Digest of the Soviet Press*, *(CDSP)* (1988), Vol. 40, no. 3: 9-10.

53. In a lecture at the University of California, Berkeley, Soviet energy specialist Aleksandr Kalinin noted that at least thirty-nine reactors had been closed or cancelled since the Chernobyl accident (Sept. 1990).

54. Decisions to close or cancel nuclear power stations have occurred at the all-union, republic and local levels. Announcements of closures and cancellations may be found in the following sources: *Archangelsk* - Radio Moscow (2/14/90) announced decision of city and oblast soviets to halt construction; *Azerbaijan* - Radio Moscow (10/28/88) announced cancellation; *Armenia* - *Kommunist* (Armenian, 10/8/88) announced decision to close station as quickly as possible; TASS (3/17/89) announced both reactors shut down; *Bashkir* - Radio Moscow (2/27/90) reported that 99% of local population voted against continued construction of AES in referendum (unknown whether this referendum implied an official decision to cancel); *Chernobyl - Literaturnaia gazeta* (12/9/87) reported

cancellation of fifth and sixth reactors; *Pravda* (6/1/90) announced that an all-union commission had been established to work out plan to halt operation of reactors 1-3 as soon as possible; *Chigirin - Radianska Ukraina* (5/24/89) reported decision to convert station to conventional energy station; *Crimea* - Council of Ministers decision (early 1990) to use Crimean AES as operator-training facility confirmed in interviews with Ukrainian energy specialist V. Yegorovna and members of Zelenyi svit secretariat (June 1990); *Gorky* - City soviet decision to halt construction of station (early 1990) noted in interviews with local Gorky activists; *Ivanova* - Radio Moscow (4/16/90) reported decision of USSR Council of Ministers to cancel station; *Karelia* - TASS (2/22/90) reported decision of Karelian Supreme Soviet Presidium to suspend construction; *Khmelnitsky - Robitnicha gazeta* (5/20/89) quoted Deputy Chairman of Ukrainian Council of Ministers, V. Fokin, as saying that construction of reactors 5 and 6 had been halted; interview with Nagulko, Ukrainian Supreme Soviet representative from Khmelnitsky, revealed that Khmelnitsky oblast soviet voted for moratorium on operation and construction of reactors 2-4 (spring 1990); *Kiev - Robotnicha gazeta* (10/21/87) noted decision to cancel; *Krasnodar* - noted above; *Kursk* - TASS (4/20/89) noted USSR Council of Ministers' decision to cancel construction of sixth reactor; *Minsk - Izvestiia* (9/7/88) announced cancellation and conversion to conventional power station; *Odessa* - Chancen (12/87) interview with V. Legasov notes cancellation; *Robotnicha gazeta* (5/20/89) interview with V. Fokin, however, indicated station to be resited; *Rostov* - Radio Moscow (7/1/90) reported Rostov oblast soviet decision to halt construction; *Rovno - Robotnicha gazeta* (5/20/89) interview with V. Fokin noted decision to halt expansion; discussion with members of Zelenyi svit, however, indicated that construction was continuing (spring 1990); *Smolensk* - TASS (4/20/89) announced USSR Council of Ministers' decision to halt construction of fourth reactor; *South Ukraine* - Interviews with members of Zelenyi svit secretariat indicated that ministerial decision to cancel expansion was issued spring 1990; *Tataria* - TASS (4/27/90) reported Supreme Soviet of Tatar Autonomous Republic decision to halt construction; *Voronezh* - Vremya (5/16/90) announced that 96% of residents opposed construction in official referendum organized by oblast soviet.

55. Two of the most interesting articles on this issue may be found in *Novyi mir*, 1989, No. 4, and *Kommunist*, 1990, No. 2. Leningrad television also broadcast a daring and memorable indictment of the Soviet nuclear power industry on the popular show *Piatoe koleso* (April 1990).

56. It would be interesting to chart the changing balance in the publication of pro- and anti-nuclear power views in the central press by means of a content analysis study. Unfortunately, such a study is beyond the scope of this project.

57. According to Bohdan Nahaylo, while Ukraine occupied only 3% of the territory of the former USSR, it was the site of 25% of the Soviet Union's reactors and produced approximately 40% of the Soviet Union's nuclear capacity. Nahaylo, "Mounting Opposition in the Ukraine to Nuclear Energy Program," *Radio Liberty Supplement* (1/88), p. 2.

58. *Literaturnaia Ukraina*, Oct. 7, 1987, translated and excerpted in Nahaylo, "Mounting Opposition in the Ukraine to Nuclear Energy Program," p. 7.

59. *Literaturnaia gazeta*, Dec. 9, 1987.

60. K. Grigorev and S. Kiselev, *op. cit.*

61. TASS announced on Dec. 31, 1987, that the Khmelnitsky AES had begun operation. Noted in *FBIS*, Jan. 4, 1988, p. 46.

62. *Literaturnaia Ukraina*, Jan. 21, 1988, translated and excerpted in Nahaylo, "Mounting Opposition in the Ukraine to Nuclear Energy Program," p. 12.

63. *Literaturnaia Ukraina*, Dec. 17, 1987, translated and excerpted in Nahaylo, "Mounting Opposition in the Ukraine to Nuclear Energy Program," p. 9.

64. Umnov, *op. cit.*

65. *Ibid.*

66. See Nikolai Lukonin, "On the Defensive and on the Attack," *Moscow News*, 1988, No. 11: 10.

67. See, for example, the discussion of nuclear power by A. Lapshin, Deputy Minister of the USSR Ministry of Atomic Energy, and other top officials published in *Pravda Ukrainy*, Feb. 21, 1988, translated in *FBIS*, March 9, 1988, pp. 47-49.

68. This treatment of the anti-nuclear scientists was vociferously protested by fellow scientists in the pages of *Literaturnaia Ukraina*, May 12 and 19, 1988.

69. During 1989, mass demonstrations, while initially meeting with significant official resistance and repression, became part of the Ukrainian activist repertoire. The first mass demonstration in Kiev, numbering in the tens of thousands of participants, was not until November of 1989. This "meeting" was sponsored jointly by several key informal groups, including Zelenyi svit. Following this key breakthrough for Ukrainian activists, mass demonstrations became a regular feature of the Ukrainian political scene.

70. See note above for details on cancellations.

71. Estimate given by Ukrainian journalist, Andrei Glazovoi.

72. A content analysis study would be needed to confirm such a hypothesis. Interestingly enough, several Soviet institutes involved in radiation hygiene are currently collecting press articles (from Ukraine and RSFSR) with just such an objective in mind.

73. The Ukrainian Supreme Soviet decision was reported by Radio Moscow, Aug. 1, 1990.

74. This was confirmed in discussions with journalists at *Robotnicha gazeta* and *Leningradskii rabochii.*

75. Cobb, Ross and Ross, "Agenda Building," p. 129.

76. In reviewing the stages of initiation, specification, and expansion in the Ukrainian case study, the questionarises as to why the scientific community lagged behind the writers' community in promoting public discussion of the nuclear safety issue. One possible explanation is that scientists have the professional authority to attempt to present their views through inside channels, and thus do not feel the need to immediately turn to outside channels. In the Ukrainian case, an officially sanctioned conference in Kiev allowed the scientific community to voice its concerns about the continued expansion of the Chernobyl plant, and the recommendations of this conference appear to have had some impact on the final decision making process. In contrast, however, the August 25, 1987 meeting at which the Ukrainian scientists recommended against the continued expansion of the Rovno, Khmelnitsky, and South Ukraine facilities, proved entirely futile and the Ministry of Atomic Energy appears to have totally ignored the advice of the local scientific community. It is only after the scientists have failed to promote the adoption of their viewpoint in August of 1987, that scientists begin to utilize paths outside the official channels of decision making and attempt to make their point of view public through the local press. If this hypothesis is accurate, then it would explain why the writers' community turned immediately to outside channels, since its members lacked recognized authority on the nuclear question, while the scientific community was able to voice its authoritative views through existing inside channels, and did not see the need to turn to outside channels until later in the game.

77. See: Nahaylo, "More Ukrainian Scientists Voice Opposition to the Expansion of Nuclear Energy Program," *Radio Liberty* (135/88).

78. Law on the Press adopted by USSR Supreme Soviet, June 12, 1990. Text published in *Izvestiia*, June 20 1990. Draft Law on Public Associations published in *Pravda*, June 4, 1990.

79. In my doctoral dissertation, Social Mobilization in Post-Leninist Societies: The Rise and Fall of the Anti-Nuclear Power Movement in the USSR, I examine the linkage between anti-nuclear protest and nationalist aspirations in Lithuania, Armenia, Ukraine, Crimea, Tatarstan and Russia. Using detailed case studies from these republics (and semi-autonomous regions), I argue that anti-nuclear and nationalist demands were intimately intertwined in all of the non-Russian territories of the former USSR investigated. The degree to which the two platforms overlapped, however, varied across republics, with the strongest linkage being found in Lithuania and Armenia. I discuss reasons for the linkage between the two causes and variations across republics.

The Quest for Rational Labor Allocation within Soviet Enterprises: Internal Transfers Before and During Perestroika

Kathryn Hendley

An essential aim of the economic reforms undertaken in the late Gorbachev period was to make the economy more efficient. One of the most critical proving grounds for these reforms was the workplace. More specifically, in order for the Soviet Union to stand any chance of competing in the world economy, the productivity of labor had to be enhanced. Prior efforts to stimulate productivity, whether through tightening labor discipline or enhancing material incentives, had proved largely unsuccessful.

There are a number of reasons why the Soviet economy has been plagued by low levels of productivity. The aging nature of the capital stock mandates a high level of manual labor,[1] and the retooling of factories has traditionally been a low priority for planners.[2] Perhaps more important has been the practice of allocating the available work force. Traditionally, Soviet managers have met demands from above for increased output by hiring more workers. All too often these additional workers stood idle most of the time and were sprung into action only when the enterprise began "storming" to meet the plan targets.[3]

Although such practices appear irrational when viewed through Western eyes, they represent a completely rational response to the incentive system under which Soviet managers operated. The basic features of this system are well known. They included evaluation in terms of gross output rather than net profits; linking the wage fund of the enterprise to the aggregate number of workers; and legal norms that favored workers' rights to retain the same job rather than management's right to allocate workers in the most rational manner.

With the onset of the most recent economic reforms in the former Soviet Union, these constraints began to fall away, to be replaced by those arguably

The research reported on in this paper was financed in part by grants from the International Research and Exchanges Board, the Department of Education and the Center for German and European Studies of the University of California, Berkeley. The author would like to thank Michael Burawoy, Richard Buxbaum, Robert Kagan, Gail Lapidus, Peter Maggs and Susan Solomon for helpful comments on an earlier version of this paper.

more conducive to the introduction of a market. Perhaps the most important change was the stipulation that increases in the wage fund were now to be permitted only when there had been an increase in output.[4] Thus, the wage fund was no longer automatically bumped up when more workers were hired. Rather, the wages for these additional workers were to come out of the existing wage fund. This, combined with the demographic data indicating that the work-age population was actually shrinking in major urban centers,[5] provided a powerful incentive for Soviet managers to use the workers they had more efficiently.

Management was also legally constrained in its ability to reallocate its work force.[6] As a general principle, the law permitted changes in the basic conditions under which a person worked only with his or her prior consent. Obtaining this consent could be time consuming; if not done properly, the courts could force management to rescind the changes and reinstate the worker to his or her former job. While hardly an insurmountable burden, managers often found it easier just to hire additional workers than to reorganize the workers they had.

With the February 1988 changes to the labor law, these legal restrictions on intra-enterprise transfers were greatly eased.[7] This statutory change was introduced as part of the much-heralded policy of "freeing-up labor resources" (*vysvobozhdenie trudovykh resursov*),[8] which was designed to rationalize the work force by allowing managers to lay off redundant workers and to redistribute those remaining in a more rational manner. Policy makers estimated at the time that, by the year 2000 as many as 40 million workers would be affected.[9] Yet the vast majority were not to be laid off, but reallocated within the same enterprise so as to enhance efficiency.[10] Thus, the ability of Soviet managers to transfer workers quickly and easily assumed critical importance to the overall success of economic reform.

On another level, the issue of intra-enterprise transfers highlights one of the basic tensions underlying perestroika, namely that of efficiency versus individual rights.[11] All societies struggle with how best to balance these competing interests. In the former Soviet Union, at least in the work place setting, concerns of efficiency have generally taken a back seat to the protection of workers' interests.[12] Indeed, some Western commentators have gone so far as to argue that this was one of the linchpins of the "social contract" between state and society.[13] However, as the successor states move toward a market economy, this balance is obviously being reevaluated and readjusted. The law governing internal transfers represented one element of this readjustment process and illustrates the overall trend toward giving greater weight to efficiency concerns.

The purpose of this article is to examine how the legal constraints on management's ability to reallocate its work force have changed and what impact the easing of the legal (and other) constraints has had in practice. I begin by outlining the law both before and after the February 1988 changes. As we will see, it was not only the substance of the law, but also the attitude of the courts in implementing that law that took on a decidedly pro-management or, perhaps more accurately, a pro-efficiency tilt with the introduction of these new statutory provisions. I then go on to assess practice. To my surprise, I found that these changes had little effect on the behavior of Soviet managers. The incidence of internal transfers remained basically the same both before and after the February 1988 amendments to the labor law. The widely-predicted massive internal rationalizations of enterprise workforces failed to materialize. This leads me to question why managers were so reticent. Both structural and cultural explanations can be advanced. While each of these is plausible, none is ultimately convincing.

Evidence of the Law

In determining the substance of the law, one must examine the three basic sources of Soviet law: statutory law, Supreme Court "guiding explanations" and decrees, and case law.[14]

Statutes. The first and most important of these sources is statutory law. Labor relations in the Soviet Union were governed by the Fundamental Labor Legislation of the USSR and the Union Republics (the "Fundamentals"), adopted in 1970,[15] and the labor codes of the union republics, most of which were adopted in 1971.[16] As the name suggests, the Fundamentals set forth the basic principles of labor law and served as the basis for the more detailed union republic codes. As a result, these codes did not vary much among republics[17] and, for the sake of simplicity, I have relied on the labor code of the Russian Republic (the "RSFSR Labor Code").[18]

Supreme Court interpretations. The "guiding explanations" (*rukovodiashchee raz"iasnenie*)[19] and decrees (*postanovlenie*) issued periodically by plenary sessions of the Supreme Courts of the USSR and the RSFSR constitute the second category of evidence. Their importance as a source of law is well recognized among Western experts on Soviet law.[20] The USSR and RSFSR Supreme Courts have each issued a series of decrees interpreting the provisions governing internal transfers of the Fundamentals and the RSFSR Labor Code, respectively.[21] As N.Iu. Sergeevna, a member of the RSFSR Supreme Court, has stated, their purpose is to instruct the lower courts as to how to resolve commonly encountered issues.[22]

Case law. Finally, I have relied on the published decisions of Soviet courts at various levels on cases of internal transfers. Objections to using case law in order to understand Soviet law can and have been raised on two grounds. Some have argued that the cases reported are too few to permit general conclusions to be drawn.[23] Decisions are reported in the bi-monthly *Bulletin of the Supreme Court of the USSR* and the monthly *Bulletin of the Supreme Court of the RSFSR*, and the actual number of cases dealing with internal transfers or even labor law issues more generally is relatively small. However, it is important to keep in mind that the cases published are carefully selected and are intended to have instructional value for the lower courts.[24] Thus, at the very least, these decisions represent an important indicator of what the law is intended to be.

I have supplemented these decisions with references to other cases described in scholarly articles. Sometimes these articles are written by judges who report on what is going on in their courts[25] and sometimes they are written by scholars who enjoy unusual access to court records.[26] Both sources provide insights otherwise unavailable to outsiders. Again, this evidence cannot be accepted unquestioningly, but it can be valuable in providing confirmation of trends in court behavior.

The value of case law has also been questioned on the grounds that, because the Soviet Union has a civil law or Romanist legal tradition, judges cannot make law. The implication is that, in contrast to countries with common law tradition, precedent carries little weight in civil law countries.[27] The first problem with this argument is its assumption that the Soviet Union is a "civil law" country. Certainly, for many years this was the conventional wisdom. However, as the dissimilarities between the Soviet legal system and the traditional "civil law" systems of Europe became more apparent, an ever-increasing number of Western scholars of Soviet law began to argue that a new designation was needed for the Soviet legal system and its progeny. They argue that these countries should be regarded as having a "socialist law" tradition.[28] Others continue to hold to the characterization of the Soviet Union as a "civil law" country, though, at this point, that is clearly the minority position.[29]

Regardless of whether the Soviet Union is categorized as a "civil law" or "socialist law" country, the unimportance of judicial decisions cannot be assumed. While on a formal level, both "civil law" and "socialist law" theory admonishes that the decision of a court is binding only on the parties and has no precedential value, in practice, reliance by other judges and litigants on prior decisions is commonplace.[30] That this is true in the Soviet context is apparent from the *Kommentarii k zakonodatel'stvu o trude*, the official commentary to the Fundamentals and the RSFSR Labor Code.[31] In support of their interpretations, the commentators consistently refer to previous court decisions.[32]

The Law Governing Transfers Prior to 1988

The law governing internal transfers was based on the fundamental principle of contract law that neither party to a contract can unilaterally change its terms. Following this logic, the Fundamentals and the RSFSR Labor Code provided that a worker could not be transferred without his or her consent.[33] The apparent simplicity of this rule was, however, deceptive, for the full implications of this single principle were greatly affected by definitional issues.

Definitional Issues

The first of these was the definition of transfer. Under the pre-1988 law, a "transfer" (*perevod*) was deemed to have occurred when management demanded that the worker perform "other work" (*drugaia rabota*) or be relocated to a different "place of work" (*mesto raboty*) not stipulated in the labor contract, or when management unilaterally changed the "essential conditions of labor" (*sushchestvennie usloviia truda*) for the worker. Such "transfers" were permitted only with the consent of the worker. Notwithstanding the fact that, according to prominent Soviet labor law scholars, the term "other work" was to be broadly construed,[34] management was by no means hamstrung by the law. Management could change the worker's "workplace" (*rabochee mesto*) or alter non-essential conditions of labor at its discretion.[35] Such changes were defined as "shifts" (*peremeshchenie*) and, in contrast to "transfers," did not require the worker's consent.[36]

Thus, the critical issue for management when contemplating a reorganization of the workplace in order to enhance efficiency was whether the changes made would be construed as "transfers" or "shifts." Management preferred the latter because no consent was required, while workers obviously preferred to have changes categorized as "transfers" because it gave them a voice in their future.

The statutory law provided a basic guideline in making this distinction. The RSFSR Labor Code provided that:

> The shifting of a . . . worker to another work place in the same enterprise . . . without a change in specialty, qualifications, position or amount of pay, privileges, advantages and other essential conditions of labor shall not be considered a transfer to other work.[37]

The RSFSR Supreme Court clarified that "a change even if in only one of these conditions is a transfer to other work demanding the consent of the worker."[38] The approach taken in this statute of having a non-exhaustive list of essential conditions in labor gave rise to two distinct lines of cases. On the one hand, there were cases in which a condition listed in the statute (a "Core Condition") had been changed. On the other hand, there were cases in which management had changed a condition not listed in the statute, but which the worker believed to be essential.

Distinguishing between the two types of cases is useful because different levels of proof were required for each. For example, a worker who claimed that management had unilaterally changed a Core Condition did not have to prove that the condition was, in fact, essential. That was assumed. In contrast, a worker who made a similar claim based on a non-Core Condition first had to prove to the court that the condition was essential. In such cases, the presumption was that it was not essential and, consequently, that the change was not a transfer but merely a shift not requiring the worker's consent.

Changing Core Conditions

Cases involving changes in Core Conditions were often fairly straightforward. In many instances, management had clearly changed the worker's specialty, qualifications and position, thus giving rise to a transfer to which the worker's consent should have been sought. For example, demanding that a hotel administrator work as a floor supervisor (*dezhurnaia*) was held to be an illegal transfer by a trial court (*narodnyi sud*) in the Tadzhik SSR and the worker was ordered reinstated to her prior position.[39] Similarly, a Moscow suburban trial court held that sending a photographer to work as a third-class laboratory assistant was an illegal transfer and reinstated the worker.[40] In these cases, it was clear that the worker was being asked to do something to which he or she had not initially agreed, amounting to an attempt by management to change the labor contract without the worker's consent.

The changes in Core Conditions need not have been this dramatic in order to warrant a finding that the labor function had been changed. A murkier case was that of a woman who had been hired in 1971 to tidy up a research laboratory and, after a co-worker had been fired in 1975, was then assigned the additional duties of cleaning up after the laboratory animals. She argued that these duties had not been stipulated in her labor contract and that management could not therefore demand them of her without her prior consent. The RSFSR Supreme Court agreed, holding this to be a change in her labor function, i.e., a transfer, and ordered her reinstated to her prior duties. In this case (as in many others), there was no detailed written contract that could be consulted.[41] Instead, the plaintiff had only an oral agreement with management. In this case, the plaintiff's allegations were buttressed by the four years of employment during which she had not been asked to care for the animals. In such cases the worker makes an allegation as to the scope of his or her duties which must then be affirmatively disproved by management. Thus, the process itself favored workers by imposing a significantly heavier burden of proof on management.

In recent years, however, management became more creative and the courts more lenient. Take the example of a design engineer who was suddenly asked to prepare technical documentation for microfilm readers. Although this task was outside the circle of tasks he normally performed, it was part of his written job description (*dolzhnostnaia instruktsiia*). Despite the fact that this document came into existence well after the plaintiff had been hired and so could not possibly have served as the basis for the plaintiff's labor contract, it was this piece of evidence that ultimately persuaded the RSFSR Supreme Court that the demands of management did not constitute a change in the labor function. The court was unsympathetic to the estoppel argument it had found so persuasive in the 1976 case described above. This would seem to represent an attempt by the court to loosen the reins on management while continuing to pay lip service to the sanctity of the labor contract.[42]

The Core Conditions consisted not only of a worker's labor function (specialty, qualifications, position), but also of wages and privileges which likewise could not be changed unilaterally by management. A good example is the case of a worker who was moved from ordinary painting work to painting done on board a vessel. Despite the identical nature of the worker's duties, the RSFSR Supreme Court held it to be a transfer requiring the worker's consent because the pensionable age at the second job was 50 while it was 55 at the first. This change in the worker's pension rights was construed as a change in her privileges.[43] The case of a worker moved from his regular duties as a stoker in the boiler room of a fish factory to the boiler room of a dormitory attached to the factory provides yet another example of this tendency. Once again, the RSFSR Supreme Court was not swayed by the identical nature of the duties. Because the worker had received 12 days of vacation at the first assignment and only 6 days at the second, the Court held that his privileges had been altered. As a result, this new assignment was deemed to be a transfer and so could be carried out only with the worker's consent.[44]

Similarly, in a reference book for labor inspectors, R.Z. Livshits, a prominent Soviet labor law scholar associated with the Institute of State and Law of the USSR Academy of Sciences, wrote that a transfer requiring the worker's consent occurred when a worker's qualification level changed or even when his title changed. Even a seemingly innocuous change from "leading" engineer to "senior" engineer was considered a transfer.[45] Although some of these examples represent only marginal changes in a worker's everyday conditions, they are, nonetheless, unambiguous examples of transfer under the pre-1988 law. When Core Conditions were involved, the law governing internal transfers was very rigid. A worker had only to demonstrate that management had changed one of these Conditions without his consent in order to prevail.[46] Management's hands were tied. The presumption that these were Core Conditions, that they were fundamental to every worker's labor contract, was not rebuttable, but rather was absolute.

This formalism operated as a constraint on management efforts to reorganize its labor force in order to enhance productivity and efficiency. This is not to say that such reorganization efforts were never undertaken or were doomed to failure; rather, that the requirement of obtaining the consent of all affected workers placed a significant burden on management. It undoubtedly contributed to the longstanding practice of hiring additional workers rather than attempting to use those already available in a more rational manner.[47] However, the demographic trends of the 1980s made these extensive methods of increasing output rather outdated,[48] and should have persuaded management to find intensive methods of stimulating growth. Their failure to do so indicated the level of resistance or perhaps just the inertia of management when confronted with the need to rationalize the labor force.

Management was not entirely to blame. Recognizing the need to reallocate the work force in a more efficient manner, Soviet policy makers could have amended the law so as to loosen the constraints on management. At the very least, the presumption that the Core Conditions were essential could have been made rebuttable. This would have allowed management to embark on wholesale reordering of the work force under appropriate circumstances without having to worry that the process could be held up or even reversed by disgruntled workers. However, such changes in the law were introduced only in February 1988.

Changing Non-Core Conditions

The dynamics were quite different when dealing with changes in non-Core Conditions. In such cases, the worker was faced with the presumption that the condition was not essential and so could be changed at the discretion of management. In order to overcome this presumption, the worker had to prove that the condition was an integral part of his contract with management. Oftentimes this boiled down to the worker's word versus that of management. As was noted above, in such instances the procedural conventions favored the worker.

Reassigning workers. This can be illustrated by examining the succession of cases involving workers who had been moved from one subdivision (*strukturnoe podrazdelenie*) of an enterprise to another. Although some Soviet labor law scholars have argued that, under the pre-1988 law, such a change was a prima facie transfer requiring the worker's consent,[49] the weight of authority suggests otherwise. Both the USSR and RSFSR Supreme Courts have stated unequivocally that such changes were not to be regarded as transfers unless the parties had specifically agreed that a worker would be placed in a particular subdivision or shop or, as a consequence of the move, the worker's labor function changed.[50] Likewise, the pre-1988 editions of the *Kommentarii k zakonodatel'stvu o trude*, the primary reference source for those involved in the implementation of labor law, set forth the general rule that moves between subdivisions were generally to be considered "shifts" (*peremeshcheniia*) not requiring the worker's consent.[51]

This rule would seem to have enabled management to reallocate its work force among its subdivisions in a more rational manner. However, in practice it was virtually impossible to move a worker from one subdivision to another without affecting one or more of the Core Conditions.[52] In fact, management might have been in a better position had it simply acknowledged that a Core Condition had been altered. At least management would have been sure of the consequences of intra-enterprise redistribution. With respect to non-Core Conditions, the pre-1988 law required a case-by-case analysis of the nature of the particular labor contract.[53]

The published case decisions provide several relevant examples. A 1981 case involved a woman who had been hired as a barmaid for the Kosmos cafe in Volzhskii. After some time, the cafe was closed and she was assigned to work as a barmaid in the Kulinarie cafe. Despite the identical nature of the work, she refused to report to the new assignment and so was ultimately dismissed on grounds of absenteeism.[54] Although the trial court sided with management, the RSFSR Supreme Court reversed the finding, reasoning that the parties had specifically agreed to the plaintiff's working at the Kosmos, and she could not therefore be reassigned without her consent. It should be noted that there was no hard evidence of the parties' agreement, only the plaintiff's word. Yet the RSFSR Supreme Court viewed this as sufficient in the absence of contravening evidence. As the plaintiff could not be reinstated to her old job, the practical import of the decision was to give the plaintiff the right to refuse any proposed reassignment.[55]

A 1987 case was also decided in favor of the worker, but a different line of reasoning was employed; one that had also been sanctioned by the USSR and RSFSR Supreme Courts. The head (*nachal'nik*) of one technical design bureau was ordered to take over another such bureau within the same enterprise. Although the Minsk trial court ordered the plaintiff reinstated to his prior job, management appealed and the decision was reversed by the Minsk city appeals court, whose decision was then upheld by the Belorussian Supreme Court. The USSR Supreme Court disagreed, holding that management had illegally transferred the plaintiff. The Court reasoned that the duties of the two positions were sufficiently different to constitute a change in the labor function, clearly an essential condition of labor.[56]

The Court went on to offer management some unsolicited advice, which is interesting in its own right. It noted that Soviet law would have permitted the plaintiff to be laid off and implied that this would have been the more prudent path.[57] Although only dicta and therefore not binding on the parties, this language appeared to represent a shift in judicial thinking in favor of management. After all, a similar recommendation could have been made in the 1981 case discussed above, but was not. In fact, it would have been more appropriate given that the cafe where the petitioner initially worked had been closed, whereas the bureau originally headed by the 1987 plaintiff continued to exist.

Excluding workers from brigades. This empathy for the predicament of management is also reflected in a series of substantive pronouncements and case decisions of the USSR and RSFSR Supreme Courts in the mid-1980s on brigade membership.[58] Typically, a work, kicked out of his brigade by the other members, would challenge his exclusion on the grounds that it constituted a change in his essential conditions of labor.[59] From the worker's perspective, there is little difference between having his work situation changed unilaterally by management or by a majority vote of his brigade.

The issue first arose in a 1984 case decided as a case of first instance by the RSFSR Supreme Court.[60] The plaintiff was a woman who worked at a samovar factory as a second-class polisher and who had been kicked out of a brigade by a vote of its members. She claimed that this constituted a change in the essential conditions and so was illegal because she had not given her consent. In particular, she argued that her exclusion would result in a 50 percent decrease in her premium. The RSFSR Supreme Court found this to be not a transfer but rather a shift because she continued to work in the place and in the position and qualification level stipulated in her labor contract.[61] The Court further held that, in itself, a decrease in wages did not signify a transfer because her wages were based on a piece-rate system and so depended on the effort she herself expended.

The importance of this decision was reflected by the decision of the editors of the *Kommentarii* to include a detailed description of it in their analysis of the statute governing transfers.[62] Soviet labor law specialists criticized it on the grounds that the RSFSR Supreme Court failed to explain why changes in the wage level and the manner of working did not give rise to a transfer requiring the worker's consent.[63] After all, wages were a Core Condition.

Despite these apparent shortcomings, the USSR Supreme Court took the same line in its 1986 plenum. The Court decreed that:

> the relocation to individual work of a worker who had been ejected from a brigade by . . . its members is not a transfer that requires his consent, provided it does not change the character of the duties that are stipulated in the terms of the labor contract.[64]

The Court went on to note that such a change should be considered a transfer only if working in a brigade had been stipulated in the labor contract.[65] The USSR Supreme Court reconfirmed this rule in 1987.[66]

Thus, the rule developed for brigade exclusions appeared to be virtually identical to that articulated for non-Core Conditions. Yet the courts' attitudes when confronted with this issue demonstrate that the similarities were merely skin deep. Prior to this, the courts tended to interpret the term "essential conditions of labor" rather broadly. They usually appeared to be searching for a way to declare management's action to be a unilateral transfer, often resorting to small and seemingly inconsequential changes to justify their decisions. With brigade exclusions, just the opposite was happening, i.e., courts were going out of their way not to see a transfer when, from a common sense point of view, it would seem to be present.

One might argue that the courts' attitudinal shift was due to their greater respect for decisions of the work collective as opposed to those of management. Such an argument would seem to be undermined by the courts' consistent failure to distinguish between brigade exclusions and transfers. Although not readily apparent at the time, in retrospect it is clear that the Supreme Courts' attitude toward the brigade cases marked a major shift away from a preoccupation with workers' rights and a marked rise in concern with management's flexibility. This nascent shift in the balance of collective and individual interests was consummated with the legislative changes of February 1988.

The Law Governing Transfers After February 1988

The Substance of the Law

In February 1988, the provisions governing internal transfers were changed in parallel fashion in both the Fundamentals and the RSFSR Labor Code.[67] When analyzed for their impact on the principle of encouraging efficiency, these changes have been described as "highly progressive" by Soviet labor law specialists.[68] Management was now to enjoy more leeway when undertaking a reorganization of its work force. Not only were management's substantive rights enhanced in theory and practice, but the statutory language was clearer, thus offering more predictability.

Definition of transfer. The substantive changes to the law were threefold. First, the definitions of transfer and shift were tightened. While the basic distinction of transfer versus shift was retained, as were the legal consequences of the distinction, the statute now provided that a relocation to another subdivision or machine was also a shift, provided that the specialty, qualification level and position remained unchanged.[69] Thus, the determination of whether consent was required was now to be based solely on whether the labor function had changed. Changes in other conditions, regardless of whether previously regarded as "essential," were not taken into consideration.[70] Livshits was most complimentary of this aspect of the new law, writing that:

> Implementation of this rule is not particularly difficult. It is clear that it is forbidden to transfer a lathe operator to the position of a metal craftsman, an engineer to the position of a technician, a doctor to the position of a laboratory assistant, etc. The difficulty arises when there is a dispute over whether

the position to which the worker is being transferred is different from his previous position.[71]

Livshits relates the case of a fifth-level lathe operator (*tokar'*) who was relocated from a repair shop to a mechanical shop within the same enterprise. In connection therewith, certain conditions of labor changed, including the level of premiums and privileges. The change was not deemed a transfer because both before and after the worker was employed as a fifth-level lathe operator.[72] There is little doubt that, under the old law, such a change would have been considered a transfer requiring the worker's consent. Yet the courts did not completely abandon workers. Obvious cases, such as one in which a kitchen worker was required to work as a supply clerk, would still be recognized as transfers.[73]

When disputes arose over whether the labor function had changed, the critical piece of evidence was not the job title, but rather the written job description (*dolzhnostnaia instruktsiia*). If it included the newly-demanded duties, then the change would not be considered a transfer, regardless of the fact that management had never before requested them of the worker.[74] Furthermore, their absence was not necessarily fatal. In contrast to past practice, demands on the part of management that a worker master more advanced technology would likewise not be deemed to be transfers.[75]

These rules obviously favored management. After all, management controlled the content of the official job descriptions. A worker might have been hired and worked for many years without ever seeing this document. While the enterprise trade union committee could be called upon to approve these job descriptions, its role was strictly consultative.[76] Changes were solely within the purview of management. On a deeper level, these rules could help management by providing a degree of stability and predictability that was previously absent.[77] No longer was there any doubt that a worker's relocation within an enterprise to another division was a shift to be undertaken at management's discretion.[78] This is not to say that management had been given free rein, but rather that the scope of permissibility was clarified, thereby giving management the freedom to plan and implement reallocations of the workforce without having to look over its shoulders constantly.

Changes in "essential conditions of labor." The second major change in the law governing internal transfers concerns the legal consequences of management's unilaterally changing the "essential conditions of labor" (*sushchestvennye usloviia truda*). As was noted above, the pre-1988 law treated such changes as transfers requiring the worker's consent. While not eliminated, the nature of the legal constraint on management was lessened. The Fundamentals and the RSFSR Labor Code now provided that:

> A change in the essential conditions of labor is permitted in connection with changes in the organization of production and labor; provided that the specialty, qualification level and position remain the same. The worker must be notified of changes in essential conditions of labor--system and amount of wages, privileges, work regime, establishment or elimination of part-time work, change in job title, etc.--at least two months in advance.[79]

Thus, change in essential conditions of labor was now a distinct legal category, much like transfer and shift.[80] From the perspective of management, it fell in between these two. While managers were no longer required to obtain the worker's consent to the change in circumstances, they were not permitted to act unilaterally.

The law placed two limitations on management's ability to change a worker's essential conditions of labor: motive and notice. As to the former, changes were permitted only in connection with changes in the organization of production and labor (*organizatsiia proizvodstva i truda*). Unfortunately, the definition of this term varied depending on the circumstances.[81] The courts interpreted this term rather broadly and even sanctioned the relocation of workers in order to eliminate a conflictual situation at the workplace.[82] Yet management was not given a complete carte blanche. Indeed, the RSFSR Supreme Court emphasized the importance of having the trial court look into the reason for the change and in appropriate cases ordered that the prior conditions be reinstated where the change was motivated by personal animosity rather than the needs of production.[83]

The two-month notice provision could also be seen as a limitation on management's freedom of action. However, in practice, the courts implemented this provision in a remarkably non-formalistic manner which tended to favor management.[84] Rather than rescinding the changes or imposing some other remedy of deterrence, the RSFSR Supreme Court instructed the lower courts simply to shift the effective date of the change so as to satisfy the notice provision.[85] For example, in a case in which a worker's wage level was changed without notice, the court ordered management to maintain the old level for two months.[86]

This provision governing unilateral changes in essential conditions of labor by management represented a significant reduction in the rights of workers. In the past, if a worker's wages were reduced or any other essential condition of labor were changed without his or her consent, the worker could sue to have the prior conditions restored. This cause of action was now open to a worker only if management had acted maliciously. In all other instances, the worker needed only to be notified of the impending change. From management's perspective, this change was positive. It loosened the constraints, thereby permitting workers to be reallocated so as to enhance productivity. Yet the law was still far from perfect. The list of essential conditions remained non-exhaustive, which created a certain level of unpredictability for management.[87]

Consequences of workers' refusal to accede to changes. The third major change in the law was closely related to the second and also resulted in a cut back in worker's rights. The law now provided that workers who refused to continue working in light of changes in their essential conditions of labor could be dismissed.[88] The fact that they could be fired was nothing new. However, in the past, such dismissals were treated as layoffs, with all the customarily attendant procedural rights. A number of workers challenged their dismissals under the transfer statute, arguing that in fact they had been laid off. However, the courts have been uniformly unsympathetic to such claims, consistently upholding the dismissal as related to the refusal to accept a transfer.[89]

There are several reasons why this seemingly meaningless distinction was important from a worker's perspective. First, when dismissed pursuant to the transfer statute, a worker did not have the right to appeal his dismissal directly to the local trial court, but had first to challenge management's action in the commission for labor disputes (*kommissiia po trudovym sporam* or *KTS*) and the trade union committee (*profkom*). Only after failing to obtain satisfaction from one of these in-house bodies did the worker have the right to press his claim in court.[90] The courts strictly enforced this obligation to exhaust all administrative remedies.[91] This tended to discourage worker complaints, both because of the time and effort necessary and because of the low level of respect commanded by the *KTS* and the *profkom* among workers.[92] In addition, *profkom* consent was required for layoffs, but not for transfer-related dismissals.[93] Although I have argued elsewhere that the *profkom* generally acted as a rubber stamp for management,[94] the fact that its consent was required forced management to justify the dismissal and might well have deterred management from acting in haste. Finally, when laying off a worker, management was legally obliged to make a good-faith effort to find him a comparable job within the enterprise. If the worker alleged that this had not been done, management was forced to reinstate the worker unless it could convince the court that doing so was impossible.[95] In contrast, no such obligation obtained when a worker was dismissed because he or she refused to continue working when the essential conditions of labor had been changed. Thus, having a dismissal categorized as transfer-related (rather than as a layoff) was very much to the advantage of management.

The Law in Action

Having outlined how the law governing internal transfers has changed in recent years, I now turn to the question of what these changes have come to mean in practice. The language of the law and the limited evidence of its implementation through published case decisions indicate that the tide was turning in favor of management. The legal constraints on management's ability to rationalize its work force were greatly eased. At the same time, the incentive system was fundamentally reshaped such that hoarding labor was no longer helpful even in the short-term. Thus, I expected to find a substantial increase in the incidence of intra-enterprise transfers beginning in 1988.

Scholarly Opinion

Obtaining information about intra-enterprise transfers was not an easy task. The relevant data are not collected in any systematic fashion[96] and getting access to enterprises in order to gather the information myself proved to be an extremely difficult and lengthy process.

In the meantime, I approached Soviet labor law specialists. As the scholarly literature indicates, the issue of intra-enterprise transfers has truly captured their imagination and they were willing and eager to discuss the merits and potential long-range implications of the law. While they all agreed that it represented a triumph of efficiency over individual interests, they differed on the need and wisdom of this shift.

Some, while finding this development lamentable, recognized it as unavoidable. They argued that if Soviet industry was to become competitive or even profitable, management would have to have the unfettered freedom to reallocate its workforce based solely on considerations of efficiency.[97]

Most, however, viewed the new law as misguided.[98] Indeed, one scholar at the Institute of State and Law described it repeatedly as a "nightmare" (*koshmar*).[99] The head of the labor law sector of this Institute has written that, "[t]his amendment has made Soviet workers practically defenseless against in-house maneuvering by management."[100] For these and other scholars, the most grating element of the new law was that it gave management permission to change "essential conditions of labor" without any input from workers. Workers who could not stomach the changes were to be cast aside. Many regarded this expansion of the rights of the state at the expense of individual rights as inappropriate and even repugnant in an era in which the Soviet Union was ostensibly reconstituting itself as a law-governed state (*pravovoe gosudarstvo*).[101]

These scholars uniformly predicted that the new provisions would be a temporary aberration, i.e., that the law would be changed back to its old form in short order. Indeed, the draft Fundamentals prepared by scholars at the Institute for Soviet Structure and Legislation provided for intra-enterprise transfers to be treated as they were pursuant to the pre-1988 law. In particular, under its terms, management would no longer be permitted to change "essential conditions of labor" unilaterally. However, when the USSR Supreme Soviet took up the question of labor law in May 1991, the legislators limited themselves to revising the existing Fundamentals.[102] Although some elements of the 1988 amendments were changed back to their earlier wording,[103] the statutory provisions governing transfers were left untouched.

Why, then, was the law governing internal transfers changed in February 1988? These amendments came in connection with a center-driven campaign to rationalize the work force which was announced in a joint decree of January 1988.[104] The decree represented a first attempt to set up a safety net for workers released on grounds of redundancy. It focused on issues of labor placement, retraining and unemployment compensation. It mentioned intra-enterprise transfers only in the context of reallocating redundant workers. When the Fundamentals and the RSFSR Labor Code were amended a few weeks later to correspond with this decree, the relevant statute was changed fundamentally.

It is possible that the reasons will never be fully known. The legislative changes came in February 1988, well before the historic elections that would transform the Supreme Soviets of the USSR and the RSFSR into at least quasi-democratic institutions. In early 1988, the Supreme Soviets were still rubber-stamp operations, passing unanimously any piece of legislation placed before them. Thus, pursuing the question by talking with legislators proved to be useless.

More profitable were conversations with the various members of the working group who had drafted the amendments to the Fundamentals submitted to and approved by the Supreme Soviets in early 1988. The group included scholars from the most prominent legal and labor policy research institutes and representatives of the official trade union and the government. The stories they told were far from consistent. Just about the only thing they agreed on was that intra-enterprise transfers was one of their most contentious issues. What they could not agree upon is how the various parties lined up when the question was being debated. Sometimes I was told that it was the state (in the form of the State Committee on Labor and Social Questions or *Goskomtrud*) versus the official trade union. In this scenario, the state favored giving management complete free rein in reallocating its workers, while the trade union wanted to continue the practice of giving workers some say in their future. Others disputed this version, telling me that representatives of *Goskomtrud* and the trade union presented a united front in favor of enhancing management's flexibility and that it was left to the legal scholars to try and hold the line. These scholars were concerned not so much with the impact that the change might have on workers, but rather with the fact that it represented a rejection of the contractual theory underpinning the law itself.

What really happened is known only to the members of the group, but it is beyond dispute that the February 1988 changes to the law were the product of compromise. As B.P. Kurashvili of the Institute of State and Law has noted:

> it would be rash and dangerous not to see the contradictory, half-way, intermediate nature of the legislation that has been adopted. It is the form of a temporary compromise between radical and conservative approaches, between the initiators of fundamental reform and the inert bureaucratic apparat of management which resorts to the phraseology of perestroika in order to maximize their conservative positions and proposals.[105]

What is also beyond dispute is that the statute governing intra-enterprise transfers was considered important enough to fight over. After all, many provisions of the Fundamentals were amended pursuant to the February 1988 changes, yet it was always the transfer law that was mentioned first when I asked which of these were particularly difficult or controversial.

Incidence of Transfers in Enterprises

Scholarly concerns and the degree of controversy over the February 1988 statutory changes led me to hypothesize that the number of internal transfers at the initiative of management would have increased dramatically during the years following implementation, and that these transfers would be a subject of controversy within enterprises. When I finally obtained access to certain enterprises, I found just the opposite. The number of internal transfers had not changed and no big increase was expected in the near future. Furthermore, the reallocation of the work force in a more rational manner was neither a top priority for managers nor of particular concern to workers.

The evidence supporting these findings can be divided into three categories. The first and most important of these is a series of interviews conducted at six enterprises in Moscow and one in Kaluga between February and September 1990. The enterprises varied in terms of size and nature of production. All but one had more than 1000 employees and some had as many as 5000. The nature of production ranged from foodstuffs to textiles to plastics to electronics. The one constant element was the high percentage of manual labor, but in this these factories did not differ from the vast majority of Soviet industrial enterprises.[106]

When I visited these enterprises, I spent most of my time talking with management officials who were involved with personnel matters. On several occasions I was able to speak with workers, sometimes in groups and sometimes individually. My access to each enterprise was subject to different conditions and so the status of the officials with whom I spoke varied.[107] In most cases, I began with the in-house lawyer (*iuriskonsul't*), who would then arrange interviews for me with other officials. These often included the head of the personnel office, the head of the wage department and the chairman of the trade union committee. Sometimes this pattern varied. For example, at one Moscow enterprise, I met only with the general director. Although we met many times and he provided me with relevant documentation, he told me that he was not comfortable asking his subordinates to talk with an American researcher.[108] My trip to the Kaluga factory was organized by the plant sociologist, who set up interviews for me with relevant managers and workers once I had arrived.

Regardless of the circumstances, the responses of management officials to my questions about internal transfers were remarkably consistent. I was told that the number of such transfers had traditionally been low and that when workers were transferred it was almost always at their request. I was also told that the incidence of intra-enterprise transfers at the initiative of management had not increased in recent years. The actual numbers quoted were usually fewer than ten per year, constituting less than one percent of the work force. Although at one enterprise, the numbers were higher (between 20 and 30), this level had remained constant for the past five years and, as a percentage of the total work force, was still only approximately two percent.

My conversations with workers revealed that internal transfers barely registered on their list of priorities. They were preoccupied with wages, housing, labor conditions, pension rights and other issues of daily survival. Internal transfers were not something they worried about or even contemplated. I was impressed by the strong sense of loyalty they felt to the shop (*tsekh*) in which they worked. For them, being transferred from one shop to another would be akin to being transferred to another enterprise. They simply did not regard it as being within the realm of the possible. This indicated that neither the workers with whom I spoke nor any of their immediate circle of acquaintances had ever been transferred at the initiative of management.

Despite the fact that this information did not support my hypothesis, it nonetheless rang true. The very fact that I kept hearing the same story in different settings was, in and of itself, convincing. In addition, in virtually every interview, when I brought up the question of internal transfers, a look of utter surprise would come across the face of the official or worker with whom I was talking, as if he could not figure out why an American had come all this way to ask them about something so unimportant. Typically, they quickly grew impatient with my detailed questions on this topic. This attitude was not present when we were discussing layoffs or unemployment.

Commissions for Labor Disputes

The records of the commission for labor disputes (*kommissia po trudovym sporam* or *KTS*) and the trade union committee (*profkom*) form the second category of evidence relating to internal transfers. I reviewed such records in four enterprises.[109] As was noted above, a disgruntled transferee had to complain first to the *KTS* and, if not satisfied, to the *profkom* before he could petition the local trial court. Thus, the incidence of appeals of transfers to these in-house adjudicatory bodies would provide some insight into the overall incidence of transfers. A direct correlation would, however, be inappropriate, given the tendency of workers not to take legal action to enforce their rights, even when they have been clearly violated.[110]

Yet the data were so lopsided that it tended to buttress the claims made by management in interviews. The docket of the *KTS* was dominated not by claims of illegal transfers, but by wage disputes. My review of the minutes (*protokoly*) of *KTS* meetings at one Moscow textile factory with more than 1700 workers revealed not a single instance of a transfer-related claim over the ten year period 1980-90. Of the annual average of only four cases, more than 70 percent involved wage disputes.[111] The *KTS* records for 1989 and 1990 at a Moscow plastics factory with approximately 4000 workers revealed only one transfer-related claim out of the few cases (12 in two years) considered. That claim was not pursued to the *profkom* level. In a Moscow electronics enterprise with more than 5000 workers, the *KTS* averaged 13 cases annually for 1986-1990, of which on average nine were wage-related and two involved transfers. No significant increase was seen in 1988-1990. Indeed, the only year when there were more than two transfer-related cases (in 1986 there were no transfer claims) was 1987 and that was due to three virtually identical petitions that the *KTS* ultimately dismissed on jurisdictional grounds.[112] If those cases are taken out of the calculation, the annual average of transfer-related cases would drop down to 1.6. Despite the fact that the *KTS* sided with management in more than half of all these transfer-related claims, not a single one was appealed to the *profkom*.

Moscow Trial Courts

The final category of evidence is composed of the actual trial records. I obtained permission from the Ministry of Justice to examine the records of Moscow trial courts. Most of my work was done in the archives of the trial court of the Proletarskii region of Moscow. A number of large factories are located in this area, including one of the largest auto plants in the Soviet Union, ZIL (*Zavod imeni Ligacheva*). My review of all labor-related cases indicated that claims of illegal transfer were very rarely filed. In 1983, only one of the 42 labor-related cases involved a transfer. In 1986, none of the 48 labor-related cases raised this issue. In 1988, two of the 52 labor-related cases involved transfers, while in 1989, no claims of illegal transfer were made.[113]

As with the information from the *KTS* records, relying on the number of cases filed to prove the presence or absence of a given phenomenon is problematic in the Soviet context. However, when taken together with evidence from interviews and enterprise records, it tended to buttress the conclusion that intra-enterprise transfers were far from common and certainly legal disputes over such transfers were rare indeed. This evidence also suggested that the incidence of such transfers had not increased significantly following the easing of legal and other constraints on management's ability to reallocate its work force.

Reasons for Management Inaction

This raises the obvious question of why management failed to redistribute workers in order to enhance efficiency and thereby increase productivity. After all, not just the legal constraints were eased, but the entire incentive system had been changed. The system was now running more or less on a profit basis. Managers were to benefit from increased productivity and, more importantly, were to be penalized for attempting extensive rather than intensive methods of increasing output. Despite all this, managers seemed reluctant to embark on mass reorganization schemes.

A number of possible explanations seem plausible. It may be that managers were unaware of their new freedoms. Certainly this was true with respect to the easing of legal constraints. Within management (with the exception of the legal staff), I found few individuals who were well versed in the post-1988 labor law. Even those actively involved in personnel matters were unaware that the law now sanctioned unilateral changes in the "essential conditions of labor." Indeed, I found that managers continued to use the law as an excuse for inaction. When I would ask them about the possibility of rationalizing their work force, they often responded by telling me that their hands were tied by the law; that the paperwork required was too time-consuming; and that their well-intentioned efforts would only be countermanded by the courts.

Yet the law was only one element of a multifaceted incentive system. These same managers who were ignorant of the legal niceties tended to be extremely knowledgeable about wage issues. They understood only too well that they could no longer boost their wage funds by hiring more workers. Furthermore, the notion that the success of economic reform was directly linked to increased labor productivity and that productivity could be increased only by a more efficient allocation of the existing labor force had hardly been hidden away in the pages of dry scholarly journals. On the contrary, the issue had been trumpeted on the front pages of the mass circulation newspapers throughout the perestroika years. Thus, management reticence is not explained entirely by lack of knowledge.

Instead, it might have been more a matter of inertia on the part of management. Feather-bedding is a time-honored tradition in Soviet industry and was not likely going to be stamped out in a few years, despite the restructuring of the incentive system. It is only human nature to stick with the tried and true rather than delve into something new. Concern with efficiency in personnel matters was new for Soviet managers and it would take time for them to become accustomed to intensive (rather than extensive) methods of increasing productivity.

However, explanations centering on inertia and lack of knowledge are undermined by the fact that production-level managers had been active in promoting new forms of corporate organization. I spent the first two months of 1991 carrying out field research at a mid-sized Moscow enterprise and found that the chiefs (*nachal'niki*) of the shops were leading the charge to become independent of the enterprise.[114] They were fairly knowledgeable about the pros and cons of the various property forms now available and were eager to make use of these new opportunities. This makes their reticence in questions of labor allocations even more puzzling.

The absence of internal labor markets in Soviet enterprises provides yet another possible explanation as to why large-scale redistributions did not take place. There was no established procedure for posting available job openings and allowing workers to bid on them. Workers tended to stay in the same shop and often on the same machine for their entire working lives.[115] Their loyalties to the shop are stronger than to the enterprise. They were usually taken aback when I asked them whether they had ever considered transferring to another shop.

This shop loyalty is certainly understandable. Workers become accustomed to the production tasks and their co-workers and so tend to resist change. In the past, there was little economic incentive for intra-enterprise transfers. Output and prices were rigidly controlled and, as a result, management had little flexibility in setting wages. However, this situation was radically transformed by the onset of perestroika. For example, in one enterprise I studied, prices had been essentially decontrolled for the output of one shop, while they had not for other shops. As a result, the shop with decontrolled prices had greater flexibility in terms of increasing wages, and average wages in that shop were much higher than in the other shops. One might have predicted a flight from the lower-paying shops to this shop with higher wages. Not only was this not the case, but the workers outside of this higher-paying shop were generally unaware of the discrepancy. This suggests that shop loyalty has outlived its economic usefulness.

Also relevant is the tendency of production-level management to think only in terms of its own situation. This trend seemed to be intensifying under perestroika. For example, in one enterprise where I spent quite a lot of time, the shop managers were obsessed with ways to become independent of the central management of the enterprise. Each had a different scheme, geared to their production profile. Some were planning to reconstitute themselves as "small enterprises" (*maloe predpriiatie*), while others were enamoured of joint-stock companies or leasing arrangements. The common feature was the desire to be able to enter into contracts, i.e., to become a "legal person" (*iuridicheskoe litso*).[116] This trend toward boutique privatization only made the possibility of reallocations of workers on an all-enterprise basis in order to enhance productivity even more remote. Once the shops became "legal persons," any reassignment from one to another would be analogous to a reassignment from one enterprise to another and so would automatically be deemed a transfer requiring the worker's consent.[117] The high level of compartmentalization that has always existed in Soviet enterprises seemed only to be becoming more institutionalized as the various constituent parts of enterprises began seeking greater independence. The likelihood of transfers between these parts becomes ever more remote and more problematic from a legal point of view.

Thus, the question remains why Soviet managers failed to take advantage of the opportunities that became available to them to rationalize their workforces. Soviet scholars are also struggling to explain this behavior. Although not much has yet been written much about this phenomenon, in private conversations, these scholars stressed one or another of the explanations advanced above. Each of the explanations advanced is plausible, but none is ultimately convincing. Even taken together, they are not entirely persuasive. Perhaps neat explanations are simply not possible during the transition to the market. After all, such a transition is unprecedented and so we have no models to structure our expectations of the behavior of managers or workers.

Conclusion

On a superficial level, the change in the law governing internal transfers would seem to promote efficiency in labor allocation. Managers were now permitted to change a worker's "essential conditions of labor" unilaterally in order to enhance productivity, whereas prior to the February 1988 amendments to the Fundamentals and the RSFSR Labor Code, such changes would have been permitted only with the worker's prior consent. As a general matter, the law now provided management with a level of security and predictability that had been absent in the earlier law, which required case-by-case determination of virtually every issue. Furthermore, it was not just the language of the statutory law that provided a basis for optimism, but also the published case opinions and Supreme Court pronouncements. When viewed from management's perspective, the courts were becoming much more lenient, tending to search for a basis to side with management, whereas before the tendency had been just the opposite.

Yet the failure of managers to take advantage of their newly-granted flexibility in labor matters could no longer be explained by pointing to an incentive system that rewarded labor hoarding and other inefficient uses of manpower. The system was being fundamentally restructured such that redistribution of the existing work force would now be the rational response. The data available to date, albeit limited, indicate that such redistributions did not take place.

The inertia among Soviet managers, though troubling, is understandable. For years, their hands were tied from above. Now that these ties have been loosened (though still not completely removed), it is hardly surprising that managers are struggling to find their place in the new and constantly changing system.

Notes

1. See Silvana Malle, *Employment Planning in the Soviet Union: Continuity and Change* (London: Macmillan, 1990), pp. 183-88; David Lane, *Soviet Labour and the Ethic of Communism: Full Employment and the Labour Process in the USSR* (Boulder, CO: Westview Press, 1987), pp. 137-38.

2. See Anders Aslund, *Gorbachev's Struggle for Economic Reform* (Ithaca: Cornell University Press, 1989), p. 71; Ed A. Hewett, *Reforming the Soviet Economy: Equality Versus Efficiency* (Washington, D.C.: The Brookings Institution, 1988), p. 215.

3. While Western economists who study the Soviet Union have long argued that the practice of labor hoarding was common among Soviet enterprises (see Joseph S. Berliner, *The Innovation Decision in Soviet Industry* [Cambridge: The MIT Press, 1976], pp. 165-69; and Philip Hanson, "The Serendipitous Soviet Achievement of Full Employment: Labour Shortage and Labour Hoarding in the Soviet Economy," in *Labour and Employment in the USSR*, ed. David Lane [Brighton: Wheatsheaf Books, 1986], pp. 85-86), in recent years their Soviet counterparts have likewise acknowledged the widespread nature of this practice: see I.I. Gladkii, "Intensivnoi ekonomike--effektivnuiu zaniatost'," *Sotsialisticheskii trud* [hereafter *Sots. trud*], 1988, No. 5: 3; A. Kotliar, "Nuzhno li nam polnaia zaniatost'," *Pravda*, Nov. 21, 1989, p. 2.

4. See the Basic Provisions on the Composition of Wages To Be Included in the Cost Price of Production (Work and Services) at Enterprises of the USSR, Decree passed by the USSR Council of Ministers on Nov. 5, 1990, *Ekonomika i zhizn'*, Jan. 1991, No. 2: 14-15.

5. For a discussion of these troubling demographic trends, see V.G. Kostakov, "Zaniatost': defitsit ili izbytok?" *Kommunist*, 1987, No. 2: 78-79; Iu. Iakovets "Trudovoi potentsial obshchestva: tendentsii i perspektivy," *Sots. trud*, 1988, No. 8: 43-44.

6. Western commentators did not agree on whether the law was a meaningful constraint on Soviet managers. Some argue that it was, e.g., John N. Hazard, *Managing Change in the U.S.S.R.* (Cambridge: Cambridge University Press, 1983), pp. 86-92; Ger P. van den Berg, "Labor Law as a Restraint on the Soviet Economy," in *Soviet Law and Economy*, eds. Olympiad S. Ioffe and Mark W. Janis (Dordrecht, The Netherlands: Martinus Nijhoff Publishers, 1987), pp. 45-50. Others disagree, arguing that law was largely meaningless in the context of the Soviet workplace, e.g., Malle, *Employment Planning*, pp. 70-79; Nick Lampert, "Job Security and the Law in the USSR," in *Labour and Employment in the USSR*, ed. Lane, pp. 256-74.

7. *Vedomosti SSSR* (1988), No. 6, item 95; *Vedomosti RSFSR* (1988), No. 6, item 168.

8. There was a joint decree announcing the new campaign: "On Securing the Effective Employment of the Population, Improving the System of Job Placement and Increasing Social Guarantees for the Working People," *Pravda*, Jan. 19, 1988, pp. 1-2, trans. in *Current Digest of the Soviet Press* [hereafter *CDSP*] 40, no. 4 (Feb. 24, 1988): 1-4. See generally "Problemy ratsional'nogo i ekonomnogo ispol'zovaniia trudovykh resursov," (Round Table), *Sovetskoe gosudarstvo i pravo* [hereafter *SGiP*], 1987, No. 8: 36-52.

9. V. Shcherbakov, the chairman of the USSR State Committee on Labor and Social Questions (*Goskomtrud*) estimated that 35-40 million workers might be laid off in connection with the transition to the market economy. "Unemployment: Search for Work Abroad," *Izvestiia*, Oct. 13, 1990, trans. in *BBC Summary of World Broadcasts*, Nov. 2, 1990, p. A7. Others believed the number would be considerably lower, around 16 million. See A. Kotliar, "Nuzhno li nam polnaia zaniatost'," *Pravda*, Nov. 21, 1989, p. 2; V.I. Nikitinskii, "Pravovye voprosy vysvobozhdeniia izlishnykh rabotnikov," *Sots. trud*, 1988, No. 9: 59.

10. The joint decree announcing the policy (see note 8) explicitly indicated that management should provide for "job placement first of all within the enterprise." This sentiment was echoed by policy makers, e.g., "To Each According To His Work," *Trud*, Aug. 30, 1986, p. 2, trans. in *CDSP*, Oct. 24, 1986, 38, No. 39: 4 [interview with V.I. Shcherbakov, chairman of *Goskomtrud*]. A survey carried out at 55 enterprises revealed that 87% of managers questioned believed laid off workers should be redistributed within the same enterprise: Gladkii, "Intensivnoi ekonomike," p. 3.

11. Soviet labor law scholars were split on how this balance was to be struck. S.A. Ivanov was troubled by the favoring of efficiency over humanism. "Problemy ratsional'-nogo ekonomnogo ispol'zovaniia trudovykh resursov," *SGiP*, 1987, No. 8: 42. On the other hand, R.Z. Livshits and V.I. Nikitinskii supported an increase in management flexibility. "Reforma trudovogo zakonodatel'stva: voprosy teorii," *Sots. trud*, 1989, No. 1: 78-80. For a more general perspective on this balancing process, see Hewett, *Reforming the Soviet Economy*.

12. See David Granick, *Job Rights in the Soviet Union: Their Consequences* (Cambridge: Cambridge University Press, 1987), pp. 1-6.

13. E.g., Peter Hauslohner, "Gorbachev's Social Contract," *Soviet Economy* 3, no. 1 (1987): 56-60.

14. See William E. Butler, *Soviet Law* (London: Butterworth & Co., 1983), pp. 39-68.

15. The Fundamentals were translated in *The Soviet Union Through Its Laws*, ed. and trans. Leo Hecht (New York: Praeger, 1983), pp. 93-130. Since this English translation was published, however, the Fundamentals were amended several times. See *Svod zakonov SSSR*, Vol. 2, pp. 184-213, and *Trud*, May 21, 1991, pp. 1, 3.

16. These codes were adopted at a time when only one organizational form, namely that of the state enterprise, was available. In the past few years, there has been a virtual explosion in organizational forms, including cooperatives, leased enterprises, small businesses (*maloe predpriiatie*), joint-stock companies (*aktsionernoe obshchestvo*) and individual labor activities. V.I. Nikitinskii, a prominent Soviet labor law expert, questioned the applicability of existing labor legislation to these new organizational forms. V.I. Nikitinskii and V. Vaipan, "Pravovoe regulirovanie truda v usloviiakh mnogoobraziia form sobstvennosti," *Sots. trud*, 1991, No. 1: 80-88. He advocated expanding the scope of labor legislation to include these new property forms. However, the Fundamentals were amended in May 1991 and these issues were left unaddressed. *Trud*, May 21, 1991, pp. 1, 3. My research centers on state enterprises, to which the existing labor legislation clearly applied.

17. R.Z. Livshits argued that this system of having the republic level codes copy the substance of the Fundamentals ought to be abandoned. He argued that the Fundamentals should be relatively short and contain only the most basic principles of the legal regulation of labor and a list of the general social rights of workers. All remaining questions should be left to the discretion of the republic legislatures. "Trudovoe zakonodatel'stvo: poisk kontseptsii," *SGiP*, 1990, No. 7: 47-56, p. 52. There was a series of similar articles in journals attempting to lay the theoretical foundation for new labor legislation. See generally, V.I. Nikitinskii, "Perestroika fundamenta sistemy zakonodatel'stva o trude," *SGiP*, 1988, No. 4: 56-64; R.Z. Livshits and V.I. Nikitinskii, "Reforma trudovogo zakonodatel'stva: voprosy teorii," *Sots. trud*, 1989, No. 1: 80-85; Iu. Volegov, "Neobkhodimy radikal'nye izmeneniia," *Sots. trud*, 1989, No. 8: 91-96. The process of drafting new labor legislation was undertaken, but behind closed doors. The USSR Supreme Soviet passed certain amendments to the Fundamentals in the spring of 1991: *Trud*, May 21, 1991, pp. 1, 3, but these fell far short of the fundamental reworking of the legislation called for by these scholars.

18. The RSFSR Labor Code was translated by Preston M. Torbert in *The Soviet Codes of Law*, ed. William B. Simons (Alphen aan den Rijn, The Netherlands: Sijtoff & Noordhoff, 1980), pp. 681-760. The RSFSR Labor Code was amended a number of

times over the past decade. For the most recent version, see *Svod zakonov RSFSR*, Vol. 2, pp. 123-189.

19. *Iuridicheskii entsiklopedicheskii slovar'*, 1984 ed., s.v. "rukovodiashchee raz"iasnenie," by Kh.V. Sheinin.

20. See Peter Solomon, "The USSR Supreme Court: History, Role, and Future Prospects," *American Journal of Comparative Law* 38, no. 1 (Winter 1990): 136; Donald D. Barry, "The USSR Supreme Court: Recent Developments," *Soviet Studies* 20, no. 4 (April 1969): 511.

21. "Guiding explanations" of the USSR Supreme Court: "O primenenii v sudebnoi praktike osnov zakonodatel'stva soiuza SSR i soiuznikh respublik o trude," *Biulleten' Verkhovnogo Suda SSSR* [hereafter *BVS SSSR*], 1974, No. 3: 19-21; "O vypolnenii sudami postanovlenii plenuma Verkhovnogo Suda SSSR ot 18 oktiabria 1971," *BVS SSSR*, 1980, No. 3: 9-14; "O primenenii sudami zakonodatel'stva, reguliruiushchego zakliuchenie, izmenenie i prekrashchenie trudovogo dogovora," *BVS SSSR*, 1984, No.3: 24-33; "O primenenii sudami zakonodatel'stva o trudovom dogovore i povyshenii ikh roli v ukreplenii trudovoi distsipliny," *BVS SSSR*, 1986, No. 6: 8-11; "O vnesenii izmenenii i dopol'nenii v postanovlenie plenuma Verkhovnogo Suda SSSR ot 26 aprelia 1984," *BVS SSSR*, 1988, No. 3: 7-12.
"Guiding explanations" of the RSFSR Supreme Court: "O nekotorykh voprosakh primeneniia norm kodeksa zakonov o trude RSFSR o perevodakh i peremeshcheniiakh rabochikh i sluzhashchikh na druguiu rabotu," *Biulleten' Verkhovnogo Suda RSFSR* [hereafter *BVS RSFSR*], 1973, No. 3: 6-8; "O nekotorykh voprosakh primineniia sudami RSFSR zakonodatel'stva pri razreshenii trudovykh sporov," *BVS RSFSR*, 1987, No. 3: 12-16; "O vnesenii izmenenii i dopol'nenii v postanovlenie plenuma Verkhovnogo Suda RSFSR ot 16 dekabria 1986," *BVS RSFSR*, 1988, No. 10: 8-9; "O nekotorykh voprosakh primeneniia sudami RSFSR zakonodatel'stva pri razreshenii trudovykh sporov," *BVS RSFSR*, 1989, No. 7: 9-15.

22. Interview, Moscow, February 1991. See also Kh.B. Sheinin, "Rukovodiashchie raz"iasneniia plenuma Verkhovnogo suda SSSR," *SGiP*, 1980, No. 9: 70-78.

23. E.g., Blair A. Ruble, "The Soviet American Comparison: A High Risk Venture," *Comparative Labor Law* 2, no. 4 (Winter 1977): 252.

24. E.g., Yuri Luryi, "The Scientific-Technical Revolution and Soviet Labor Legislation," in *Soviet and East European Law and the Scientific-Technical Revolution*, eds. George Ginsburgs, Peter B. Maggs and Gordon B. Smith (New York: Pergamon Press, 1981), p. 217.

25. E.g., V. Ershov, "Rassmotrenie sporov, sviazannykh s perevodami na druguiu rabotu," *Sovetskaia iustitsiia* [hereafter *Sov. iust.*], 1989, No. 1: 21-22 [the author is chairman of the Zheleznodorozhnyi district people's court of Moscow]; V. Kovalev and

S. Ryzhkov, "Sudebnaia praktika primeneniia zakonodatel'stva o trude (obzor)," *Sov. iust.*, 1989, No. 15: 7-9 [the authors are members of the Rostov oblast court]; V. Gliantsev, "Spornye voprosy rassmotreniia del, sviazannykh s perevodom i peremeshcheniiem rabotnikov," *Sov. iust.*, 1989, No. 18: 5-7 [the author is a member of the RSFSR Supreme Court]; G. Shabalina, "Spory o vosstanovlenii na rabote (obzor kassatsionnoi i nadzornoi praktiki)," *Sov. iust.*, 1990, No. 13: 19-21 [the author is a member of the Kirov oblast court].

26. E.g., A.I. Stavtseva, "Kommentarii sudebnoi praktike po trudovym sporam," in *Kommentarii sudebnoi praktike za 1979 god*, eds. E.V. Voldyreva and A. Pergament, pp. 3-35; R.Z. Livshits, "Izmenenie trudovogo dogovora," *Sots. trud*, 1988, No. 8: 55-60; I. Orlo and Kh. Siigur, "Primenenie v sudebnoi praktike zakonodatel'stva, reguliruiushchego trudovoi dogovor," *Sovetskoe pravo*, 1985, No. 5: 333-41.

27. E.g., Blair A. Ruble, "Full Employment Legislation in the U.S.S.R.," *Comparative Labor Law* 2, no. 3 (Fall 1977): 181-82.

28. E.g., John Quigley, "Socialist Law and the Civil Law Tradition," *American Journal of Comparative Law* 37, no. 4 (Fall 1989): 781-808; Harold J. Berman, "What Makes 'Socialist Law' Socialist?" *Problems of Communism* 20, no. 5 (Sept.-Oct. 1977): 24-30.

29. *Ibid.* Given the rapid unravelling of the Soviet bloc and, indeed, the Soviet Union itself over the past few years, scholars may well abandon the category of "socialist law" and return the Soviet Union and the countries of Eastern Europe to the "civil law" fold.

30. John Henry Merryman, *The Civil Law Tradition*, 2d ed. (Stanford: Stanford University Press, 1985), pp. 34-38; Martin Shapiro, *Courts* (Chicago: Chicago University Press, 1981), pp. 126-56. See generally, John P. Dawson, *The Oracles of the Law* (Ann Arbor: University of Michigan Press, 1968).

31. *Kommentarii k zakonodatel'stvu o trude* (Moscow: Iuridicheskaia literatura, 1988). Previous editions of the *Kommentarii* were published in 1976, 1980, 1984 and 1986. Unfortunately, there has not been an edition that takes into account the February 1988 amendments to the Fundamentals and the RSFSR Labor Code.

32. The commentator for the sections dealing with internal transfers is V.I. Nikitinskii, a well-respected authority on Soviet labor law from the Institute of Soviet Legislation.

33. Article 13, Fundamentals; Article 25, RSFSR Labor Code.

34. R.Z. Livshits and V.I. Nikitinskii, *An Outline of Soviet Labour Law* (Moscow: Progress Publishers, 1977), p. 47.

152   *Kathryn Hendley*

35. For a helpful analysis of the difference between "place of work" (*mesto raboty*) and "workplace" (rabochee mesto), see V.I. Krivoi, "Mesto raboty po sovetskomu trudovomu pravu," *SGiP*, 1989, No. 11: 56-58.

36. For a discussion of how this definitional issue has developed over time, see L.Iu. Bugrov, "Perestroika i razvitie sovetskogo zakonodatel'stva o perevodakh na druguiu rabotu," *SGiP*, 1988, No. 12: 38-39.

37. Art. 13, Fundamentals; Art. 25, RSFSR Labor Code.

38. *BVS RSFSR*, 1974, No. 3: 6. Similar language can be found in the 1974 decree of the USSR Supreme Court. *BVS SSSR*, 1974, No. 3: 20. This language was reprinted in the 1976 edition of the *Kommentarii k zakonodatel'stvu o trude*, p. 51. Interestingly, it is not in the 1986 edition of the *Kommentarii*, p. 39, perhaps indicating a more restrictive view.

39. "Primenenie sudami zakonodatel'stva pri rassmotrenii trudovikh sporov: Obzor sudebnoi praktiki," *BVS SSSR*, 1980, No. 6: 7.

40. A. Kniazev, "Razreshenie sudami sporov o vosstanovlenii na rabote (obzor nadzornoi praktiki)," *Sov. iust.*, 1983, No. 12: 11 [the author is a procurator].

41. *BVS RSFSR*, 1976, No. 10: 2.

42. *BVS RSFSR*, 1984, No. 2: 1.

43. Livshits and Nikitinskii, *An Outline of Soviet Labour Law*, p. 48.

44. *BVS RSFSR*, 1974, No. 2: 1-2.

45. R.Z. Livshits, *Spravochnik pravovogo inspektora truda* (Moscow: Profizdat, 1979), pp. 58-60.

46. A group of Soviet labor law experts have argued that, "[t]he consent of an employee is a sine qua non of any transfer to other permanent work. It is even necessary when the new job is better paid or carries a higher status." V. Glazyrin, V. Nikitinskii, N. Maksimova, A. Yarno, *Soviet Employee's Rights in Law*, trans. James Riordan (Moscow: Progress Publishers, 1987), p. 30. A worker may convey his consent to a transfer in written or oral form or by voluntarily complying with the demands of management. However, if a worker files a complaint but follows management's orders, this is not considered evidence of consent. E.g., V. Ershov, "Rassmotrenie sporov, sviazannykh s perevodami na druguiu rabotu," *Sov. iust.*, 1989, No. 12: 21; *BVS RSFSR*, 1973, No. 1: 3.

47. See generally "Problemy ratsional'nogo i ekonomnogo ispol'zovaniia trudovykh resursov," *SGiP*, 1987, No. 8: 36-52.

48. See generally Kostakov, "Zaniatost': defitsit ili izbytok?" *Kommunist*, 1987, No. 2: 78-82; Iakovets, "Trudovoi potentsial obshchestva: tendentsii i perspektivy," *Sots. trud*, 1988, No. 8: 46-48.

49. E.g., Krivoi, "Mesto raboty," p. 58; I. Orgo and Kh. Siigur, "Primenenie v sudebnoi praktike zakonodatel'stva, reguliruiushchego trudovoi dogovor," *Sovetskoe pravo*, 1988, No. 5: 335.

50. *BVS SSSR*, 1977, No. 4: 41; *BVS SSSR*, 1974, No. 3: 20; *BVS RSFSR*, 1974, No. 3: 6. See generally Livshits, *Spravochnik*, p. 67.

51. *Kommentarii* (1976), p. 53; *Kommentarii* (1986), pp. 39-40; *Kommentarii* (1988), pp. 43-44.

52. L.Iu. Bugrov, *Sovetskoe zakonodatel'stvo o perevodakh na druguiu rabotu* (Krasnoiarsk: Izdatel'stvo krasnoiarskogo universiteta, 1987), pp. 55-56.

53. In 1980, the USSR Supreme Court reported that the lower courts had found 69.9 percent of transfers to other work to be illegal and attributed this to the lack of clarity in the law and the need for case-by-case analysis. *BVS SSSR*, 1980, No. 6: 7. Iu.A. Dmitriev has also criticized the law on these grounds. *Poniatiia "normal'nye," "vrednye," "opasnye," "tiazhelye," "sushchestvennye" usloviia truda i ikh pravovoe znachenie* (Leningrad, 1984), pp. 19-21.

54. Art. 17, pt. 4, Fundamentals; Art. 33, pt. 4, RSFSR Labor Code.

55. "Obzor sudebnoi praktiki po grazhdanskim delam," *BVS RSFSR*, 1981, No. 7: 10-11.

56. *BVS SSSR*, 1987, No. 2: 11-12.

57. Art. 17, pt. 1 Fundamentals; Art. 33, pt. 1 RSFSR Labor Code. For a discussion of layoffs, see Kathryn Hendley, "The Ideals of the *Pravovoe Gosudarstvo* and the Soviet Workplace: A Case Study of Layoffs," in *Toward the "Rule of Law" in Russia?: Political and Legal Reform in the Transition Period*, ed. Donald D. Barry (Armonk, NY: M.E. Sharpe, Inc., 1992).

58. Work brigades existed for much of Soviet history, but only in the late 1970s and early 1980s did they begin to be organized on a formal basis and to be used as a tool to increase productivity. See generally Peter Rutland, "Productivity Campaigns in Soviet Industry," in *Labour and Employment in the USSR*, ed. David Lane (Brighton, UK: Wheatsheaf Books, 1986), pp. 200-202.

59. The rules governing the creation of, and the exclusion of members from, production brigades are set forth in "Tipovoe polozhenie o proizvodstvennoi brigade, brigadire, sovete brigady i sovete brigadirov," *Biulleten' Goskomtruda*, 1984, No. 7.

60. *BVS RSFSR*, 1984, No. 7: 12-13.

61. The Court was able to conclude that the plaintiff's place of work (*mesto raboty*) had not changed because its analysis stopped at the level of the shop (*tsekh*). A shop is composed of several sub-units (*uchastki*) and, while the plaintiff continued to work in the same shop, following her ejection from the brigade she was assigned to a different sub-unit. Before, she had worked in the decorating sub-unit, whereas afterwards she was assigned to the sub-unit that polishes samovars before nickel-plating. Thus, the Court had to work very hard to come to the conclusion that a transfer had not occurred.

62. *Kommentarii* (1986), pp. 40-41.

63. E.g., Bugrov, *Sovetskoe zakonodatel'stvo*, pp. 55-57.

64. "O primenenii sudami zakonodatel'stva o trudovom dogovore i povyshenii ikh roli v ukreplenii trudovoi distsipliny," *BVS SSSR*, 1986, No. 6: 10-11. The 1988 edition of the *Kommentarii* (p. 45) refers to this decree rather than to the 1984 decision of the RSFSR Supreme Court.

65. *BVS SSSR*, 1986, No. 6: 11.

66. "Primenenie sudami zakonodatel'stva o trudovom dogovore: obzor sudebnoi praktiki," *BVS SSSR*, 1987, No. 2: 40.

67. *Vedomosti SSSR*, 1988, No. 6, item 95; *Vedomosti RSFSR*, 1988, No. 6, item 168.

68. Livshits and Nikitinskii, "Reforma trudovogo zakonodatel'stva," p. 78.

69. For a helpful discussion of the implications of these changes, see Krivoi, "Mesto raboty," pp. 53-60.

70. See Livshits, "Izmenenie trudovogo dogovora," pp. 56-58; V. Kovalev and S. Ryzhov, "Sudebnaia praktika primeneniia zakonodatel'stva o trude (obzor)," *Sov. iust.*, 1989, No. 15: 8.

71. Livshits, "Izmenenie trudovogo dogovora," p. 56.

72. *Ibid.*, p. 58.

73. Kovalev and Ryzhov, "Sudebnaia praktika," pp. 7-8.

74. E.g., Livshits, "Izmenenie trudovogo dogovora," p. 56; V. Gliantsev, "Spornye voprosy rassmotreniia del, sviazannykh s perevodom i peremeshheniem rabotnikov," *Sov. iust.*, 1989, No. 18: 5.

75. Gliantsev, "Spornye voprosy," p. 5.

76. As a part of my field research, I examined the minutes of trade union committee (*profkom*) meetings at three Moscow enterprises. At only one of these enterprises did I find instances of changes in the official job descriptions having been submitted to the *profkom* for approval.

77. E.g., Livshits, "Izmenenie trudovogo dogovora," p. 59; Bugrov, "Perestroika i razvitie sovetskogo zakonodatel'stva," p. 38.

78. Livshits and Nikitinskii were critical of the fact that the law seemed to allow management to reassign a worker to another shop even where the labor contract specified the original shop. "Reforma trudovogo zakonodatel'stva," p. 80.

79. Art. 13, part 3, Fundamentals; Art. 25, part 3, RSFSR Labor Code.

80. Krivoi, "Mesto raboty po sovetskomu trudovomu pravu," p. 58, n. 21.

81. Kh. Siigur and I. Orgo, "Ob izmeneniiakh v kodekse zakonov o trude Estonskoi SSR," *Sovetskoe pravo*, 1988, No. 5: 337.

82. Gliantsev, "Spornye voprosy," p. 6.

83. *BVS SSSR*, 1988, No. 3: 11. Gliantsev, a member of the RSFSR Supreme Court, described a case in which the Court overturned a trial court decision on the grounds that the court failed to verify management's motives in light of evidence that its action had been prompted not by the production interests, but rather by the personal interests of the institute director. "Spornye voprosy," p. 6. Along similar lines, Livshits described a case of truck drivers having been "shifted" from one type of truck to another with less horsepower, resulting in lower wages. Management argued that its action had been linked to efforts to improve production. The workers contended that it had been prompted by ill will between the parties. The court sided with the workers and ordered their prior conditions reinstated. "Izmenenie trudovogo dogovora," p. 58.

84. This contradicted the usual tendency of Soviet courts to be very formalistic when it came to procedural requirements imposed by statutory law. A good example of this was the requirement that the enterprise trade union committee consent to all dismissals. If it were absent, the court would automatically reinstate the worker, a practice which often led to criticism on the grounds of formalism. See generally, A. Pavlov, "Bez soglasiia profkoma," *Sovetskie profsoiuzy*, 1990, Nos. 1-2: 56-57; R.Z. Livshits, *Trudovoe zakonodatel'stvo: nastoiashchee i budushchee* (Moscow: Nauka, 1989), pp. 58-60.

156 Kathryn Hendley

85. *BVS RSFSR*, 1989, No. 7: 12-13.

86. *Ibid.*, pp. 58-59.

87. A. Fatuev and E. Chezhina, "Stat'ia 25 KZoT RSFSR: problemy i suzhdeniia," *Sots. trud*, 1990, No. 7: 86; Kh. Siigur, "O trudovom dogovore v usloviiakh intensivnogo razvitiia ekonomiki i polnogo khozrascheta," *Sovetskoe pravo*, 1988, No. 4: 261.

88. See generally, Fatuev and Chezhina, "Stat'ia 25 KZoT RSFSR," p. 89.

89. E.g., Gliantsev, "Spornye voprosy," pp. 5, 7.

90. For a general overview of the procedure, see Livshits and Nikitinskii, *An Outline of Soviet Labour Law*, pp. 196-207.

91. E.g., *BVS RSFSR*, 1989, No. 5: 1-2; Shabalina, "Spory o vosstanovlenii na rabote," p. 19.

92. Livshits was highly critical of the *KTS*. "Trudovoe zakonodatel'stvo: poisk kontseptsii," *SGiP*, 1990, No. 7: 51. In a February 1991 interview in Moscow, he advocated the complete elimination of the *KTS*, thereby allowing all labor disputes to be heard immediately by the courts. In May 1991, the law governing the resolution of individual labor disputes was changed, but the basic procedural structure was retained. *Trud*, May 17, 1991, pp. 1, 3.

93. A number of Soviet labor law experts argued that *profkom* consent should have been required for all transfers-related dismissals. E.g., Krivoi, "Mesto raboty po sovetskomu trudovomu pravu," p. 60; Siigur and Orgo, "Ob izmeneniiakh v kodekse," p. 338.

94. Hendley, "The Ideals of the *Pravovoe Gosudarstvo* and the Soviet Workplace."

95. *Ibid.*

96. V.I. Nikitinskii documented the difficulties in obtaining information relating to the effectiveness of labor law. *Effektivnost' norm trudovogo prava* (Moscow: Iuridicheskaia literatura, 1971), pp. 6-8.

97. E.g., Livshits and Nikitinskii, "Reforma trudovogo zakonodatel'stva," pp. 78-80; Gliantsev, "Spornye voprosy," pp. 5-7.

98. E.g., Fatuev and Chezhina, "Stat'ia 25 KZoT RSFSR," pp. 90-93; Krivoi, "Mesto raboty po sovetskomu trudovomu pravu," pp. 59-6; Bugrov, "Perestroika i razvitie sovetskogo zakonodatel'stva," pp. 41-42.

99. Interview with A.A. Shugaev, Moscow, November 1989.

100. S. Ivanov, "Labor Law in Socialist Countries: Three Issues of General Theory," *Comparative Labor Law Journal* 11, no. 1 (Fall 1989): 84.

101. A.S. Pashkov, "O kontseptsii obnovleniia trudovogo zakonodatel'stva," *Pravovedenie*, 1990, No. 2: 20-22. For a discussion of the concept of *pravovoe gosudarstvo* in the Soviet context, see Harold J. Berman, "The Rule of Law and the Law-Based State *(Reshtsstaat)*," *The Harriman Institute Forum*, No. 1 (1990); Mark R. Beissinger, "The Party and the Rule of Law," *Columbia Journal of Transnational Law* 28, no. 1 (1990): 41-50.

102. *Trud*, May 21, 1991, pp. 1, 3.

103. A good example of this was the provision dealing with the consent of the enterprise trade union committee to dismissals. In February 1988 the law was changed such that the consent no longer had to be preliminary. In May 1991, the word "preliminary" *(predvaritel'no)* was reinserted into the statute. *Trud*, May 21, 1991, p. 1.

104. "On Securing the Effective Employment of the Population, Improving the System of Job Placement and Increasing Social Guarantees for the Working People," *Pravda*, Jan. 19, 1988, pp. 1-2, trans. in *CDSP* 40, no. 4 (Feb. 24, 1988): 1-4.

105. Quoted in Livshits and Nikitinskii, "Reforma trudovogo zakonodatel'stva," p. 79.

106. S.A. Ivanov, head of the labor law sector of the Institute of State and Law, claimed that 40 percent of all Soviet industrial workers were engaged in manual labor (55 percent in construction). "Krizis sovetskogo trudovogo prava," *SGiP*, 1990, No. 7: 44. However, E. Kotliar, a prominent labor economist, while not disputing that the level of manual labor acts as a brake on economic development, argued that the imprecise method of calculating it leads to misstated and perhaps overestimated assessments. "Metodicheskie voprosy sovershenstvovaniia ucheta ruchnogo truda," *Sots. trud*, 1988, No. 12: 55-57.

107. In no case was I ever granted "official" access to an enterprise. I was officially attached to the labor law *kafedra* of the law faculty of Moscow State University. The members of this *kafedra* found my desire to spend time at enterprises quite bizarre and not at all scholarly. Their official line was that this was "completely impossible" *(sovsem nevozmozhno)* and they surreptitiously deleted all references to this field research from the "scientific plan" *(nauchnyi plan)* that I was required to prepare. As a result, I was forced to prevail on friends in order to obtain access to enterprises and the scope of this access varied greatly based on the sort of connections my friend had with a given enterprise.

108. When one of his colleagues would interrupt us or some other situation would arise that necessitated his explaining my presence, he would always introduce me as a relative of his Georgian wife, presumably to justify my accented Russian.

109. V.I. Nikitinskii, a prominent Soviet labor law scholar associated with the Institute of Soviet Legislation, decried the slackness in record-keeping in Soviet enterprises. He also criticized the failure to collect statistical data on a systematic basis. *Effektivnost' norm trudovogo prava*, pp. 5-7.

110. Hendley, "The Ideals of the *Pravovoe Gosudarstvo* and the Soviet Workplace." note 57.

111. This factory, as with all of the factories whose records I examined, had a higher than normal number of disputes under consideration by the *KTS*. Livshits claimed that, on average, 1.3 or 1.4 disputes were heard per year. He contrasted this with the hundreds of thousands of complaints sent to the "central organs" on labor. "Trudovoe zakonodatel'stvo," p. 52.

112. The *KTS* did not have the right to consider claims brought by certain categories of management personnel. Instead, such claims had to be pursued through the ministry. See generally V.V. Shkuro, "O rasshirenii sudebnoi zashchity trudovykh prav grazhdan," *SGiP*, 1989, No. 8: 48-49.

113. I was able to review only 18 of the 54 labor-related cases brought in 1989 because many of the files had still not been transferred to the archives.

114. Michael Burawoy and Kathryn Hendley, "Strategies of Adaptation: A Soviet Enterprise Under Perestroika and Privatization," *Berkeley-Duke Occasional Papers on the Second Economy in the USSR*, Paper No. 29, June 1991.

115. *Ibid.*, pp. 5-6.

116. *Ibid.*, pp. 15-34.

117. Kovalev and Ryzhov, "Sudebnaia praktika," pp. 7-8.

The Eurasian Imperative in Early Soviet Language Planning: Russian Linguists at the Service of the Nationalities

Michael Smith

Introduction

"Vulgar tongues," wrote the Italian political theorist and linguist Antonio Gramsci, "are written when the people become important once again."[1] He was referring to the city communes of early modern Italy where the native, "vulgar" Italian gained in literary prestige at the expense of the ornate Latin language of Imperial Rome. At the time, in celebration of native identity and community, renaissance humanist thinkers from Dante Alighieri to Leonardo Bruni praised the beauty of their native Italian, spoken and written, and wrote panegyrics to the promenades and panoramas of Florence, their native town. Their perspective reveals an eloquent truth: that the people may occupy a space in language as much as in the world around them.

Throughout the 1920s, a decade of revolutionary expression and experiment in the USSR, cultural leaders of the Caucasus and Central Asia similarly promoted the development and reform of their native languages as one aspect of nation building. In this spirit, S.A. Agamalioglu--one of the foremost cultural and political leaders of Soviet Azerbaijan--spoke out against clerical Islam as an obstacle to modernization, comparing the old Arabic script to "all those narrow, curving streets and small mudhouses, together with those cumbersome mausoleums, minarets and medresses--symbols of the defenders of backwardness." It was Agamalioglu's goal to promote a new Latin script for his own Azerbaijani people first, and for the neighboring Turkmen, Kazakhs, Kirgiz and Uzbeks of Central Asia second. A Latin script, he believed, was much better suited to the native sound systems of the Turkic peoples, to pan-Turkic tasks, and to Western technology than either the Arabic or Cyrillic (Russian) scripts then in use or under consideration. His Latinization project was designed to promote a cultural renaissance for the Turkic peoples of the Caucasus and Central Asia.[2] By the mid-1920s, Latinization of scripts was implemented with Moscow's approval not only for the Turkic peoples, but for almost all of the peoples of the USSR (with the exception of the Russians, Georgians, Armenians and several "small peoples" of the RSFSR).

Agamalioglu's project was part of a broader linguistic and cultural movement which took shape in the 1920s as the nationalities of the USSR created and recreated themselves, on the basis of language planning, by way of the codification and standardization of the basic foundations of literacy: alphabets, orthographies, grammars and literary and scientific-technical languages (what linguists call corpus planning). The creation of newspapers, books, advertisements, school texts and instruction manuals (what linguists call status planning, or the delimitation of language usage and function) was not possible, after all, without these foundations.

This chapter is about the work of several Russian linguists, from the late Imperial period to the early Soviet period, who understood language as a field for experimentation and the improvement of a modern literate society. These linguists worked together with political and cultural leaders in the 1920s and 1930s to create new speech communities and literary cultures for the USSR. In carrying out these tasks, Russian linguists not only made crucial advances in their science but refined an ideology of service. Inspired by what I call a "Eurasian imperative" in Soviet language planning, they set out for the lands of the Soviet East, specifically the Caucasus and Central Asia, with a commitment to the development of the Russian and "non-Russian" languages.[3]

The Eurasian imperative suffered from its own twisted contradictions. Soviet leaders legitimized the development and use of both the Russian and non-Russian languages, yet in practice reserved a place for Russian as a "first among equals." This created tensions for linguists whose ostensible task was to serve primarily the non-Russian languages. Moreover, the language reforms of the early Soviet period (1919 to 1939) were implemented under the tutelage of Lenin and Stalin's nativization (*korenizatsiia*) programs, which meant to "root" the authority of the Bolshevik party-state in the life of the non-Russian nationalities by patronizing native cultures and languages. Even without these contradictions, the demands made on the young science of linguistics were immense: how to accomplish in a few years of central planning what had taken centuries of sporadic creation and spontaneity to develop.

Western studies of Soviet language and nationality policies in the 1920s and 1930s, rich in detail and insights though they are, have tended to subscribe to one of two models: the "pendulum model," according to which language planning and nationality policy swung alternately from centrifugal (nativization) to centripetal (russification) forces, or the "gyrocompass model," according to which russification was the magnetic pole to which nativist deviations invariably returned, subdued.[4] Though valuable for the analysis of shifts in party-state ideology and avowed policy, in my view these constructs have become so simplified as to risk being caricatures. For example, historians today generally identify nativization of the 1920s as a constructive moment in the development of the native non-Russian languages, particularly by comparison with the policy of russification which is alleged to have begun to swamp language policy in the 1930s. But the pendulum model has tended to obscure the extent to which the process of russification was also at work during the earlier period, and nativization during the later.

In describing the policies of nativization and russification, scholars have tended to confine their attention to the machinations of an all-powerful party-state apparatus, one always intent on "dividing and conquering" the peoples of the Soviet East. What is lost is a historical appreciation for the range of groups and processes involved and of the subtle interplay between them. True, the Communist party-state defined the limits of debate and policy within which linguists and cultural leaders operated, but these leaders were also given some latitude during the 1920s (and beyond) to decide on specific policy questions. Party-state leaders depended on linguists and their scientific innovations--unavailable even a few decades earlier--for success on the language-reform front. They also depended on nationality leaders to help implement cultural and language reforms on native terms and according to native interests. Within all of these constraints and freedoms, party-state leaders, linguists and nationality leaders worked together to bring the non-Russian peoples of the USSR to literacy.[5]

So the reality of early Soviet language planning is much more dynamic than any of these models, formulas and theoretical approaches allow. There was no sudden or irrevocable turn between nativization in the 1920s and russification in the 1930s; rather the two policies existed in a fascinating symbiotic relationship, much in the way that apparently contradictory cultural and political trends coexisted in the same periods. Further, the "gyrocompass" model and the "divide and conquer" formula exaggerate the power and performance of the party-state; they underestimate real cultural processes at work among the native peoples.

Soviet language reform in the 1920s, and specifically Latinization of alphabets mentioned above, offers us the opportunity to explore two processes at work in that decade--national renewal through language and Russian service to this task. The processes have been at work again over the last few years. The renaissance in language and culture first promoted during the 1920s is enjoying a revival today as the Russian and non-Russian peoples bring new life to cultural programs and policies from the distant pre-stalinist past, a past which lay buried by the ideological dictates of the party-state. Today the peoples of the new independent states are reshaping their national identities and destinies. Language laws adopted for the USSR union and autonomous republics (decreed between 1989 and 1991) attest to the importance of language reform as a field for cultural creation and as a crucible of national identity. These laws and declarations, which reconfirmed native languages as state languages, were in fact some of the first signs of national revival.

The resurgence of nationalism in the USSR and its successor states over the last few years has brought with it not only a new status for native languages, but a new momentum for reforming the codes and standards (structures) of these languages--the reforms of alphabets, orthographies, grammars, literary languages and scientific-technical terminologies. In the Gorbachev era, alphabet reform for the Turkic peoples entailed either a revision of existing Cyrillic-based scripts (first imposed upon most languages after 1937); or a return to Latin-based scripts (in use between 1919 and 1939); or a return to Arabic scripts which were in use by several peoples before 1917. The choice of script would take these peoples in new cultural and political directions, carrying as well the potential for both separatist and assimilationist tendencies between them. Thanks in large part to Turkey's 1992 campaign among the new Turkic successor states in the Caucasus and Central Asia, the momentum has now shifted decidedly in favor of the Latinization of existing Cyrillic-based scripts. As in the case of the early 1920s, Azerbaijan has again taken the lead in turning to Latin.[6]

How have Russian leaders begun to relate to their new neighbors to the South and East? The old Communist party-state ideological formulas of *rastsvet* (the "flowering" of languages and nations), *sblizhenie* and *sliianie* (the "rapprochement" and "merging" of languages and nations, into Russian) have been discredited. In the Gorbachev era, two new concepts emerged: "reciprocal bilingualism" and "Soviet language union." These concepts, which respected the development of the minority languages of the USSR, yet which retained a preference for Russian as the leading language, "first among equals," were discussed in several forums, both scholarly and political. Linguists and pedagogues (Russian and non-Russian alike) in the Ministries of Education of the RSFSR and USSR and in the Academy of Pedagogical Sciences of the USSR undertook a campaign (largely through the journal, *The Russian Language in the USSR*) to promote the real development of reciprocal bilingualism (and the complementary notion of "language union") in education. They called for a "system of interrelated instruction of the native and Russian languages in general education schools." These pedagogues rejected the traditional study of genetic language families as mechanical and formalistic; in the "mixed" schools, both the Russian and non-Russian languages were to be taught together, in order to highlight how they have interacted and enriched each other through language contact, as participants in "language union." The Communist party accepted these new formulas as renovative and useful in its own discussions and platforms on the nationalities question.[7]

In fact, alphabet reform, reciprocal bilingualism and language union are not new phenomena on the Soviet stage. It is no coincidence that in recent years Russians began to celebrate the advances of a range of linguists--N.S. Trubetskoi, E.D. Polivanov and N.F. Iakovlev--and their service to the nationalities during the 1920s.[8] For the Russians, as for us in the West, the appeal to these and other primary sources reflected the attempt to gain a better understanding of the difficult choices from both the past and present.

The Heritage of Linguistic Science

Official language policy in the late Imperial period has been rightly characterized as chauvinistic at its worst, patronizing at its best.[9] But we also need to make the distinction between official policy and academic avant-gardes. For already during the late Imperial period, scholars were heading in the direction that future Soviet reformers would take. After the 1880s, the Moscow School of F.F. Fortunatov and the Petersburg School of Ia.A. Baudouin de Courtenay began to define language in new "structuralist" terms: as an integral system of sounds, signs and meanings, open to scientific analysis and conscious manipulation. Their object of study became language as a structure of phonological, morphological and syntactical systems and subsystems, governed by a whole series of functional relations within and between them. These new methods had more than laboratory or academic application. They were the basis for the grand experiment in language reform that would be attempted in the USSR in the 1920s and 1930s.

Fortunatov revived the tradition of *russistika*, the study of Russian in all of its dialect variations, levels of sound and meaning and literary styles. He was a master of comparative phonetics and morphology, best known for his structural or "formal" approach to morphology: the study of "language forms" and the "search for objective (or as they were then called 'formalist') criteria of differentiation" within language. Together he and his students were known as the "armoured Muscovites" for their scientific severity and strict methods of linguistic analysis.[10]

Baudouin is credited (along with Ferdinand de Saussure) for delineating linguistics, the autonomous study of language as a system of signs, into that part which studies language as an abstract system of interdependent elements (*langue*) and that part which studies the actual speech of individuals and groups (*parole*). Baudouin made the further distinction between the linguistic study of the static system of language (synchrony) and the study of its changes over time (diachrony). He and his students also came to some of the first definitions of modern phonology, or the study of the concept of the phoneme, the sound unit in speech which distinguishes meaning and which is the basis for the rational creation of alphabet systems.[11]

Baudouin exemplified the humanism of his generation. He believed devoutly in the capacity of people to control and perfect language. "Language," he wrote, "is neither a self-contained organism nor an untouchable fetish; it is a tool and an activity," one which demands improvement. As Victor Shklovskii (one of his students) wrote, Baudouin "was a man who gave the future tasks, not riddles," for he sought to apply "the results of science to everyday needs." Baudouin understood just how important linguistics was in cementing national cohesion and in helping the growth of literacy. Linguistics, he knew, was a field for both inquiry and application to the extent that "only a clear knowledge of the sounds of language" and of the "origin and structure of words" could make for "a good method of teaching children (and adults) to read and write in a given language." By helping to create a popular language and literature, such a science was thus an effective means for national and "social intercourse," providing a "link between successive generations."[12]

Both Fortunatov's and Baudouin's students filled the Society for the Study of Poetic Art (1914-1923); the Moscow Linguistic Circle (1915-1923); and Moscow Linguistic Society (1918-1923). In these associations, they engaged in open and noisy debates in the spirit of the revolutionary times; afterward they joined the new research and educational institutions of Soviet Russia. Here in these first groups they devoted themselves to "new methods of linguistic analysis" and to the elucidation of a "synchronic" (*staticheskoi*) linguistics, based on the teachings of Fortunatov and Baudouin at home and on the theories of Ferdinand de Saussure from abroad. They discussed the "poetic functions" of language (in sounds and sound units), the sociological and dialogical characteristics of language, and the application of linguistic methods to art. These linguists shared semiotic insights with avant-garde Futurist and Constructivist artists of the war, revolution and reconstruction (NEP) periods. They applied some of the same techniques and methods to language reform that Cubist painters applied to their canvasses by way of geometric shapes; or that Futurist poets applied to the creation of "transrational poetry" (*zaum*) by way of disjointed sounds. This meant breaking down language or painting into their component forms in order to rebuild them in artistically creative and socially useful ways.[13]

Thus Iakovlev's mathematical formula for the construction of rational alphabets or Polivanov's scientific rationales for language reform, both of which we explore below, were not purely scientific constructs, but were also meant to serve new social tasks, in the spirit of the Moscow and Petersburg schools and in the manner of the Futurist and Constructivist values. Here was linguistic research not only directed to social ends, but created and nurtured by linguists who were in some cases poets themselves, or at the very least creators of new literary and scientific cultures. Polivanov and Iakovlev drew from Baudouin's concepts of sound and word function to create a powerful analogy: if language as a system of signs was functional between people, it could also be made to function better between people in society. Hence they came to what they called a "teleological" insight about language: that it was purposeful (served certain ends) both within itself (as sign system) and without (as social communication).

The "armoured Muscovites" and Baudouinists also discussed how their methods might be applied to the study of the many peoples and nationalities living in and around Russia. A.A. Shakhmatov, one of Fortunatov's most successful students, shared his mentor's appreciation for the study of linguistics as a "moral pathway." Known as "one of the few Russian humanists of his day,"

Shakhmatov dedicated his life to the study of the Russian language, in all its rich history and dialects, as a service to the Russian people.[14] In fact, a new scholarly and ideological perspective first congealed among the students of the Moscow school in the years before and during World War I. Here a group of classmates, including R.O. Jakobson, N.S. Trubetskoi, P. Bogatyrev and N.F. Iakovlev, studied dialects and folklore as part of their work on the Moscow Dialectological Commission during 1915 and 1916. The stated tasks of this commission were to study the Russian language, both in space (synchronically) and through time (diachronically) in connection with ethnography, archeology and history; and to study the "interaction between the Russian language and its neighbors." In the Moscow Linguistic Society they and others heard and debated G.G. Shpet's ideas on a new, value-free "ethnic psychology" and on the objective, "semasiological" or semiotic interpretation of cultures--ideas which may very well have been at the source of Roman Jakobson's and Claude Levi-Strauss's later explorations into structuralist ethnography.[15]

Baudouin, a "proletarian intellectual" as he liked to refer to himself, was especially successful in inspiring his students to explore non-Russian cultures and languages. True, he was a specialist in Indo-European linguistics and believed that the Indo-European languages were the "most highly advanced in their morphological, flexional structure," that "their speakers have formed the most civilized and influential nations in world history." Yet he was also a determined opponent of outdated views, namely traditional philology and its pretentious study of only the noble languages of Sanskrit, Greek, Latin and Old Church Slavonic. He was a proponent of the "democratization of linguistic thought," which meant providing the masses with the language reforms and language teaching sufficient to make them fully literate.[16]

Baudouin was a moderate Polish patriot and an arch-opponent of Great Russian or any other chauvinism. A graduate of Warsaw University in 1856, he was prevented from teaching there due to Tsarist russification policies; again in 1874 he was forced to move from St. Petersburg to Kazan because of russification. A decade at Dorpat (1883-1893) ended when its university was russified; at that point, he moved to Krakow University (1893-1899), where his Slavicism was ill-received by its Austrian-Hungarian patrons and where he became entangled in nationality disputes once again.

Most noteworthy were his days in St. Petersburg between 1899 and 1914 where he valiantly defended his ideas on the cultural and language rights of the non-Russian nationalities of the empire against the forces of Russian domination. His progressivism and internationalism aimed for a maximum of development and unification of peoples within the Russian empire, but with a minimum of disruption of their native traditions and languages. He campaigned to ensure the fuller political and language rights of the minority peoples of the empire within a restructured Russian federation. In a prescient assessment of imperial travails, he even predicted that the Tsarist government would surely "perish" without such reforms. For his proposals on this score, published in a 1912 booklet, *The Territorial and National Mark in Autonomy*, and exacerbated by his public protests against Great Russian chauvinism and "Black Hundredism," he spent some months in a Russian prison in 1914--whose air, he was fond of saying, was easier to breathe than the air of Russian "freedom."[17]

E.D. Polivanov first acquired both his interests in the sounds and signs of language and his political convictions from Baudouin. As he wrote in later years, "from the second year of my studies, my world outlook was conditioned by the very comprehensive influence on me by my teacher, Baudouin de Courtenay--by conviction an internationalist-radical." Baudouin's political tract of 1912 and subsequent imprisonment inspired Polivanov's own call to action. At the beginning of World War I, he wrote a short tract of his own opposing the war, for which he was arrested and jailed for a week. "My international platform became clear for me," he later wrote, "I was a pacifist; I then came to internationalism." By 1919 Polivanov, a socialist by conviction and a Bohemian by temperament, had joined the Bolsheviks.[18] P.S. Kuznetsov, a young member of Fortunatov's school and a future Marxist ideologue in linguistics, recounted in his unpublished memoirs that Baudouin inspired the young Kuznetsov to study linguistics. In his youth, Kuznetsov had read a popular novel in which one of the heroes took an expedition to Siberia to study its unknown languages--a linguist-hero whom Kuznetsov considered to be Baudouin himself.[19]

Baudouin passed on to these students not only a sense of the plasticity and perfectability of language, but also an appreciation for its intricacies and varieties. He was a scientist always intent on improving his methods and results. Yet Baudouin was also an advocate of the development of minority national cultures and languages on native terms. This duality set a tone for the work of his school in the 1920s. For Baudouin called on his students to help construct language systems for the non-Russians based on scientific principles. Build language bridges between people, he preached, but always with a deference to their own languages, cultures and national aspirations. Here was a dual mission which, in the context of the 1920s and 1930s, became something of a curse for the Baudouinists sent into the Soviet East to reform languages.

The Eurasian Imperative and Russian Linguists

The Eurasianists Abroad

During the first decades of the twentieth century, Russians experienced something of a crisis in identity. Writers, poets and philosophers began to ruminate upon Russia's special role as a "Eurasian" country, partly for the shock value of such pronouncements, partly because of their disgust with the decadent West, partly for the sense of power and destiny associated with such a role for Russia. This movement first took shape in the philosophical and literary writings of Vladimir Solovev, Andrei Belyi and Alexander Blok. They were, in a sense, precursors to the Eurasianist cultural and political movement of the 1920s.[20]

As a specific linguistic school, Eurasianism was centered in the emigre "Prague circle," a product of Fortunatov's Moscow Dialectological Commission. R.O. Jakobson and N.S. Trubetskoi, by 1921 living in exile in Prague, sought to help resolve this crisis of identity by combining, in one unitary formula, linguistic theory with a new ideology about the Soviet East. Drawing from their perspective on the structural (semiotic or systematic) and functional (social) aspects of language, they experimented with new ideas about language mixing and language union. Both concepts were earlier developed by Baudouin, who understood the importance of studying how languages interact with each other, both in space and through time. Polivanov came to interesting insights regarding language mixing as well, theorizing about the connections between the sound (phonetic) systems of the Germanic and Ural-Altaic language groups, Chinese and Korean, and Japanese and Malay-Polynesian.[21] Jakobson and Trubetskoi developed these early stirrings into the more sophisticated idea of "Eurasian language union." This theory complemented the traditional study of the genetic relations within language families with the new study of the spatial relationships and existing geographic, cultural and linguistic interconnections between the Russians and their Eastern neighbors. Such an enthusiasm for spatial over temporal study has been cited by Krystyna Pomorska as a peculiarly "futurist" characteristic of modern linguistics--whereby, as in the case of Einsteinian relativity and Cubist painting, "time and space are discussed as structure determinants."[22]

Trubetskoi applied the futurist impulse to explore spatial sequences in his own study of the Turkic languages (which are quintessentially "Eurasian"), a study which reinforced his own understanding of language as a system and structure. In his view, the Turkic or Turanian "linguistic type is characterized by schematic regularity and a consequent realization of a small number of simple and clear principles which fuse language into a single whole." Trubetskoi was simply fascinated by the symmetry and balance in Russia's neighboring Turkic languages.[23]

These concepts of Eurasian language union and Turanian man were part of a broader ideology of Eurasianism which Jakobson and Trubetskoi helped to create and which constituted a new way of looking at the cultures and languages of the East. Jakobson and Trubetskoi rallied against all forms of chauvinism and for objective ethnographic studies of the Eastern nationalities. As founders of the Prague Circle, they fought against "scholarly isolationism" and a "narrow-minded fear of teamwork." They worked rather to build up "international ties" by way of "collective tasks." Despising chauvinism and aggressive communist internationalism for their pervasive influence on scholarship, they campaigned for a balanced treatment and appreciation of the non-Russian peoples of Eurasia.

To complement this mode of scholarship, Trubetskoi and some of the Eurasianists envisioned a political federation with Russian as the dominant language of communication, bounded by the native languages of the periphery which were to enjoy substantial rights to development and assimilation within their own language groups. He even approved of recent Soviet measures to reorganize the old empire. In Eurasian terms, Jakobson and Trubetskoi sought to revive the "symphonic" relationship between the brother nations of "Russia-Eurasia" (*Rossiia-Evraziia*). The "Eurasian language union" was thus a concept derived in part from the special character of Russia's relations with the East, for as Russia expanded eastwards it created a unique kind of empire, being conquered as much as conquering.[24] The Eurasianists sought to salvage something of this old pseudo-imperial order, creating a "Rossiia-Evraziia" which would offer a more equitable relationship between West and East, such that these spatial distinctions would no longer even be made.

The Soviet Eurasianists

The Prague Eurasianists were not alone in their conceptualizations, for they always considered their Soviet classmates and colleagues--also students of Fortunatov and Baudouin--as part of their "circle," as scholarly collaborators of a kind. This Soviet cadre of expert linguists was equipped with a knowledge of the non-Russian languages of the USSR and with novel theories and methods about language system and structure: E.D. Polivanov on Turkic and Chinese; N.F. Iakovlev on the languages of the North Caucasus; L.I. Zhirkov on Tajik, Persian, and the languages of Dagestan; D.V. Bubrikh on Finno-Ugric; R.O. Shor on Turkic and the languages of Dagestan.[25] Thus a vibrant linguistic science was at work in the USSR during the first decades of Soviet power, informed by new structural methods and a Eurasian imperative, trying to give shape to the key language reforms of the day. Science offered well-developed studies of the sound systems of the several language groups of the Soviet East, as well as its own ideological motives to aid in the development of national literary cultures and speech communities.

Two of the Soviet linguists, E.D. Polivanov and N.F. Iakovlev, are especially important for our discussion. They may be seen best as a kind of advance guard of a Soviet type of Eurasianism which was still international in scope, but without the less palatable components in its emigre ideology (anti-communism). Polivanov was enamored with the languages of the East. He was a specialist in Turkic (namely Uzbek), Chinese and Japanese; he was experienced with Abkhaz, Azeri, Ainsk, Dungan, Georgian, Kirgiz, Korean, Malaysian,

Mordvinian, Tajik and Tatar, among other languages. He was adamant not only that Russians learn these langauges and help to teach them but also that the methods of modern structural linguistic science be applied in their study, codification and standardization.[26] He had high hopes of raising the peoples of the Soviet East to new cultural levels. As head of linguistic work in the RANION (the Russian Association of Scientific-Research Institutes for the Social Sciences) in the 1920s he even planned a series of books under the general title, *The Languages of the National Minorities of the USSR*, to study the social and territorial dialects of the Turkic, Finnic and Caucasian peoples; his classic work, *Introduction to Linguistics for the Eastern Universities* (originally meant to be published in four volumes) helped to establish the contours of structural linguistic science for the languages of the Soviet East.[27]

Polivanov's résumé is a stunning example of the rich and exciting lives which Soviet linguists could lead. Both his knowledge of the languages of the Soviet East and his Bolshevik convictions qualified him for a number of diverse posts. In 1917 he worked in the Office of the Military Press of the All-Russian Soviet of Peasant Deputies, in charge of literacy education; he was a plenipotentiary of the Peoples' Commissariat for Foreign Affairs, in charge of relations with the East, helping to translate and publish the secret treaties of the Tsarist regime. In 1918, he taught the Russian language and revolutionary politics to Chinese communists in Petrograd, helping to organize the Union of Chinese Workers, the Chinese Soviet of Workers' Deputies and the Chinese section of the Russian Communist Party; in 1921 he was assistant director of the Far East section of the Communist International. He edited the first Chinese Communist newspaper, and was a teacher at the Communist University of the Workers of the East.

After the Bolshevik revolution, Polivanov was not only a teacher in the Japanese and Chinese Divisions of the Central Institute of Living Eastern Languages in Petrograd, but also founder and chair of the party "collective" at the institute. Through this latter organ, he fought against the traditionalists within the field. During an April 1921 meeting of the collective he denounced the "White Guard professors" entrenched at the institute, declaring them unfit to properly train political workers for the East. He even charged that some of them brought a "counter-revolutionary attitude" to their work: supporting the recent Kronstadt uprising, wrecking political instruction and the political use of Eastern languages at the Institute, or teaching traditional rather than contemporary Arabic or Indian. Polivanov labelled this an open "betrayal of the Soviet government" and called for reform and purge within the institute.[28]

Both in theory and in application, N.F. Iakovlev's linguistic work followed in the spirit of Jakobson and Trubetskoi. In an April 1927 lecture to Chechen and Ingush students in Moscow he encouraged them to study their fragile pasts so as to strengthen their sense of identity. This meant to study ethnography in terms of everyday life, "the documents and monuments of past material culture," and contemporary literature and oral traditions. History, philosophy and linguistics are just as important as engineering and economics, he noted, for "one cannot build an economy without culture, without education."[29] Such ideas were markers of Iakovlev's Eurasianist mentality, which helped to inform language planning in the Soviet East in the 1920s and 1930s.

He brought his "Easternist" outlook to the Moscow Linguistic Circle, of which he was chair beginning in March 1923. Part of the plan of the Circle, as promoted by Iakovlev, was to study theoretical and applied linguistics from a structural point of view; to examine the interaction of language and society; and to study the non-Russian nationality languages of the USSR. Iakovlev gave reports before the circle on Kabardin phonology, on Ingush phonetics and phonology in relation to the neighboring languages of Chechen and Kabardin. L.I. Zhirkov, Iakovlev's close colleague, delivered reports on Avar grammar. Together they made plans to take expeditions to Cherkessia and Ossetia, Georgia, Armenia and the Finno-Ugric areas of the USSR.[30] Between 1920 and 1924, Iakovlev continued his work in the service of the non-Russian nationalities in the Committee for the Study of the Languages and Ethnic Cultures of the Northern Caucasus Peoples (attached to the Russian Academy of Sciences), which he was instrumental in transforming into the Scientific-Research Institute for the Study of the Ethnic and National Cultures of the Peoples of the East (by 1926), now devoted to the study of the North Caucasus, Turko-Tatar and Finno-Ugric peoples.[31]

The Imperative at Work: Latinization of Alphabets

Shortly after the 1917 Revolution and their reconquest of the former imperial periphery, the Bolsheviks offered the nationalities a nativization program of language equality within union and autonomous republics and regions. This policy reflected political needs as well as Lenin's own consistent willingness to accommodate to minority language cultures, together with his disapproval of an official state language.[32] Thus with the relative stability of the 1920s, the non-Russian nationalities not only retained formal language rights but actually began to enjoy these rights through the development of presses and publications, cultural organizations and educational establishments. In some regions, especially where national communists were in power and where circumstances dictated--Tatarstan, for example--the native language competed with Russian as the main language of the party and state.[33]

If Bolshevism made language reform possible through its new nativization policy, only linguists like Polivanov and Iakovlev, in service to the new Bolshevik regime, could make language reform successful. Linguistic science played a central role in the nativization program, for the undeveloped periphery of the USSR needed not only "engineers, doctors, pedagogues, and party and soviet workers," but above all those who had mastered "the respective national languages" of these regions. The trouble was that many of the literary languages of the RSFSR and USSR were still in their "formative stages," requiring linguistic study to determine dialects, sound systems, grammars and the like--problems which were to plague the USSR into the 1930s and beyond. To address these tasks, dozens of academic and scientific-research institutes were now oriented to fulfilling the needs of nativization policy and its component policy of language planning.[34] Between 1925 and 1927, educational leaders in the RSFSR recognized the importance of linguistics as the primary scientific base upon which further national development rested. In the Commissariat of Enlightenment (Narkompros), its Main Directorate for Professional Education (Glavprofobr) and its Council for the Education of the Non-Russian-Speaking Peoples (Sovnatsmen)--largely under the direction of I.V. Davydov, a deputy director of Sovnatsmen and a school inspector for Narkompros--sought to establish nationality linguistics departments in higher pedagogical institutes throughout the RSFSR and to organize and centralize linguistic work in general.[35]

In 1929, the linguist D.V. Bubrikh even called on party-state leaders "to create, under state authority, a strong scientific center for the study of the languages and cultures of the national minorities" within Russia. With boldness and self-assurance, he creatively manipulated the current party formula--that the USSR was a country "national in form, proletarian in content"--claiming that work in the realm of "proletarian by content" was far less important than work in the realm of "national by form." For only decisive language reforms among the nationalities, he believed, would strengthen the base for the introduction of proletarian ideology in the future.[36]

The Latinization movement which Bubrikh, Iakovlev, Polivanov and other linguists served offers an especially instructive case study into the character of the nativization program, the Eurasian imperative, and the intricacies of nationality policy. This movement was not simply a device used by the Communist party-state to maintain power, as scholars commonly maintain, but was also a means for the non-Russian nationalities to modernize and unify their own peoples. Although the party-state was a key player in the Latinization reforms, its role tends to be exaggerated. One tendency in the existing scholarship stresses the political angle, often reducing language policy and Latinization to generic terms. Such a view holds that Moscow and the party-state employed a conscious and premeditated policy of "divide and conquer" by way of Latinization, allowing the many and varied languages of the Soviet East to develop separate Latin alphabets freely (in masked terms of "flowering" or *rastsvet*) as a means of reinforcing central control, or at least as a means of heightening the value of Russian as a language of inter-nationality communication.[37]

There is no denying that in many respects the creation of nations in the USSR was politicized, done by way of a "painful process of trial and error"; that the demarcation of nations and boundaries was often rigged as a means of divide and control; or that Latinization was used as a tool to destroy Islam, traditional cultures, and the unity of the non-Russian peoples, especially the Turkic nations.[38] But to consider the party-state as the sole agent of these developments is to oversimplify the process. To be sure, the policy of "divide and conquer" played an important role in Russian and Soviet history and is a legitimate subject for scholarly study. But it must also be placed in its proper context. The issues of boundary-drawing and nation-making need to be clearly distinguished from those of language reform, for they were different processes. In some cases, as we explore below, some non-Russian nationalities used language planning to negate the very divisions which the Bolsheviks had wrought by way of boundary-drawing.

Fragmentation among the nationalities was not simply the result of a pernicious party policy of "divide and conquer," but of the clear wishes of the nationalities themselves (which the party itself helped to unleash with the revolution and its ideology of national development).[39] Language planning proceeded not only by way of the divide and conquer formula but also by way of the national republics' own demands for fully native scripts and literary languages. Moscow did not need to impose fragmentation; it was already in place, as one by-product of national development. "Mass" scripts and literary languages were necessary to help local masses come to literacy as quickly as possible; written languages needed to represent local sound systems as closely as possible. One corollary of the divide and conquer thesis has held that the separate Latin alphabets which were developed during the 1920s destroyed the former unity of the Arabic script, which was for the most part common for all Turkic and North Caucasus languages. This is true. But by the early 1920s these peoples were already creating separate Arabic scripts for themselves precisely because of the need to create their own mass languages.[40]

Serious debate about Latinization of the Russian-Cyrillic script began shortly after the Bolshevik revolution, enjoying brief attention between 1917 and 1919, and more sustained effort some ten years later. Why was a Latin script so alluring? One explanation is the Eurasian imperative. For the most idealistic of Bolsheviks and their allies, Latinization of the Russian-Cyrillic script was to serve as a means to bridge West and East--through Russia. In 1919, Narkompros (more specifically its Scientific Department and its Department for the Education of the National Minorities) appealed to scholars throughout Russia to come to its aid in discussing the possibility of Latinization of the Cyrillic and Arabic scripts of the former Empire, this as the "next logical step along the path that Russia has already set out upon" (given the turn to the metric system and a new Western calendar). One Narkompros report noted that a turn to Latin would complete Russia's recent turn to Europe, finally doing away with Peter the Great's "Slavonic-Latin script" and Russia's "script separatism" from Europe. A similar report referred to Latin as the best means available for a "rapprochement" (*sblizhenie*) between the peoples of the new Soviet federation and as the best script to fit the "phonetic features of each republic's language." The North Caucasus peoples (notably the Ossetians and Komi), the report continued, had already embarked upon Latinization of their Cyrillic-based scripts. Russia, so the argument went, need not fall behind.[41]

One of the most forceful propagandists for a new Latin script for the Russian people was none other than N.F. Iakovlev, who in fact helped to create a streamlined Latin project for the Russian-Cyrillic script in 1928. At the Third Plenum of the All-Union Central Committee of the New (Latin) Alphabet in 1929, Iakovlev--as one of the leading linguists on the Scientific Council of the Committee--told an interesting story, one that revealed his Eurasian mentality in no uncertain terms. He referred to what in the West had become known as the "yellow peril," an inordinate racist fear of the encroaching East which had received some currency in Russia at the turn of the century along with the notion of "Eurasia." The West was correct to fear the yellow peril, Iakovlev believed, but it was wrong to think that the invasion would be violent, in the manner of Genghis Khan and Tamerlane. No, Iakovlev noted, the new Mongol invasion would be carried out by men armed with books, not weapons. And the books would be written in the new Latin alphabet of the Soviet East, the new weapon with which to conquer the technology and culture of Europe.[42]

Unlike the Soviet Russians, almost all of the non-Russian peoples of the USSR--who were either altogether without scripts, or used Cyrillic-based scripts, or used the Arabic--chose new Latin scripts after 1917. Most notably, several sub-languages of the North Caucasus (Adygei, Kabardin, Cherkess, Abazin, Abkhaz), Chechen-Ingush and Dagestani, Ossetian, and several Turkic sub-languages (Azeri, Karachai-Balkar, Nogai, Kumyk, along with Iakut in Siberia) were given new Latin scripts in the 1920s. In the Volga-Urals and Central Asia, the Turkic sub-languages (Tatar, Bashkir, Kazakh, Kirgiz, Turkmen, Uzbek) and Tajik (an Iranic language) were subject for the most part to a second wave of Latinization after 1926.

The first of the non-Russian peoples to convert to the Latin alphabet were the Iakuts in 1917, whose language was previously written in a modified-Cyrillic script. With the inspiration of Baudouin de Courtenay and E.D. Polivanov, the Iakut intellectual S.A. Novgorodov--then a student in the Faculty of Eastern Languages at Petrograd University--chose the International Phonetic Alphabet (IPA) as a basis for the new Iakut script. With Polivanov's help, Novgorodov was able to compile a reading primer by December 1917, modifying the IPA to match with the special sounds of Iakut (using diphthongs rather than diacritical marks to represent special Iakut sounds).[43]

Polivanov, fully displaying his respect for national cultures and aspirations as received from Baudouin, did not rudely intervene in Novgorodov's project but hailed it as a great service to Iakut national identity. As Polivanov knew from his own work with phonetics and phonology, Novgorodov did not apply the phonemic principle in sufficient ways to modify the IPA to the specific needs of the Iakut language. Such a principle would have limited the size of the alphabet to the sound-sign correspondences which distinguished meaning (phonemes) rather than bloat it with the many phonetic distinctive features of one and the same phoneme. So Novgorodov's result was more of a transcription system than an alphabet, for it represented an extreme number of native sounds and signs. But this result was intentional: the new alphabet was designed for mass use according to the radical phonetic principle "write as you hear," with very simplified forms (diphthongs, no capital letters, no punctuation marks).[44]

Although it became widely popular in the 1920s in Iakutia, the script also drew complaints from language professionals who found it difficult to adapt to the needs of print culture and pedagogy. Over the next decade, especially after Novgorodov's premature death in 1924, polemics and debates ensued in conferences and the press by those who favored a revision of the transcription into a new, streamlined, Latin phonologized alphabet (among them E.D. Polivanov); or by those who favored a Iakut alphabet based on Russian characters (among them, V.N. Leontiev, chair of the Iakut research society, and the linguist N. Poppe).[45]

Along with Iakutia, the North Caucasus represents one of the first crucibles of experimentation with Latin scripts. Lacking strong native traditions of literacy and scholarship, its peoples came to depend more than perhaps any other on linguistic science--namely in the person of N.F. Iakovlev--for aid in their Latinization projects. By 1922, the short-lived Mountain ASSR (1920-1924) began to be whittled away as autonomous regions (*oblasti*) were created within it: the Karachai-Cherkess and Kabardin-Balkar Autonomous Oblasts (AOs) in early 1922; the Adygei AO, South Ossetian AO and Chechen AO later in that year; the North Ossetian and Ingush AOs in 1924. The party-state's policy of nativization meant that separate languages and scripts were now created for these newly-separated peoples. Hence out of a common Circassian language group came several new sub-languages: West Circassian or Adygei; East Circassian or Kabardin-Cherkess; Abkhaz; and Abazin. At first, alphabets were revised or created using the Arabic script, as was the case with Kabardin-Cherkess (1920-1923) and Adygei (1918-1926). Among the first to Latinize was the Ossetian language in 1918 and 1919; Karachai-Balkar in 1921; Ingush in 1922-1923 (Chechen followed in 1925). Soon afterward, the base Circassian languages (Kabardin, Cherkess, and Adygei) turned to Latin as well, partly following the lead of their Turkic neighbors, partly with the aid of Iakovlev. Two Education Congresses for the Mountain Peoples (Piatigorsk in 1923 and Rostov-na-Donu 1925) passed resolutions approving the creation of Latin alphabets.[46]

These Latin alphabets were created rather spontaneously and without coordination, resulting in the "discord" (*raznoboi*) which would plague the North Caucasus for years to come. Although the Piatigorsk conference of 1923 approved Latinization, it stopped short of calling for unification of alphabet projects, preferring that each nationality create its own project.[47] The degree to which these decisions were either forced by the party leadership or achieved by native leaders themselves is as yet unclear. My own conclusion is that this momentum for Latin was not simply a function of divide and conquer politics but was also a natural process of development of the languages and sub-languages of the area. For during the very first stirrings of self-government in 1917 and 1918, leaders had already made provisions for the development of the sub-languages of the North Caucasus. The logic of literacy-building was such that the sub-languages and dialects of mass speakers needed to be studied, codified and standardized in order to introduce mass literacy.[48] To this extent, even the differences (some linguists would say substantial ones) between the closely-related languages of the Circassian peoples demanded their separate study and organization.

By the late 1920s, North Caucasus leaders were already establishing projects for the unification of their Latin alphabets and thus for the assimilation of their peoples. By way of a unified Latin script, they aimed to overcome the very political divisions imposed by the Bolsheviks, along with the discord which resulted from the creation of different Latin scripts. They now hoped to regain the unity lost during the years of demarcation by way of language reform. The maximal ideal was the New Mountain Alphabet to unite the scripts of the peoples of the North Caucasus. Although extra letters were recognized as necessary for the different sound systems of the different languages, the base alphabet was to be the same. In minimal terms, leaders understood the first steps toward this goal to be the unification of alphabets and terminologies of related languages: Circassian (Adygei, Kabardin, Cherkess); Abkhaz and Abazin; Chechen and Ingush, the Dagestani languages; Ossetian; and the Turkic languages (Karachai, Balkar, Nogai, Kumyk). Remarkably, the most vocal spokesmen for this project were not only two of the North Caucasus's most visible Turkic leaders--D. Korkmasov and Umar Aliev--but the Muscovite linguist, N.F. Iakovlev himself.[49]

Iakovlev consistently campaigned and worked for the centralized planning and unification of the Latin alphabets for the North Caucasus peoples through the Mountain Region Scientific Research Institute at Rostov-na-Donu and several pedagogical institutes in the region. In his view, the "theoretical linguist" and "practical pedagogue" were now armed with the scientific methods necessary to systematize language and promote literacy. They also had the ability to coordinate alphabet projects and thereby aid in the assimilation of peoples, which Iakovlev understood as a rational and welcome development, founded on the "graphic agreement" between scripts and on the new insights of phonemic theory.[50] He was perhaps best known for his mathematical formula for the creation of alphabets, a project for the "systematization of the sound phenomena" of the North Caucasus languages which was inspired by Baudouin's and Saussure's structural linguistic theories. Presented before the Second Conference on the Education of the Mountain Peoples of the Northern Caucasus (1925) and the First Turkological Congress at Baku (1926), it applied new structural insights in phonology to the rational and economical creation of alphabets for the Northern Caucasus peoples.[51]

With Azerbaijan at the lead, which by its own accord had converted its Arabic script to Latin beginning in 1921, the Latinization movement gathered momentum with the Baku Turkological Congress of 1926. At this point, the movement entered into a new stage. The party-state now charged most of the remaining non-Russian peoples of Central Asia and the Far East with the task of creating Latin alphabets for their languages (except for the Russians, Armenians and Georgians). Between 1926 and 1933, the All-Union Central Committee for the New Alphabet met in a series of plenums and sessions to decide on how to unify existing Latin alphabets and indeed how to Latinize all non-Russian alphabets in the USSR. Along with Iakovlev, Bubrikh and others, Polivanov joined the work of the Latinization Committee with passion and dedication. An active member of the new scientific and academic institutions of Turkestan and Uzbekistan between 1921 and 1926, he was a proponent for Latinization of scripts and unification of all Latinization projects for the Turkic peoples.[52]

Russian linguists, for all their good intentions to aid in Latinization, now became ever more entangled in heated disputes between the nationalities over group loyalties and ethnic identities. Battles erupted among linguists and nationality leaders over such issues as alphabets, grammars, scientific-technical and literary languages. To decide on these issues, after all, meant to decide which dialect, language or culture would dominate a region or republic. There were highly divisive disputes about working principles. In simplified terms, a battle between the phonetic and phonological principles was at the heart of the Latinization campaigns of the 1920s. The phonetic principle (write as one hears), with supporters in the nationality regions (the Tatars and Iakuts especially), stressed native sound and sign differences. The phonological principle (write to keep related words and word parts spelled the same in the interests of economy and rationality), supported by structural linguists in Moscow and Leningrad, stressed the integration of sounds and signs, even projecting the unification of both alphabets and orthographies. Linguists and nationality leaders also disputed capital letters: the Muscovite linguists, as well as Tatar and Azerbaijani representatives, were largely in favor of them as links to Western culture; the Iakut, Turkmen, Uzbek, Kazakh and Kirgiz representatives were largely against them as complicating the learning process.[53]

The Eurasian contingent of linguists, thanks to their enthusiasm for nation-building through Latinization, tended to be overbearing. As the leaders of the Scientific Council of the All-Union Central Committee of the New Alphabet, they were consistent voices for more centralized work and rule. Iakovlev and Zhirkov argued at the First Plenum of the Committee for a powerful, centralized scientific council. Polivanov even suggested, half-jokingly, the benefits of making a "Nikolaevan" (autocratic) decision on alphabet unification, given all the bickering in 1926-27. By the Second Plenum, Polivanov wanted to turn the Central Committee into a "war-revolutionary committee, or perhaps just a revolutionary committee, for the graphic revolution in the East."[54]

There is no doubt that these linguists had the best interests of the non-Russians in mind when they advised and argued with them, but their good intentions often showed through as patronizing benevolence. M. Pavlovich, an Orientologist and cultural leader in the Soviet regime, probably expressed this benevolence best when he wrote in 1923 that if Tsarist Russia had been a conqueror and commercializer of the East, Soviet Russia would be a "teacher." And Moscow in turn would become the new "Mecca and Medina" for the peoples of the East. Linguists were often just as colorful in their language, with their hubris and sense of superiority showing through. Iakovlev once voiced his despair with all of the bad linguists among the non-Russian peoples. Zhirkov made the remark that nationality leaders should appear before the Scientific Council to ask for help. For if "Muhammed does not go to the mountain, then the mountain should go to Muhammed."[55] If Zhirkov's quip did not hurt religious sensibilities, it was surely a step beyond good taste and professional demeanor.

With such lapses in judgement, and given that among themselves they were in general agreement about linguistic principles, these Muscovite scholars formed a solid target for all those nationality leaders who were bickering among themselves, who were angry and frustrated with the whole process of Latinization, and who presumed to know better what to do with the sounds and signs of their own local langauges. A Turkmen representative once attacked the "professors" and their self-styled "authority" for their indecisions about capital letters.[56] The Azerbaijani leader, Agamalioglu, lost his patience many times with the "professors" and other nationality leaders for talking and debating endlessly about language reform rather than acting on it. He even accused the Russian linguists of wanting to create alphabets artifically, by their own decisions, without waiting for cultural and economic conditions to do their work. He portrayed them as having their heads stuck in their books, obsessed with Latinization "project-mania."[57]

In fact, criticisms of the Scientific Council and its Russian linguists are to be found in abundance throughout the documents of the time. Native leaders resented outside interference, no matter how well-intentioned. Polivanov,

Iakovlev, Zhirkov and Bubrikh understood their work mainly as consultative, one part of a grand project in language planning, but all too often the natives saw in this shades of dominance and russification. Thus embroiled in controversies partly of their own making, these linguists revealed the Eurasian imperative in all its paradox: yes, service to the peoples of the Soviet East, but either at the command or with the approval of the Bolshevik regime, and with no little patronizing benevolence on the part of linguists themselves.

Between 1919 and 1939, the Latin script became the norm for most of the languages of the USSR, instead of the Arabic or Cyrillic, for a variety of reasons: national desires for development and modernization (especially in Azerbaijan and the North Caucasus); Communist party-state patronage (especially in Central Asia); the ease with which the new script promoted literacy; its flexibility in adapting to national, "mass" language demands and pan-Turkic tasks; the support of linguistic science. This last reason was altogether problematic, for even simple letters and grammatical forms became highly disputative markers of group allegiances and national identities--markers which by then had lost the simple power and rationality which linguists had assigned to them.

Between Nativization and Russification

The first stages of the Latinization movement marked a high point in the nativization campaign. For at least a few short years in the 1920s, Russian linguists and nationality leaders worked together, without undue party-state interference, to solve urgent problems of cultural life. Yet the nativization campaign still suffered from the ambiguities of the Eurasian imperative and the rather condescending good will of Russian linguists. Worse yet, all through the campaign to raise the native non-Russian languages to new social and political levels, both Russians and non-Russians continued to value the power and role of the Russian language in the life of Soviet society and state.

The policy of nativization itself was hardly "Bolshevik." The prospects and problems related to the development of native languages and cultures had already been identified and a new path marked out at several educational conferences in 1916 and 1917. They resolved that the nationalities be given the right to form their own schools; and that the methods of teaching Russian in the nationality schools be established on the basis of the study of the specific features of the native languages (requiring structural investigation and diagramming). Each citizen, the congresses resolved, had the "right to think, feel, speak and learn in the native language," a right which demanded the "urgent abolition of all national constraints in the field of education." Subjects were now to be established and taught in all native languages. Where Russian was not the native language, it was to have a "purely auxiliary character."[58]

Thus these educational conferences, not the October Revolution, first announced the new "language union" between the Russian and non-Russian peoples, the new cooperative relationship of the "veracious Russian language in fraternal collaboration [*sodruzhestvo*] with the languages of the other nationalities."[59] During the last years of the tsarist empire, as during the Soviet 1920s and 1930s, raising the non-Russian languages did not mean devaluing the central functions of Russian. For the formation of national languages (corpus planning) was approved only in the context of the higher status (power and place) of Russian.

Bolshevik architects of nationality policy inherited these noble aims--and contradictions--from humanist educators in the late war years, refitting them for their own tasks. "It is impossible to construct socialism without the nationalities," said Davydov, deputy director of the National Minorities Council (Sovnatsmen) of Narkompros. In crudest, contradictory terms this meant that the dissemination of the Russian language (and socialism) depended precisely on the development of the non-Russian languages (and the nationalities). Inherent in this state policy was the working assumption that different languages needed to be treated differently, a basic component of structural linguistics and Eurasian theories. Davydov was a consistent supporter of the study of the specific "features" (*osobennosti*) of the national minority languages, of studying the "structures" of both the Russian and non-Russian native languages--as a means, for example, to create rational alphabets or scientific grammars. As Narkompros general directives to the national schools of the RSFSR proclaimed: we need to teach the Russian language differently based on the different internal features and external circumstances of the native languages.[60]

During the rather open and liberal 1920s, the "comparative study of languages" (meaning the study of the "language union") and the need to study "scientifically" and "rationally" the comparisons and parallels between Russian and its neighbor languages was hailed as a complement to Soviet nativization policy.[61] In its narrowest of meanings, of course, nativization also meant establishing party-state cadres in the national and national minority regions of the USSR to help lead local masses. S.M. Dimanshtein--one of Stalin's chief deputies in the conduct of language and nationality policy--understood this task well. He also postulated the need to teach party workers both the native languages and Russian according to a "differential approach"--that is, depending on the language and its circumstance.[62]

Dimanshtein employed E.D. Polivanov as a central party adviser on matters of teaching the native and Russian languages in the party schools, whose specific task was to help establish norms for language teaching in the different republics and regions. The problem, as Polivanov saw it, was that party-school students thought like communists in the Russian language, not in their native tongues. Hence the aim of the party schools was to teach party workers to speak to the masses in their own languages, something they were not always willing to do given the difficulty of expressing Russian concepts in languages with poorly-developed lexicons. Polivanov defined his methods in this way: to begin with lessons preparing political and scientific terminologies for each language (by way of translation from Russian or from comparisons with Latin and Greek root words); to continue with the study of the dialects of the given language (the "key to the psyche of the given collective") in order eventually to establish a standard literary language (if one did not exist already); and finally to move on to the study of what he called "differential grammar," or the "comparison of the grammatical facts of two or more dialects" of the same language.

This latter exercise was crucial, so Polivanov believed, to help the student take control over his or her whole language by way of "descriptive linguistics" or what he also called the "control (and especially self-control) over language." For languages like Chechen, which did not even have a standard dialect, "differential grammar" was obligatory; it was otherwise useful in helping the native non-Russian learner discover the intricacies of his or her own language as a means of learning Russian more easily. Polivanov was one of the first linguists to create such scientific rationales for new state policies.[63]

Polivanov was thus not merely a patron of the native non-Russian languages but also a passionate supporter of spreading Russian as the language of inter-nationality communication in the USSR. By 1928 he was quietly extolling, albeit always in conjunction with respect for native non-Russian languages, the "all-union" (*obshche-soiuznii*) and "international" role of Russian "as the literary language of Soviet culture." Drawing upon work he first completed as a member of the Futurist circle, the Left Front for the Arts (LEF), Polivanov also championed teaching the Latin and Greek roots of political and scientific terms as a means of bringing Russians and non-Russians to international culture. Such teaching was especially important for the party schools and universities, he believed, where the Russian language was studied as the "language of Soviet culture."[64]

This was in keeping with Leninist principles. Although himself an architect of the nativization policies of the 1920s, Lenin had not devalued the roles and functions of the Russian language and Russian-Soviet culture in the USSR. He simply believed that the Russian language should not be used in any coercive way which might alienate the non-Russians. Rather, by dismantling imperial russification policies then in effect he hoped to make peace with the national-ities, helping them to develop their languages and cultures. He sought in this circuitous way to convince them of the value and utility of Russian language and Russian-Soviet culture.

Throughout the 1920s, the classical epoch of Bolshevik nativization policy, what the historian finds in the daily documents of educators and policymakers in the RSFSR, what one finds even in the writings of all kinds of scholars and administrators, is not a valuation of native languages at the expense of Russian but often a sincere appreciation of the need to bolster the study, teaching and functions of both. Language professionals of different stripes in the RSFSR in the 1920s stressed a balanced need to develop the Russian and non-Russian native languages.[65]

Russian was definitely the language of prestige throughout the early Soviet era, a phenomenon expressed in all kinds of debates. In discussing the need for reform of the Russian writing system, educators regularly referred to Russian as "the language of the international proletarian revolution," a language which linguists ought to simplify in order to "facilitate the mastering of the Russian language by the proletariat of the East and West." Other scholars and administrators wrote freely about Russian as the official language of communication in the USSR, about Russian as the language of Lenin, of civilization, socialism, science and technology, as the fulcrum of "great-Russian proletarian culture."[66]

Thus with the advent of the Soviet regime a new language union began to take shape which promised the revitalization of most of the major (and many of the minor) languages of the new state, both non-Russian and Russian. True, Russian was no longer a "state language," but it was a "general language," the "language of the federation" and the "first among equals" in Davydov's words (for the RSFSR directly and the USSR indirectly). Hence a consistent priority for Soviet educators through the 1920s and 1930s was how best to disseminate the Russian language from the center into the non-Russian peripheries.[67] That these cultural leaders and linguists defined the development of the non-Russian languages as a necessary means for this dissemination is perhaps the best testimony to the paradoxes of the "Eurasian imperative."

Conclusion

The contours of early Soviet language planning in Russia, the Caucasus and Central Asia, defined as they were both by central state policies and by underlying cultural processes, offer scholars challenging research frontiers. They can help us explore the structures and codes of languages and cultures in and around Russia in all their intricacies and varieties. They can help us recognize how the demands of the Russian center intersected with those of the non-Russian peripheries, how the new theorems of linguistic science became so awkwardly intertwined with all kinds of political, ideological, social and nationality demands. And they can help us to appreciate the power of language as a means of national identification and self-control, as a medium for inter-nationality communication and foreign domination.

These contours also offer Turkic nationality and cultural leaders today an important historical ground and reference point, one long denied them under the Soviet system. For as the Turkic peoples begin to transform their Cyrillic-based scripts into new Latin alphabets, several issues of corpus planning (script and grammar unification and terminological reform) will remain open to discussion and dispute. Language planning, as a function of ethnic and national politics, will represent a crucial field for cultural and political re-creation in the coming years. The transformation of part of the USSR into independent Turkic successor states has thus set the stage for a convergence of interests. The revival of "Russian and Eurasian studies" in the West, liberated from the traditional concerns of Sovietology and rededicated to the study of the varieties of peoples, cultures and histories, can now complement the renaissance of cultural and national identity in the successor states. This revival, at least in some measure, is a celebration of the best values of the Eurasian imperative.

Notes

Archival Abbreviations (in use before 1992): AAN (Arkhiv Akademii Nauk SSSR); TsGA RSFSR (Tsentral'nyi gosudarstvennyi arkhiv); TsGALI SSSR (Tsentral'nyi gosudarstvennyi arkhiv literatury i iskusstva); TsGAOR SSSR (Tsentral'nyi gosudarstvennyi arkhiv oktiabr'skoi revoliutsii).

f. (*fond* or collection)
o. (*opis'* or inventory)
d. (*delo* or file)
l. and ll. (*list[y]* or page[s])

1. Antonio Gramsci, *Quaderni del carcere*, vol. 1 (Turin, 1975), 3/76.

2. See his comments in *Stenograficheskii otchet vtorogo plenuma vsesoiuznogo tsentral'nogo komiteta novogo tiurkskogo alfavita* (Baku, 1927), p. 3.

3. The term "Eurasia" has become fashionable with the end of the Soviet era, as witnessed by the editorial comments in *Slavic Review* 51 (Spring 1992). I use the term in relation to the historical context of the first decades of Soviet power when, as I argue, it was charged with sometimes considerate, sometimes chauvinistic values. The terms "Soviet East" and "non-Russian" are drawn from the debates of the time period; in this paper they refer to the native peoples and languages of the Caucasus (with the exception of Georgia and Armenia) and Central Asia. For detailed reviews of language reforms in different regions and republics, see William Fierman, "Nationalism, Language Planning and Development in Soviet Uzbekistan, 1917-1941" (PhD Dissertation, Harvard University, 1981); *Sociolinguistic Perspectives on Soviet National Languages*, ed. Isabelle Kreindler (Berlin, 1985); and *Language Planning in the Soviet Union*, ed. Michael Kirkwood (London, 1989).

4. For a discussion of these models, see Jonathan Pool, "Developing the Soviet Turkic

Tongues: the Language of the Politics of Language," *Slavic Review* 35 (1976): 425; Isabelle Kreindler, *The Changing Status of Russian in the Soviet Union* (Jerusalem, 1979), pp. 1-2; and Wolf Moskovich, "Planned Language Change in Russian Since 1917," in *Language Planning*, ed. Kirkwood, pp. 85-99. For studies which perpetuate the relevance of these closed, ahistorical models, see *The Nationalities Question in the Soviet Union*, ed. Graham Smith (London, 1990), p. 6; Gerhard Simon, *Nationalism and Policy Toward the Nationalities in the Soviet Union* (Boulder, 1991); Alexander Motyl, *Sovietology, Rationality, Nationality* (New York, 1990), p. 170; and a recent comparativist and theoretical offensive against the old Sovietology, *Thinking Theoretically about Soviet Nationalities*, ed. Alexander Motyl (New York, 1992), pp. 86-87, 109.

5. A study by David Laitin, *et al.*, "Language and State: Russia and the Soviet Union in Comparative Perspective," in *Thinking Theoretically*, ed. Motyl, offers an interesting comparativist and "game-theory" approach to these issues, but bases its premises and conclusions on traditional historical studies which more comprehensive archival research, in my view, does not substantiate.

6. For a review of the revival in Turkological studies, which includes discussion about history, folklore, culture and language reform (alphabets, grammars, and terminologies), see the issues of *Sovetskaia tiurkologiia* (Baku) especially after 1989. Radio Liberty's *Report on the USSR* and *RFE/RL Report* offer regular updates on questions of alphabet reform in the Caucasus and Central Asia. These questions were widely discussed in the Western media in 1992, particularly after the Turkic-speaking countries of the former USSR agreed in June to begin converting to Latin scripts with Turkey's patronage. Tajikistan (whose people speak an Iranic language) prefers the Arabic script.

7. See the remarks by N.M. Shanskii, a leading administrator in bilingual education, in V.I. Bespalov, "Sovershenstvovat' prepodavanie rodnykh iazykov, razvivat' dvuiazychie," *Russkii iazyk v natsional'noi shkoly*, 1989, No. 6: 3-7. This journal, renamed *Russkii iazyk v SSSR* in 1990 and placed under the new editorship of M.I. Isaev, devoted many articles and commentaries (especially after 1989) to questions of teaching the Russian and non-Russian native languages in the schools. See also remarks by G.A. Yagodin (chair of the USSR State Committee on Public Education and member of the Ideological Commission of the Central Committee of the CPSU), "Ideological Problems of Ethnic Relations (Session of the Ideological Commission of the CC CPSU held May 5, 1989)," in *Current Politics of the Soviet Union* 1, no. 1 (1990): 73.

8. Trubetskoi's works (formerly banned) were published in Russian in 1988, and have provoked much interest and discussion. See, for example: V.P. Neroznak, "Slovo o N.S. Trubetskom," *Izvestiia ANSSSR. Literatura i iazyka* 2 no. 49 (1990): 148-151; "100-letie so dnia rozhdeniia N.S. Trubetskogo," *Vestnik Moskovskogo Universiteta. Seriia 9. Filologiia* 5 (1990), pp. 83-85; and "Vsesoiuznaia konferentsiia 'N.S. Trubetskoi i sovremennaia filologiia,'" *Izvestiia ANSSSR. Literatura i iazyka* 50/2 (1991), pp. 188-191. Note also the following publications: *N.F. Iakovlev i sovetskoe iazykoznanie: sbornik nauchnykh trudov*, ed. Iu.D. Desheriev (Moscow, 1988); and the study and collection, E.D. Polivanov, *Izbrannye trudy po obshchemu i vostochnomu iazykoznaniiu* (Moscow,

1991). Polivanov's work has actually been a continuing topic of study ever since he was rehabilitated in the early 1960s.

9. See Isabelle Kreindler, "The Non-Russian Languages and the Challenge of Russian: the Eastern Versus the Western Tradition," in *Sociolinguistic Perspectives*, ed. Kreindler, pp. 345-46; Serge Zenkovsky, "Kulturkampf in Pre-Revolutionary Central Asia," *American Slavic and East European Review* (February 1955): 15-41; A.A. Rorlich, "Islam Under Communist Rule," *Central Asian Survey* 1, no. 1 (1982): 12. Cyrillic scripts were created for the native languages of several target peoples--the Bashkir, Volga Tatars, Chuvash, Kirgiz-Kazakh, Gagauz, Iakuts, Ossetians, Mari, Komi and Udmurts among them--who stood at key entry points along Russia's frontier with Asia, where in several cases Islam (and therfore the Arabic script) were already under seige by Orthodox missionaries.

10. The Moscow School included V.K. Porzhezinskii, D.N. Ushakov, A.A. Shakhmatov, A.M. Peshkovskii, M.N. Peterson, R.O. Jakobson, N.S. Trubetskoi, R.O. Shor, N.N. Durnovo, G.O. Vinokur, N.F. Iakovlev, L.I. Zhirkov, R.I. Avanesov, V.N. Sidorov, A.A. Reformatskii, and P.S. Kuznetsov. See R.O. Jakobson and K. Pomorska, *Dialogues* (Cambridge, 1983), pp. 10-11; and A.A. Reformatskii, *Selected Writings* (Moscow, 1988), pp. 30-31.

11. The Petersburg School included L.V. Shcherba, L.P. Iakubinskii, D.V. Bubrikh, N.V. Iushmanov, S.I. Bernshtein, V.V. Vinogradov, and E.D. Polivanov. Phonology is the sub-field of linguistics which studies phonemes.

12. V.B. Shklovsky, *Zhili-byli* (Moscow, 1966), p. 89; and *A Baudouin de Courtenay Anthology*, ed. and trans. Edward Stankiewicz (Bloomington, IN, 1972), pp. 50-52, 141-42.

13. See the reports of the Moscow Linguistic Circle of 1923 in TsGALI, f.2164, o.1, d.1, l.2; and TsGAOR, f.2307, o.2, d.431, ll.4-5; TsGA RSFSR, f.2307, o.2, d.431, l.4; and R.O. Jakobson's comments in *Selected Works*, vol. 2 (The Hague, 1971-1988), p. 518. In the context of these activities and debates, I would argue, M. Bakhtin's school appears as altogether derivative and conventional. I discuss these and other issues of language theory and language planning in more detail in a book manuscript in progress, "Soviet Language Frontiers: Linguistic Theories, Language Reforms and the Nationalities Question in the USSR, 1917-1953."

14. Among other accomplishments, Shakhmatov was editor of the multi-volume *Diction-ary of the Russian Language* between 1891 and 1916 and author of the *Outline of the Contemporary Russian Literary Language* of 1913. See V.V. Vinogradov, *Aleksei Aleksandrovich Shakhmatov* (Petrograd, 1922); and Shakhmatov's correspondence with Fortunatov in *Perepiska A.A. Shakhmatov s F.F. Fortunatovym i F.E. Korshem, 1885-1914*, eds. E.S Istrina and V.R. Leikina-Svirskaia (Leningrad, 1948), p. 37.

15. See I. Golanov and N. Durnovo, "Moskovskaia dialektologicheskaia komissiia (1904-1924)," *Slavia* 3 (1924-1925): 749-56; and R. Jakobson and P. Bogatyrev, "Slavianskaia filologiia v rossii za gg. 1914-1921," *Slavia* 1, 2-3, 4 (1922): 171-84, 457-69, 626-34. For Shpet's report, "The Object and Tasks of Ethnic Psychology," see AAN, f.696, o.1, d.155, ll.7-88; or his later book, *Vvedenie v etnicheskuiu psikhologiiu* (Moscow, 1927).

16. Stankiewicz, *Baudouin Anthology*, pp. 65-66, 241. During his stay in Kazan, Baudouin promoted the study and teaching of the local Turkic and Finnic languages.

17. Ia.A. Boduen de Kurtene, *Natsional'nyi i territorial'nyi priznak v avtonomii* (St. Petersburg, 1913), p. 83; and V.I. Chernyshev, "Vospominanii," in V.I. Chernyshev, *Izbrannye trudy* (Moscow, 1970), pp., 685, 688. On Baudouin's "itinerant career," see Henry Walsh, "The Early Development of the Concept of Phonemes in Russian Linguistic Science" (PhD Dissertation, University of North Carolina, 1970), p. 7.

18. Victor Shkolvskii called Polivanov "a man of broad linguistic knowledge and a wreckless life." He was a founding member of the Society for the Study of Poetic Art, the center for avant-garde experimentation in Petrograd, and an amatuer poet in his own right. A Futurist thinker and Bohemian, his scholarly friends unanimously testified to his "eccentricities and extravagances," which included an opium habit he acquired during his travels and language studies in the Far East and Central Asia. See Shklovskii, *Zhili-byli*, p. 95; A.A. Reformatskii, "Petr Savvich Kuznetsov," in *Iazyk i chelovek* (Moscow, 1970), p. 23; V.A. Kaverin, *Petrogradskii student* (Moscow, 1976); and archival materials quoted by A.A. Leontiev in his "Introduction" to E.D. Polivanov, *Selected Works*, compiled by A.A. Leontiev and trans. by Daniel Armstrong (The Hague: Mouton, 1974), pp. 12-13. For poetry selections, see V. Lartsev, *Evgenii Dmitrievich Polivanov. Stranitsy zhizni i deiatel'nosti* (Moscow, 1988).

19. As discussed in Reformatskii, "Petr Savvich Kuznetsov," p. 19.

20. On the precursors and variations of Eurasianism, see Nicholas Riasanovsky, "Prince N.S. Trubetskoi's 'Europe and Mankind,'" *Jahrbucher für Geschichte Osteuropas* 12, no. 2 (1964): 207-20; and Dmitry Shlapentokh, "Thermidor or Mongol Empire: History as Political Model in Russian Emigre Thought," *Cahiers du monde russe et sovietique* 32, no. 3 (1991): 379-408.

21. Boduen de Kurtene, "O smeshannom kharaktere vsekh iazykov," *Izbrannye trudy*, vol. 1 (Moscow, 1963), p. 371; L.V. Shcherba, "O poniatii smesheniia iazykov," *Izbrannye raboty*, vol. 1 (Leningrad, 1958), pp. 40-53; V.V. Ivanov, "Lingvisticheskie vzgliady E.D. Polivanova," *Voprosy iazykoznaniia*, 1957, No. 3: 68-69. Polivanov even partly appreciated the concept of language union as outlined below, although he was opposed to Eurasianist political ideology.

22. See Roman Jakobson, "K kharakteristike evraziiskogo iazykovogo soiuza," in *Selected Writings*, vol. 2, pp. 144-201; and N.S. Trubetskoi, "Vavilonskaia bashnia i

smeshenie iazykov," *Evraziiskii vremennik*, 1923, No. 3: 107-24; and Krystyna Pomorska, "The Utopian Future of the Russian Avant-Garde," in Daniel Armstrong, et al., *Roman Jakobson: Echoes of His Scholarship* (Lisse, 1977), pp. 371-72. Trubetskoi's "Gedanken über das Indo-Germanen Problem," in *Acta Linguistica* (1939) argued against the traditional Indo-European "proto-language" thesis of language identity and origin, positing rather that the Indo-Germanic languages influenced each other by way of language contact, not by formal origin or identity.

23. See N.S. Trubetskoi, "O turanskom elemente v russkoi kul'ture," *Evraziiskii vremennik*, 1925, No. 4; and the discussion in Jindrich Toman, "Trubetzkoy Before Trubetzkoy," in Hans Aarsleff, et al., *Papers in the History of Linguistics* (Amsterdam-Philadelphi, 1987), pp. 636-37.

24. The Eurasianists appreciated Soviet federalism but despised communist internationalism. See *Evraziistvo (formulirovka 1927 g.)* (Moscow, 1927); and *Evraziistvo: deklaratsiia, formulirovka, tezisy* (Prague, 1932). Also, Marc Raeff, "Un empire comme les autres?", *Cahiers du monde russe et sovietique* 30, Nos. 3-4 (1989); and Guy Imart, "A Unique Empire," *Central Asian Survey* 6, no. 4 (1987). For English translations of Trubetskoi's works on these themes and a biographical and historical essay by Anatoli Liberman, see N.S. Trubetskoi, *The Legacy of Genghis Khan* (Ann Arbor, 1991), notably p. 243.

25. On Jakobson's and Trubetskoi's appreciation for the work of Polivanov, Iakovlev, Bubrikh and Zhirkov, see *N.S. Trubetskoi's Letters and Notes* (Berlin, 1975), pp. 87, 121, 143, 150, 200, 229.

26. See A. Leontiev, "E.D. Polivanov i obuchenie russkomu iazyku v natsional'noi shkole," *Russkii iazyk v natsional'noi shkole* 2 (1966): 55-56.

27. See TsGA RSFSR, f.4655, o.1, d.45, l.13; ll.45-47. The typographer mysteriously lost part one of volume two of the *Introduction* during 1928-1929. Only volume one survives. See also E.D. Polivanov, *Za marksistskoe iazykoznanie* (Moscow, 1931), p. 267; TsGA RSFSR, f.4655, o.1, d.389, ll.10-11, 12, 71; d.407, ll.1-2; d.415, ll.6-10, 11-26; and AAN f.468, o.3, d.21, ll.1, 20; d.22; d.28.

28. TsGAOR, f.1318, o.1, d.706(1), l.3--"Protocol No. 6 of the Committee of the RKP(b) of the Second City Region."

29. N.F. Iakovlev, *Voprosy izucheniia chechentsev i ingushei* (USSR, 1927), pp. 46-47.

30. See the 1922-1924 reports of the Circle in TsGA RSFSR, f.2164, o.1, d.1, ll.2-19; and TsGA RSFSR, f.2307, o.2, d.431, ll.4-5.

31. See D. Zelenin, "Obzor sovetskoi etnograficheskoi literatury za 15 let," *Sovetskaia etnografiia*, 1932, No. 5-6: 250. Iakovlev took the lead in the organization and develop-

ment of these institutions—see TsGA RSFSR, f.2307, o.10, d.275, ll.37-39; d.278, ll.161-162. In these organizations Iakovlev worked closely with N.Ia. Marr and L.I. Zhirkov. The latter institute provided an early haven for Iakovlev's, Zhirkov's, Bubrikh's and Polivanov's work with the non-Russian languages. Polivanov joined the Institute's work with studies of Tajik grammar and lexicon, Bubrikh with comparative studies of Finnish and German grammar, Zhirkov with studies of Avar and Dagestani phonology and grammar. See "Nauchno-issledovatel'skii Institut etnicheskikh i natsional'nykh kul'tur narodov vostoka SSSR," *Etnografiia*, 1927, No. 1: 202-205; and TsGA RSFSR, f.4655, o.1, d.289, ll.54-59.

32. See Isabelle Kreindler, "A Neglected Source of Lenin's Nationality Policy," *Slavic Review* 36, no. 1 (March 1977): 86-87; and Michael Bruchis, "The Effect of the USSR's Language Policies on the National Languages of its Turkic Population," in *The USSR and the Muslim World*, ed. Yaacov Roi (London, 1984), pp. 129-32.

33. See Bruchis, "Effect," pp. 132-33; Stephen Blank, "The Origins of Soviet Language Policy, 1917-1921," *Russian History* 15, no. 1 (1988): 77; M. Mamakaev, "Za bolshevisticheskie tempy korenizatsii apparata protiv nedootsenki roli rodnogo iazyka," *Revoliutsiia i gorets*, 1930, No. 11: 65-67.

34. See A. Grintovt, "K planovoi organizatsii nauchno-issledovatel'skoi raboty," *Prosveshchenie natsional'nostei*, 1931, No. 1: 61-67; and K. Barkhin, "Novoe v podgotovke pedkadrov," *Prosveshchenie natsional'nostei*, 1930, No. 6: 47-48. The Bolshevik revolution opened up new opportunities for the study and reform of the languages of the Soviet East. Several institutions, to name but a few, were either created or revived for these tasks: the Central Institute of Living Eastern Languages, established in Petrograd in 1920 with the aim of preparing leadership cadres for practical work in the East; the Institute of Orientology in Moscow and Leningrad with similar aims; the All-Union Association for Orientology; the Communist University of the Workers of the East, where party workers were the focus of attention. See TsGAOR, f.1318, o.1, d.62(b), l.34; d.64; and "Khronika," *Sovetskaia etnologiia*, 1932, Nos. 3-4: 206-31; and 1934, No. 3: 108.

35. See TsGA RSFSR, f.296, o.1, d.118, ll.1-2,12. Between 1925 and 1931, Davydov and his colleagues called time and time again for the establishment of a "Committee on the Language Cultures of the Eastern peoples" and for the centralization of linguistic work within Narkompros in order to deal with the primary scientific questions of alphabet and language reform. TsGA RSFSR, f.296, o.1, d.116, ll.113-114(b); d.72, ll.85-93; and TsGA RSFSR, f.296, o.1, d.470, ll.175-176.

36. D.V. Bubrikh, "Neobkhodim revoliutsionnyi pochin," *Prosveshchenie natsional'nostei*, 1929, No. 1: 73-74.

37. The "divide and conquer" thesis is pervasive in much of the otherwise valuable scholarship: Aiaz Ishkaki, *Idel'-Ural* (Paris, 1933; reprint ed., London, 1988), pp. 52-

54; Olaf Caroe, *Soviet Empire* (London, 1953), pp. 154-59; Alexandre Bennigsen, *Islam in the Soviet Union*, p. 250; Ronald Wixman, *Language Aspects of Ethnic Patterns and Processes in the North Caucasus* (Chicago, 1980), pp. 122-25; S. Enders Wimbush, "The Politics of Identity Change in Soviet Central Asia," *Central Asian Survey* 3, no. 3 (1985): 73; Nadir Devlet, "A Specimen of Russification: the Turks of Kazan," *Central Asian Survey* 2, no. 3 (1983): 80; Michael Rywkin, *Moscow's Muslim Challenge* (Armonk, 1990), p. 92; Richard Pipes, *Russia Observed* (Boulder, 1989), p. 205; H.B. Paksoy, *Alpamysh: Central Asian Identity Under Russian Rule* (New Britain, 1989). Audrey Alstadt's *The Azerbaijani Turks* (Stanford, 1992), pp. 95 and 124, offers a more balanced appreciation for Latinization as both native cultural process and Soviet policy.

38. As the sources in the above note maintain, particularly Bennigsen, *Islam*, p. 126; and Wixman, *Language Aspects*, pp. 146-47.

39. The nationalities of Central Asia had been developing self-consciousness ever since the late 1800s, not only in reaction against Tsarist policies but as a result of the activities of indigenous peoples. See Edward Allworth, *Central Asia: A Century of Russian Rule* (New York, 1967); Serge Zenkovsky, *Pan-Turkism and Islam in Russia* (Cambridge, 1960). Essays by Simon Crisp and Shirin Akiner in *Language*, ed. Kirkwood; and by Martha Brill Olcott and Isabelle Kreindler in *Sociolinguistic Perspectives*, ed. Kreindler, have explored the early developing nationalism of the Caucasus and Central Asian peoples.

40. In 1922, G.I. Broido, a deputy director of the Commissariat for Nationalities, complained in a report to the Central Executive Committee of the Russian Communist Party (RKPb) of the troubles which arose because each of the Central Asian peoples needed their own Arabic scripts--an obstacle to setting up typographies. In TsGAOR, f.1318, o.1, d.214(2), l.105. There were several reforms of existing Arabic scripts: by Baitursunov in Kazakhstan, Sharaf in Tatarstan, and Arabaev in Kirgiziia. Arabic scripts were also revised for the Karakalpak, Uigur, Karachai-Balkar, and Dagestani languages. See *Opyt sovershenstvovaniia alfavitov i orfografii iazykov narodov SSSR*, ed. K.M. Musaev (Moscow, 1982), pp. 46, 89, 108, 140; and D. Validov, *Ocherk obrazovannosti i literatury Tatar do revoliutsii 1917 g.)* (Moscow, 1923), pp. 156-57.

41. See the reports of 1919-1920 in TsGA RSFSR, f.2306, o.19, d.125, ll.7-8.

42. See Iakovlev's remarks in *Stenograficheskii otchet tret'ego plenuma VTsKNTA* (Kazan: VTsKNTA, 1928), pp. 10-11--greeted with applause and a flourish by the orchestra.

43. E.D. Polivanov, "Osnovnye formy graficheskoi revoliutsii v turetskikh pis'men- nostiakh SSSR," *Novyi vostok* 23-24 (1928): 316-20. See also S.A. Novgorodov, *Pervye shagi iakutskoi pis'mennosti* (Moscow, 1977). Novgorodov purposely did not choose a transcription system then in use by Russian scholars (the Russian Linguistic Alphabet, whose main adherent was V.V. Radlov).

44. Polivanov, "Osnovnye formy," pp. 316-20; Novgorodov, *Pervye shagi*, pp. 8-9.

45. See A.G. Danilin, "Etnograficheskaia rabota v iakutskoi ASSR," *Etnografiia*, 1927, Nos. 1-2: 185-92; and S. Donskoi, "Po etapam iakutskoi pis'mennosti," *Revoliutsiia i pis'mennost'*, 1932, No. 3: 40-43.

46. The ostensible authors of these script projects were, for the most part, native representatives of the North Caucasus peoples. For a history of Latinization projects in the North Caucasus, or how the "light of the Latin alphabet" was helping these peoples to modernize, see Umar Aliev's report in TsGAOR, f.1318, o.1, d.1700, ll.3-4. See also Musaev, *Opyt*, pp. 99, 156, 161-62.

47. Kh.D. Oshaev, "K voprosu ob unifikatsii," *Izvestiia 1-go i 2-go severo-kavkazskikh pedagogicheskikh institutov* 2, no. 11 (1934: 223.

48. The First North Caucasus Peoples' Congress of 1917 and government of the Union of Mountaineers of the North Caucasus agreed not only to form one nation, but also to recognize the right of all languages to development and study through the schools. See N. Samurskii, *Dagestan* (Moscow, 1925); B. Baytugan, "The North Caucasus," *Studies on the Soviet Union* 11, no. 1 (1971): 12-13; R. Karcha, "The Status of Popular Education in the North Caucasus," *Caucasian Review* 7 (1958): 110-24.

49. See Umar Aliev, "Latinizatsiia pis'mennosti," *Revoliutsiia i gorets*, 1928, No. 1: 34; Umar Aliev, "Polnaia pobeda novogo alfavita na severnom kavkaze," *Revoliutsiia i gorets*, 1928, No. 2: 69-72; A. Khadzhiev, "Ob unifikatsii gorskikh alfavitov," *Revoliutsiia i gorets*, 1930, No. 4: 46-51; M. Milykh, "O plane rabot kraikoma novogo alfavita," *Revoliutsiia i gorets*, 1933, Nos. 1-2: 93-96.

50. See N.F. Iakovlev, "Voprosy natsional'noi gramoty," *Zhizn' natsional'nostei* 18 (1922): 4-5; and N.F. Iakovlev, "Razvitie natsional'noi pis'mennosti u vostochnykh narodov sovetskogo soiuza i zarozhdenie ikh natsional'nykh alfavitov," *Revoliutsionnyi vostok*, 1928, No. 3: 217-21.

51. N.F. Iakovlev, "Matematicheskaia formula postroeniia alfavita (opyt prakticheskogo prilozheniia lingvisticheskoi teorii)," *Kul'tura i pis'mennost' vostoka*, 1928, No. 1: 41-64, reprinted in *Iz istorii otechestvennoi fonologii*, ed. A.A. Reformatskii (Moscow, 1970), pp. 123-48. See also N.F. Iakovlev, *Tablitsy fonetiki kabardinskogo iazyka* (Moscow, 1923), p. 5; and N.F. Iakovlev, "Voprosy natsional'noi gramoty," pp. 4-5.

52. D. Polivanov, *Problemy latinskogo shrifta v turetskikh pis'mennostiakh (po povodu novogo iakutskogo alfavita, azerbaidzhanskoi azbuki jeni jol i uzbekskogo alfavita* (Moscow, 1923), p.i, and *Proekty latinizatsii turetskikh pis'mennostei SSSR k turkologicheskomu s"ezdu II* (Tashkent), 1926.

53. On disputes over working principles, see *Pervyi vsesoiuznyi tiurkologicheskii s"ezd.*

190 Michael Smith

Stenografcheskii otchet (Baku, 1926); and *Stenografcheskii otchet pervogo plenuma vsesoiuznogo tsentral'nogo komiteta novogo tiurkskogo alfavita (VTsKNTA)* (Moscow, 1927). On disputes over capital letters, see *Stenografcheskii otchet tret'ego plenuma VTsKNTA* (Kazan, 1928), pp. 115-16, 130-31, 134-35, 138, 148-49, 154-56, 161.

54. See *Stenografcheskii otchet pervogo plenuma*, pp. 81-82, 85; and *Stenografcheskii otchet vtorogo plenuma VTsKNTA* (Baku, 1929), p. 46.

55. Iakovlev, "Voprosy natsional'noi gramoty," p. 5; and *Stenografcheskii otchet V plenuma VTsKNA* (Moscow, 1932), p. 67.

56. See *Stenografcheskii otchet tret'ego plenuma*, pp. 141-42.

57. *Stenografcheskii otchet vtorogo plenuma*, pp. 10, 56, 75-78; See also Agamaly-Ogly's attack on Polivanov in his "Novyi tiurkskii alfavit v tiurko-tatarskikh respublikakh soiuza," *Sovetskoe stroitel'stvo*, 1927, No. 7: 60-63.

58. See "S"ezd prepodavatelei russkogo iazyka," *Rodnoi iazyk v shkole*, 1917, No. 6: 259-61; A. Artiushkov, "Pervyi vserossiiskii s"ezd slovesnikov v Moskve v 1916-1917 g.," *Rodnoi iazyk v shkole*, 1927, No. 5: 293-98, on the First All-Russian Congress of Teachers of the Russian Language in the Middle Schools (December 1916 to January 1917); and "Vserossiiskii s"ezd deiatelei srednei shkoly," *Rodnoi iazyk v shkole*, 1917, Nos. 8-10: 426-28, on a conference held on May 12-15, 1917.

59. "Pered novoi zhizn'iu," *Rodnoi iazyk v shkole*, 1917, Nos. 8-10: 357-58.

60. See Davydov's 1929 report in TsGA RSFSR, f.296, o.1, d.434, l.33; and d.470 for his remarks at a 1931 Narkompros conference on the national minorities of the RSFSR.

61. See P. Khadzaragov, "Zabytyi uchastok," *Prosveshchenie i natsional'nosti*, 1930, No. 6: 96. D.V. Bubrikh (1890-1949), for example, completed a comparative study of Russian and Mordvinian sounds, stresses, words, word formations and commbinations. This was something of a classic in the genre of language union studies, applauded for its scientific study of such interactions between the languages and for being most useful to Mordvinian students learning Russian. See his report, "The Russian Language and its Distinctions from Mordvinian," and Academician B.M. Liapunov's comments on it in TsGA RSFSR, f.296, o.1, d.447, ll.1-18.

62. See S.M. Dimanshtein, "Partprosveshchenie sredi natsional'nostei i natsmen," and "Tesizy ob osnovakh prisposobleniia programm natsional'nykh sovpartshkol k usloviiam natsional'nykh osobennostei (priniatye soveshchaniem natsovpartshkol i natsotdelenii po dokladu tov. Dimanshtein) (utverzhdeno APO TsK VKPb)," in *Voprosy natsional'nogo partprosveshcheniia* (Moscow, 1927), pp. 19-24, 151-55; and S.M. Dimanshtein, "Printsipy sozdaniia natsional'noi terminologii," in *Pis'mennost' i revoliutsiia*, ed. D. Korkmasov (Moscow, 1933), pp. 32-34.

63. See E.D. Polivanov, "Rodnoi iazyk v natsional'noi partshkole," *Voprosy natsional'nogo partprosveshcheniia*, pp. 111-22. Polivanov wrote methodological tracts comparing the phonological and grammatical forms between the Russian and other non-Russian languages. He further refined the new method of teaching Russian to non-Russians by first diagramming the features of the native non-Russian languages, this to allow students to draw the crucial analogies between the structures of their own languages and Russian. See E.D. Polivanov, "Osnovnye formy," in *Za marksistskoe*, pp. 315, 321. With L.I. Pal'min, Polivanov was co-author of an early Russian language primer for Turkic children, *'Mak.' Russkii bukvar' dlia nerusskikh detei Turkestana* (Tashkent, 1925), as well as author of a text on teaching Russian to Uzbek speakers, *Opyt chastnoi metodiki prepodavaniia russkogo iazyka uzbekami*, part 1 (Tashkent, 1935). See also Leontiev, "Polivanov," pp. 56-59; and E.D. Polivanov, "Chtenie i proiznoshenie na urokakh russkogo iazyka, v sviazi s navykami rodnogo iazyka," in *Voprosy prepodavaniia russkogo iazyka v shkolakh vzroslykh (trudy vserossiiskoi konferentsii prepodavatelei slovesnikov shkol politprosveta 1928 g.)*, part II, eds. G. Danilov and I. Ustinov (Moscow-Leningrad, 1928), p. 31.

64. See G. Polivanov, "O prepodavanii terminologii," *LEF* 3 (1925), pp. 109-17; and E.D. Polivanov, "Inostrannaia terminologiia kak element prepodavaniia russkogo iazyka," in *Za marksistskoe*, pp. 67-72. I am assuming that the former article was Polivanov's, notwithstanding the different first initial, which may have been a mistake, or a practical joke.

65. My argument is based on a preliminary review of documents from the archives of \the Sovnatsmen and Narkompros, for example: TsGA RSFSR, f.296, o.1, d.72, ll.131-135, 168-171; d.118; d.386, ll.16-18.

66. See "Predvaritel'noe predlozhenie orfograficheskoi podkomissii Glavnauki," *Uchitel'skaia gazeta* 148 (Dec. 21, 1929): 3. Similar notions were expressed in *Proekt reformy pravopisaniia*, eds. K. Barkhin et al. (Moscow, 1930), p. 9; and *Proekt Glavnauki o novom pravopisanii*, eds. N.E. Kremenskii and V. Maminov (Moscow, 1930), pp. 23-26. See also V.I. Strazhev, *Ocherk po izucheniiu iazyka* (Moscow, 1931), pp. 10-11; and a report of the State Academic Council from 1929 in TsGA RSFSR, f.298, o.2, d.76. N. Samurskii, national communist leader of Dagestan, became a proponent of teaching Russian--rather than the native languages--to the small nationalities of the North Caucasus, not as a "state language" but as a Leninist language. See Samurskii's comments in the debates of the Commission for the Study of the National Question (in the Communist Academy), AAN, f.361, o.2, d.6, ll.33-34.

67. See Davydov's 1929 reports in TsGA RSFSR, f.296, o.1, d.169; and d.434, ll.117-123.

Social Areas under State Socialism: The Case of Moscow

Ellen Hamilton

Introduction

From the very beginning, one of the highest priorities of the Soviet leadership was the equitable distribution of social goods. Among the most important of those goods was housing. A wide range of policies and institutions were put to the service of ensuring universal and low cost shelter for Soviet citizens. To what extent did those policies result in equitable distribution?

In the West, the housing market is an important mechanism that distributes different kinds of housing to various social groups, usually in distinct regions of a city. Have Soviet policies had a different result? A reliable assessment of this question must be grounded in empirical evidence on residential differentiation. Such evidence will also enable analysts to pinpoint more clearly the forces that shaped the distribution of social goods in the past, and to appreciate the extent to which those same forces may affect distribution now that a market is emerging in the former Soviet Union.

The very notion of residential differentiation in a non-market society raises some interesting questions. In Western cities, institutions such as banks, developers and local governments exert significant constraints on consumer choice in the housing market by influencing such matters as the type, quantity and location of housing. Residential differentiation in Western cities cannot be adequately understood without considering these institutional constraints. This study tests the hypothesis that in a non-market urban space, in this case the city of Moscow, Soviet institutions played a similar role in structuring the distribution of housing.

The Role of the State and State Institutions

The political economy of the Soviet Union functioned very differently from that of a developed market society. The Soviet state participated in urban life to a much greater degree than its Western counterparts, using the tools unique to centrally administered or command economies. The state would set priorities-- for example, providing housing for all citizens--and then through the planning process channel economic resources to realize state priorities. It was this control of both political and economic life, which resulted from the attempt to replace the market, that differentiated the role of the state in state socialist societies from those in developed market societies.[1]

In recent research, Sovietologists began to question the classic view of the Soviet state as entirely monolothic or totalitarian, suggesting instead that pluralist models might be more appropriate to the analysis of Soviet social processes. They found that diverse institutions, including the government, the Party, and economic entities, played roles in Soviet society; for example, it was argued that local institutions, such as local governments, often pursued goals at variance with those of central institutions, for example, central government or all-Union ministries.[2]

Much recent work on the roles of various institutions and the frequently conflicting aims of central and local bodies focused on urban areas.[3] Researchers described two basic sources of conflict. The first was the tension between governmental authorities and the major ministries, more specifically the non-subordination of ministerial organizations to governmental authorities, except at the highest level. This tension was reinforced by the coexistence of two types of planning in the city: urban or general plans, and branch or economic plans. The principal tension between these two plans derived from their dual purposes. Urban or general plans would be drawn up for a particular city, in this case the city of Moscow, while economic or five-year plans covered particular branches of the economy (i.e., the ministries). The historical primacy of economic planning over regional planning ensured a certain amount of autonomy for important ministries, permitting them to flout instructions from local authorities, while still complying with central policies as embodied in the economic plans.

Another stress point was located among different levels of either the same or different institutions: the municipal or local government, for example, lacked the power to control effectively the actions of non-subordinate (or all-Union) ministerial enterprises. But at the same time, municipal authorities might pursue ends somewhat different from those envisioned by the central government.[4] Scholars found that Party officials often acted as brokers among governmental and ministerial organizations at the same, and different, levels.[5] Thus, to understand urban processes in the late Soviet period, one must consider the roles of the major institutional participants, especially the governmental and ministerial bodies, at both the local and central levels.

The tensions among institutions and the two planning processes dated back to their creation and implementation in the 1920s and 1930s, when both governmental and economic institutions built most of the physical infrastructure in Moscow (including housing, roads, water lines, stores and factories). In general, governmental and ministerial institutions built the city in accordance with larger goals expressed in either general or economic plans. Therefore, any spatial differentiation found in the built environment could be attributed to the actions of governmental and ministerial institutions.

Residential Differentiation in Moscow

Scholars suggest that for residential differentiation to take place, three aspects of social and spatial differentiation must exist. First, the population must be socially stratified. If a society is socially homogeneous, social groups cannot be territorially delimited. Second, the housing stock must be differentiated by region. If all housing were the same, or if different housing types were randomly spread throughout the city, residential differentiation of social groups would not occur. Finally, different social groups must be able to gain access to different types of housing. If housing were distributed through a random lottery, for example, the luck of the draw would determine who received what kind of housing. Any residential differentiation would be the result of random processes.[6]

If residential differentiation existed in Moscow, one would expect these three requirements to have been fulfilled. The first aspect, social stratification, has been well documented by Western and Soviet researchers, who, in general, found three main groups: the elite (including Party officials, important managers, high-level academics and prominent artists), lower social status groups (including low-skilled manual workers and workers in routine clerical, office and service jobs), and "middle class" groups (including the more skilled manual workers and many pink and white collar jobs).[7]

The second prerequisite for residential differentiation, variation in quality and location of Moscow's housing stock, has not been adequately investigated. To explore this issue, we must examine the dominant role of state institutions in the construction of the built environment, and to determine which institutions were building what type of housing, when, where, and for whom.

The final prerequisite for residential differentiation is a mechanism which links social status to housing quality and location. In the West, land and housing markets serve this role.[8] In the Soviet Union, however, all land belonged to the state and a housing market, in the western sense of that term, did not exist.[9] State institutions (municipal and ministerial) not only built but also allocated virtually all housing in Moscow. Since rents were low and standardized, if residential differentiation is found, the housing allocation process must have served as the primary mechanism to link social stratification to housing differentiation. A number of researchers have suggested that, indeed, the allocative mechanism discriminated for and against certain social groups; for example, many members of the elite (such as high-ranking Party members, academics, recipients of honorifics, high-level military and KGB officials) were legally entitled to more and better housing.[10] Central directives ensured that municipal and ministerial authorities provided more housing to some social groups. To date, few scholars have examined the allocation system much less its territorial consequences. This study seeks to fill that gap.

Geographic Scale of Analysis

Moscow, a city of about 9 million people, is divided into 33 administrative districts, which range in size from 85,000 to 660,000 inhabitants (Figure 1). The large size of some of the districts, as well as their ring-radial placement, may obscure social differentiation among the districts. Large districts probably are less homogeneous than small districts. The wedge-shaped central districts include buildings from several periods ranging from pre-revolutionary mansions of the nobility to apartments built during the 1950s and 1960s when rapid construction was emphasized at the expense of quality. More housing built recently fills the periphery.

Despite the large size and less than ideal shape of the districts, the thirty-three districts are amenable to analysis that provides some insights into understanding residential differentiation in a non-market society. They may be used to characterize in broad terms the attributes of different areas of the city.

Characteristics of the Population

In order to determine whether there was any spatial differentiation of social groups in Moscow, I have examined four variables that relate to social status (Table 1). Since data that allow measurement of social status are very scarce in the Soviet Union, I use direct and indirect measures, and where possible use variables analogous to those used in western research on residential differentiation, for example, the rate of completion of higher education and the share of children (aged 0-14) in the population. Data limitations, however, make it impossible to replicate western research.

The first variable, the number of people who have completed degrees and certificates from higher educational institutions[11] per 1,000 population aged 15 and over, is probably the strongest measure of social status. People with higher education tended to belong to higher status occupational groups, for example management or scientific researchers, and, in general, earned higher incomes. Furthermore, education and Party membership were found to be highly correlated.[12] I hypothesize that higher education correlates positively with social status.

The second variable, the rate of car ownership, provides an important indicator of material well-being in a society where a car represented a significant investment of both time and money. In 1989, a new car could well have cost

Figure 1. **Moscow Administrative Districts, 1989**

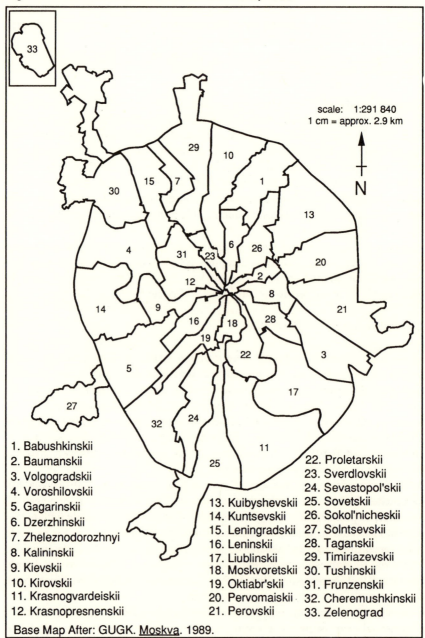

scale: 1:291 840
1 cm = approx. 2.9 km

N

1. Babushkinskii
2. Baumanskii
3. Volgogradskii
4. Voroshilovskii
5. Gagarinskii
6. Dzerzhinskii
7. Zheleznodorozhnyi
8. Kalininskii
9. Kievskii
10. Kirovskii
11. Krasnogvardeiskii
12. Krasnopresnenskii

13. Kuibyshevskii
14. Kuntsevskii
15. Leningradskii
16. Leninskii
17. Liublinskii
18. Moskvoretskii
19. Oktiabr'skii
20. Pervomaiskii
21. Perovskii

22. Proletarskii
23. Sverdlovskii
24. Sevastopol'skii
25. Sovetskii
26. Sokol'nicheskii
27. Solntsevskii
28. Taganskii
29. Timiriazevskii
30. Tushinskii
31. Frunzenskii
32. Cheremushkinskii
33. Zelenograd

Base Map After: GUGK. Moskva. 1989.

Table 1

Summary of variables used to describe social status

Variable Name	Description
Higher education	Number of people who have completed higher education per 1,000 population ages 15 and over
Car ownership	Number of cars per 1,000 population
Criminals	Number of residents convicted of a crime per 1,000 population ages 15 and over
Children	Number of youths under 15 per 1,000 population

Sources: *Itogi vsesoiuznoi perepisi naseleniia 1989 g. po g. Moskve: demograficheskaia, natsional'naia, kul'turnaia, sotsial'no-ekonomicheskaia kharakteristika naseleniia, chislo i sostav semei* (Moscow: Goskomstat RSFSR, Moskovskoe gorodskoe upravlenie statistiki, 1990); Goskomstat 1989.

10,000 rubles or more, a substantial sum since the average worker was earning about 250 rubles a month. Despite the cost, people routinely waited for years to obtain a car at state prices. A new car increased significantly in value once it was driven out the factory door. Car ownership, then, is a surrogate measure of income. An average worker living on several hundred rubles a month would not likely have been able to save for a car. The rate of car ownership should correlate positively with social status.

The third variable, the number of residents who have been convicted of a crime per 100,000 population aged 15 and over, also relates to social status. In general, criminals are less educated than the population as a whole. In Russia, as in the west, criminals were disproportionately of lower socioeconomic status, earning less money and working in lower status jobs.[13] The proportion of residents in a district who have been convicted of a crime should be negatively associated with social status.

The final measure of social status, the share of children in the population, should be negatively associated with social status. Larger families generally have lower per capita incomes, because fewer income earners support relatively more dependents. Since more highly educated couples tend to be of high social status and generally to have fewer children than their less educated counterparts, the number of children in a family should relate negatively to both social status and income.[14]

Characteristics of the Housing Stock

To determine the characteristics of Moscow's housing stock, I employed a number of variables, listed in Table 2, which describe housing quality, housing tenure, and the attractiveness of living in different districts.

Historically, housing was in extremely short supply in the Soviet Union, so floor space per capita serves as the most important measure of housing quality. Researchers have found that different social groups had significantly different amounts of living space per capita.[15] Furthermore, the law provided for some groups (i.e., elite workers in Party, governmental and economic organizations, academics, Heroes of Labor and other recipients of honorifics, high-level military officers, and artists) to receive extra housing because of their contribution to society.[16] To examine whether the provision of housing differed among districts in present-day Moscow, I used two measures of housing space: "useful" space which is the entire floor area of the apartment, and "living" space, which includes living rooms and bedrooms, but excludes kitchens, bathrooms, hallways and storage areas.

Housing quality was also related to housing tenure in the Soviet Union. To summarize briefly, socialized housing included housing belonging to the local soviets or councils (municipalized housing), and departmental housing, which belonged to extra-territorial bodies such as state institutions, enterprises, organizations, trade unions and other co-operative entities. In addition, some housing in Moscow was cooperative or built by housing construction cooperatives. Finally, a small amount of housing in Moscow belonged to private individuals.

Are There Social Areas in Moscow?

If residential differentiation existed in Moscow, then one would expect to find different social groups in different parts of the city. In prerevolutionary Moscow, this was certainly true. The central western districts housed people of higher social status, while the poor lived on the periphery.[17] During the 1920s and 1930s, a high proportion of manual workers[18] lived in Proletarskii and Stalinskii districts, where many of the largest industrial enterprises were located.

Table 2

Summary of variables used to describe housing

Variable Name	Description
Useful space	Useful space (square meters) per capita
Living space	Living space (square meters) per capita
Socialized housing	Proportion of all housing in district that belongs to the state (i.e., municipalized and departmental housing)
Municipalized housing	Proportion of all housing in district that belongs to the city council
Departmental housing	Proportion of all housing in district that belongs to departments (i.e., ministries)
Cooperative housing	Proportion of all housing in district that belongs to cooperatives
Private housing	Proportion of all housing in district that belongs to private individuals

Source: *Statisticheskii spravochnik: O zhilishchno-kommunal'nom (zhilom i nezhilom) fonde goroda moskvy po sostoianiiu na 1 ianvaria 1989 goda* (Moscow: Gorodskim biuro te inventarizatsii ispolkom Mossoveta, 1989).

To determine whether these patterns have been maintained or altered, I begin by exploring the spatial distribution of social groups at the beginning of 1989.

The four variables used to describe social status (Table 1) should vary among the districts, and should vary in the same way, if residential differentiation occurs. The coefficient of variation, which compares the relative variability of the four variables, provides a useful summary measure of the degree to which

Table 3

Coefficient of variation for variables identifying social status

Variable Description	Mean	Standard Deviation	Coefficient of Variation (%)
No. people with completed higher education/1000 pop. 15 and over	279	67.3	24.1%
No. cars/1000 population	59	8.8	14.8
No. residents convicted of a crime/100,000 population 15 and over	298	47	15.8
No. juveniles under 15/ 1000 population	183	19.4	10.6

districts vary (Table 3). The coefficient of variation permits direct comparison of variability since it standardizes the standard deviation relative to the mean, so variation in variables with different means can be compared. The coefficients of variation for the four variables range from a high of 24.1% for the share of people who had completed higher education to a low of 10.6% for the share of juveniles in the population. The proportion of residents convicted of a crime and the rate of automobile ownership fall in the middle with coefficients of variation of 15.8% and 14.8% respectively. All four variables varied among the districts of Moscow. Higher education varied roughly twice as much as the share of juveniles, which varied the least.

Correlation coefficients permit us to investigate the second hypothesis, that the variables vary in the same way among districts. Correlation coefficients indicate the strength of the association among the variables. The four variables that identify social status are all significantly ($p \leq .01$) intercorrelated (Table 4). As hypothesized, car ownership rates correlated positively with the proportion of residents who had completed higher education ($r = 0.80$). The proportion of residents convicted of a crime and the share of juveniles also fit the expected

Table 4

Pearson correlation coefficients for social status variables

Variable Name	CARS	HIGH	CRIMS	MINOR
Car ownership rate (CARS)	1.00			
Higher ed/1000 pop. (HIGH)	.80	1.00		
Residents convicted of a crime/100,000 (CRIMS)	-.66	-.76	1.00	
Juveniles/1000 (MINOR)	-.68	-.75	.60	1.00

All correlation coefficients are significant (p ≤ .01), N = 33.

pattern and correlated positively (r = .60). Higher education and the rate of automobile ownership correlated negatively with the share of juveniles and residents convicted of a crime. Districts with high rates of car ownership and large shares of residents who had completed higher education tended to be districts with few residents who had been convicted of a crime or who were juveniles.

Factor Analysis Results

The high levels of association among the variables suggest that they might be summarized using factor analysis. Factor analysis calculates a new variable, known as a factor, that summarizes the relationships among the four original variables, by describing their common variance.[19] This technique permits the four variables to be summarized by one underlying factor or variable which best describes the common variance among the four original variables. Due to their different scales of measurement, the four variables were standardized for the factor analysis.

Table 5

Results of factor analysis on variables
describing social status

Variable description	Factor loading
No. residents age 15 and over who have completed higher education	.946
Car ownership rate	.879
No. residents age 15 and over convicted of a crime	-.742
Share of juveniles under 15 years of age	-.775

Eigenvalue	2.82	
Percent of total variance	70.5	

One significant factor, accounting for 70.5% of the variance, emerged (Table 5). The level of explained variance was high, comparing favorably with the levels reported in other studies.[20] The loadings for all four variables were also large and in the expected directions. The factor measured social status, with positive loadings for the proportion of residents aged 15 and over who had completed higher education and the rate of car ownership, and negative loadings for the proportion of residents convicted of crimes, and the proportion of residents who were juveniles under 15 years of age. Districts with well educated residents and many cars had proportionally fewer residents convicted of crimes and proportionally fewer juveniles.

A factor score indicates a value for each district on the derived factor, which allows us to compare the social status of the districts directly. The scores ranged from -1.92 for Solntsevskii to 1.84 for Leninskii.[21] Since standardized variables were used in the factor analysis, the mean for the factor scores is 0. Districts with high positive scores were places with high social status (i.e., many

Table 6

Mean, standard deviation and range for elite, average and lower social status groups of districts

	N	Mean	Standard Deviation	Minimum Score	Maximum Score
Elite	10	1.16	0.40	0.70	1.84
Average	13	-.03	0.32	-0.5	0.47
Lower	10	-1.06	0.42	-1.92	-0.69

residents with higher education and cars, and few residents convicted of crimes and juveniles). The recently incorporated dacha community of Solntsevskii scored the lowest in this respect, while Leninskii district, home of the Kremlin and Moscow State University, scored the highest.

To illustrate the spatial distribution of social status, districts were ranked on the basis of their factor scores and then divided into three groups: districts with scores from 0.50 to -0.50, or districts within one-half standard deviation of the mean, were classified as average status districts; districts with factor scores greater than .50 were classified as elite; and districts with factor scores less than -.50 were classified as lower social status.

Table 6 provides summary information about the three groups. Ten districts were classified as elite with factor scores greater than .50, with a mean score of 1.16 and a standard deviation of .40. The thirteen average districts had a mean score of -.03 and a standard deviation of .32. The mean score for the ten lower social status districts was -1.06 and the standard deviation was .42.

Examination of the maximum and minimum scores for the three groups suggests they were clearly differentiated from one another. The minimum score for an elite district was .70, while the maximum score for an average district was .47. The minimum factor score for an average district was -.50. Since the maximum score for a lower social status district was -.69, average and lower social status districts could also be distinguished clearly from one another.

Figure 2 shows the spatial distribution of the three groups of districts. As expected, elite, average and lower social status districts generally conformed to

Figure 2. **Spatial Distribution of Social Status Groups in Moscow, 1989**

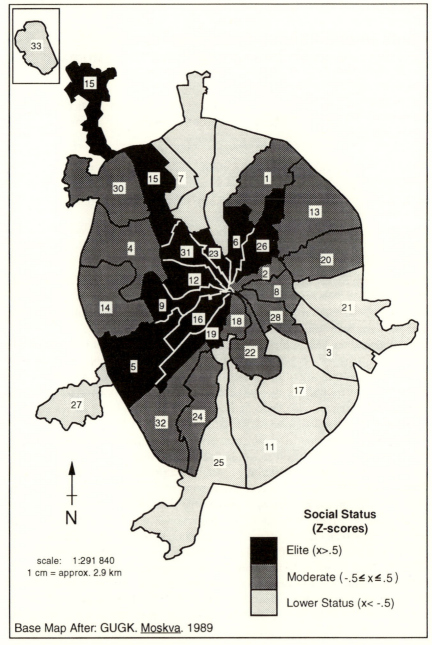

scale: 1:291 840
1 cm = approx. 2.9 km

Social Status (Z-scores)

Elite (x>.5)

Moderate (-.5≤ x ≤.5)

Lower Status (x< -.5)

Base Map After: GUGK. <u>Moskva</u>. 1989

Note: See Figure 1 for district names.

the patterns of the individual variables. Elite districts were clustered in the western part of the central city, extending in a band from the center along the Leningrad highway to the northwestern border, and in a wedge to the southwestern border. In the central part of the city, elite districts included Oktiabr'-skii [19], Leninskii [16], Kievskii [9], Krasnopresnenskii [12], Frunzenskii [31], Sverdlovskii [23], Dzerzhinskii [6] and Sokol'nicheskii [36].

It is interesting to note that the spatial distribution of the elite reflected traditional, historic patterns. In pre-revolutionary Moscow, the well off lived in the western sector of the city. It should be recalled that, following the Revolution, the central leadership[22] concentrated construction and reconstruction efforts in the central part of the city, especially the western part, which they intended to exemplify the achievements of the Soviet state. By 1931, the better educated non-manual workers (*sluzhashchie*) were concentrated in the reconstructed western part of the city.[23] In the center to the northeast, both Dzerzhinskii [6] and Sokol'nicheskii [28] districts have been identified here as elite. Dzerzhinskii district was the home of the KGB, among other institutions, and was one of the most prestigious extra-territorial departments in the Soviet Union. The KGB was housed in quarters built or reconstructed during the first general plan, from 1935-50. Before the Revolution, Sokol'nicheskii district was a prestigious resort for the elite. It, too, was an area where significant resources were invested in the 1930s, largely to develop Sokol'nicheskii Park. In the northwest, Leningradskii district [15] encompassed the second pre-revolutionary resort area for the elite as well as the beginning of the highway to Leningrad (now St. Petersburg), the second most important city in the Soviet Union and the former capital. Finally, to the southwest lies Gagarinskii [5], which stretches to the Ring Automobile Highway. Gagarinskii adjoins Leninskii [16], the district with the highest social status and the home of both the Kremlin and Moscow State University, as well as Oktiabr'skii [19] and Kievskii [9].

Lower status districts were clustered in the north and in the southeastern sectors of the city where many industrial enterprises are located. In the north, the districts of Zheleznodorozhnyi [7], Timiriazevskii [29] and Kirovskii [10] formed one distinct group. Zheleznodorozhnyi is the home of major chemical and machine building enterprises, as well as a center for the Moscow Department of Railroads, from which its name is derived.[24] Timiriazevskii [29] is the site of machine building and electronic producing enterprises as well as many construction organizations. In the southeast, the lower status districts of Sovetskii [25], Krasnogvardeiskii [11], Liublinskii [17], Volgogradskii [3] and Perovskii [21] formed another block. These districts make up the heart of heavy industry in Moscow, and house many extremely large factories including the second largest car factory and the Frezer instrument making factory.[25] Both districts outside the Ring Automobile Road (Solntsevskii [27] and Zelenograd [33]) were of lower social status. Until its recent incorporation into the city,

Solntsevskii [27] was primarily a dacha community. Most dachas lacked even basic amenities such as running water, and the year-round residents in dacha communities frequently were either peasants, who are of low social status, or people who did not qualify for a Moscow residency permit. These people, too, generally are of lower social status. Zelenograd, which is not even contiguous with the rest of Moscow, is primarily industrial.

The remaining districts fell in the middle range in terms of social status. One group of average districts (Cheremushkinskii [32], Sevastopol'skii [24], Moskvoretskii [18], Proletarskii [22], Taganskii [28], Kalininskii [8], Baumanskii [2], Pervomaiskii [20], Kuibyshevskii [13] and Babushkinskii [1]) formed a buffer zone dividing the elite districts in the central city and to the southwest from the heavily industrial southeast. These districts were diverse. In the southwest, Cheremushkinskii [32] and Sevastopol'skii [24] belong to the scientific-research group of districts, while the other districts in this group tended to be the older industrial districts. A second cluster of average districts was found between the two prongs of elite districts that stretch to the periphery in the west (Kuntsevskii [14], Voroshilovskii [4] and Tushinskii [30]). The western cluster has been developed only since the 1960s. Until then the land was used primarily for recreation.

Differentiation in the Housing Stock

Although data limitations prohibit establishing a direct correlation between social status and housing quality, the available information about housing does suggest that the housing stock was differentiated and the housing allocation system provided different social groups with access to different types of housing. These findings support the hypothesis that residential differentiation exists in Moscow.

The quality of the Moscow housing stock varies in part as a result of differences in housing tenure, or who built and owned housing. In Moscow, 89.5% of all housing was socialized, consisting of municipalized housing, owned by the city council, and departmental housing, owned by extra-territorial organizations, such as state institutions, enterprises, organizations, trade unions or other cooperative bodies. Cooperative housing built by housing construction cooperatives and private housing built by individuals accounted for the remaining stock. As of January 1, 1989, 73.4% of housing in Moscow was municipalized, 16.1% departmental, 9.9% cooperative and .4% private.[26]

In market economies, private housing is generally more desirable and of better quality than governmental housing; in Moscow the opposite was true. The most "desirable" housing was neither private nor cooperative, but socialized. As in the west, the most highly subsidized housing was publicly owned, in this case by city councils and extra-territorial departments. On average, rent covered only 25% of the maintenance costs for socialized housing. The state absorbed the remaining 75%.[27] People who lived in socialized apartments paid less for housing than those living in identical cooperative or private housing. Cooperative housing members had to pay the full costs of construction and maintenance themselves, although they received some subsidies such as long-term, virtually interest-free loans for 70-80% of the total cost of construction. Since cooperatives largely financed themselves, cooperative apartment dwellers paid 6 to 8 times more for housing and communal services than did socialized apartment dwellers who occupied an equivalent apartment.[28] Private sector housing, of which there was very little in Moscow, cost relatively more and had even fewer amenities. Private houses usually were to be found in former dacha or summer home communities that had been incorporated into the city.

Low rents meant that socialized apartment dwellers received a higher subsidy than those living in cooperative or private dwellings. Since rent was geared to living space, the more floor space an individual had, the greater the subsidy. Furthermore, the allocation of additional living space (paid for at the same rent) to high status groups meant that the groups who could most afford to pay for housing received the largest subsidy from the state. Some evidence suggests that they lived in better quality buildings as well, and thus benefitted doubly at the state's expense.[29]

Housing quality, as measured by the provision of different kinds of amenities, was related to housing tenure. Private housing ranked far below other types of housing for all amenities except the provision of gas for cooking. According to the 1971 general plan, electric stoves were preferable to gas because they were considered more sanitary.[30]. Presumably residents used either gas or electric stoves for cooking, but not both. Virtually all socialized and cooperative apartments had either gas hookups or electric stoves, but only 63% of private dwellings were so equipped. Private housing also lagged far behind socialized and cooperative housing in other amenities: only 50% of private housing had central heating, only 31% had running water and just 19% had sewerage. Clearly, then, private housing was of much lower quality than other forms of housing in the Soviet Union.

Cooperative apartments were better equipped than either private or socialized apartments. Virtually all cooperative apartments were provided with heating, running water, sewerage, a gas or electric stove, a bath and hot water. The high quality of cooperative housing reflected both its age and its cost. Almost all cooperative housing was built after 1962; cooperative housing built before 1937 was confiscated by the state in that year and no more cooperative housing was built until 1958.[31] Since newer housing has more services, and since cooperative housing had to attract prospective members who were willing and able to pay the costs of circumventing the waiting list for housing, cooperative housing tended to be of a higher quality than other kinds of housing.

Finally, socialized housing was well provided with all amenities except hot water; but if we distinguish between municipalized and departmental housing, some differences emerged. Municipalized housing had more amenities than departmental housing, with the largest difference in the provision of hot water. More than 92% of municipalized housing units had hot water, but only 80.6% of the departmental fund was so equipped. In addition, more municipalized apartments had electric stoves than departmental apartments: 80% of the latter had gas stoves, while only 65% of municipalized apartments were so equipped. The differences between departmental and municipalized housing were small, however, when compared with those differences between socialized and private housing. But the differences were important, since most people (89.5%) lived in these two types of housing.

Different types of housing tenure were favoured at different periods of development, contributing to the differences in their quality. Very little private housing was built after 1965; the median year of construction for private housing is 1947. After nationalizing all cooperative housing in 1937, the central government prohibited its construction until 1958.[32] As a result, most cooperative housing was built after that year. The median year of construction was 1973. The departmental housing stock was somewhat older than the municipalized stock. The median year of construction was 1965 for departmental housing, and 1969 for municipalized housing. The age of departmental housing reflected shifts in housing policy from the Stalin era and the Khrushchev period. Under Stalin, the extra-territorial departments were responsible for the bulk of housing construction as part of the "City Beautiful" period in Moscow. After Stalin's death, the central government concentrated on providing housing to everyone deemed in need, giving the city council responsibility for most housing construction.[33]

Figure 3 illustrates the spatial distribution of departmental housing based on location quotients. The location quotient expresses the ratio between a district's share of one kind of housing (for example departmental housing) and the district's share of all housing. On this map, dark shading identifies districts with location quotients greater than one, or districts with a higher share of departmental housing than other types of housing; light shading identifies districts with location quotients less than one.

Two clear groups of districts emerge on Figure 3. The majority of districts with location quotients greater than one lie in the eastern sector of the city. All of the most important industrial districts, except for Taganskii [28], had more departmental housing than expected. These include Kuibyshevskii [13], Pervomaiskii [20], Perovskii [21], Volgogradskii [3], Liublinskii [17], Proletarskii [22] and Kalininskii [8]. The high location quotients for the eastern industrial districts except for Taganskii were not surprising given the importance of departmental housing for major industries. Taganskii, with a location quotient of .98, had slightly less departmental housing than its share of all housing. One

Figure 3. **Distribution of Departmental Housing in Moscow, 1989.**

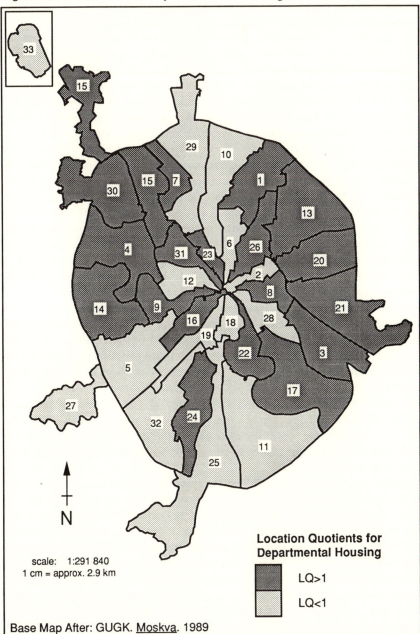

Location Quotients for
Departmental Housing

LQ>1

LQ<1

scale: 1:291 840
1 cm = approx. 2.9 km

N

Base Map After: GUGK. <u>Moskva</u>. 1989

Note: See Figure 1 for district names.

of the major sites of industrial development during the 1930s, Taganskii district experienced rapid population growth at the same time. Much of the poor quality housing built in this period of rapid growth was razed after the adoption of the 1971 general plan. Taganskii underwent significant reconstruction during the time when the city council predominated in housing construction, which would explain its location quotient.

The second cluster of districts with high location quotients in the west includes industrial and non-industrial districts. Tushinskii [30] and Zheleznodorozhnyi [7] are important industrial districts. We would expect most departmental housing in these districts to have belonged to industrial or construction departments. Leningradskii [15], Frunzenskii [31], Kievskii [9] and Leninskii [16] are not important industrial districts. In Leningradskii [15] and Leninskii [16], the departments that likely played the most active roles include institutes of higher education and research and government bodies.

In the Soviet context, living and useful space per capita probably served as the most important measures of housing quality, since demand for housing far exceeded supply. As of January 1, 1988, an estimated 880,000 people were on the official waiting lists for housing. The average waiting period was 6-7 years. Many people lived in cramped conditions. As of January 1, 1988, about 550,000 people lived in apartments where they averaged fewer than 5 square meters of living space per person; 1.1 million people lived in apartments where they averaged 5-7 square meters of living space per person; and 1.5 million people averaged 7-9 square meters of living space per person. Since the norms at the time provided for 9-12 square meters of living space per person, a total of 2.65 million people or 31% of the 1988 population would have needed additional housing to achieve the minimum norm of 9 square meters per person.[34]

For the city as a whole, living space averaged 11.2 square meters per capita and useful space 17.5. Per capita living and useful space correlated closely; the more per capita living space, the more per capita useful space.[35] Thus, people with relatively more living space benefitted doubly because they also had more total or useful space.

Figures 4 and 5 portray respectively the spatial distribution of useful space and living space per capita. The darkly shaded districts belong to the top third in terms of housing provision per capita; moderately shaded districts belong to the middle or average third; lightly shaded districts belong to the bottom third and are districts with relatively little housing space per capita. As the high correlation between total and living space per capita suggests, the two maps are quite similar. Two clear trends emerge. First, the older central districts had more per capita useful and living space on average than the peripheral districts. Many residential buildings in the central districts were built during the 1930s, when the central leadership emphasized construction of communal apartments (*kommunalki*), large apartments to be shared by more than one family. At around

Figure 4. **Useful Space per Capita, Moscow, 1989**

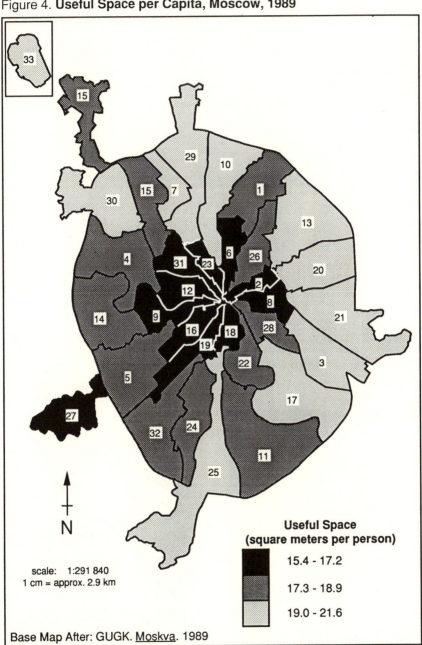

Base Map After: GUGK. <u>Moskva</u>. 1989

Note: See Figure 1 for district names.

Figure 5. **Living Space per Capita, Moscow, 1989**

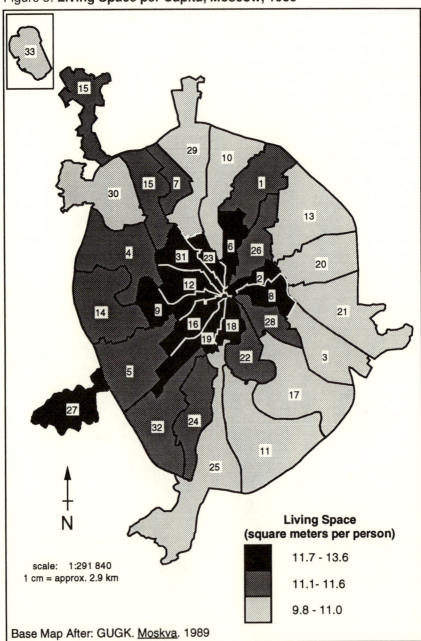

Note: See Figure 1 for district names.

the same time, the central government sought to transform Moscow into a showplace for socialism. As a result, many of the residential buildings built in the center, especially the western part, were intended for the elite, and were of much higher quality than buildings intended for industrial workers.

Only two districts on the periphery had large amounts of living and useful space per capita, Sol'ntsevskii [27] and Leningradskii [15], but their anomalous position can be explained. Sol'ntsevskii had a high proportion of private housing, since the district had only recently been incorporated into the city. As mentioned earlier, residents of private housing tended to have more space, but the housing was of much lower quality than either cooperative or socialized housing. An exception to the general rule, the large amount of useful and livng space per capita in Solntsevskii is a poor indicator of housing quality. Despite Leningradskii's [15] peripheral location, much of the housing in the district was constructed during the 1930s. Leningradskii's location along the road to Leningrad may have provided the impetus to transform this district into an example of monumental city architecture; blocks adjoining the road to Leningrad were explicitly named as sites for major construction in the 1935 general plan.[36]

The amount of useful and living space per capita in a district also varied between the eastern and western parts of the city. In the center, the western districts had large amounts of living space per capita, while three districts in the eastern half had only average amounts per capita (Proletarskii [22], Taganskii [28] and Sokol'nicheskii [26]). In the central northeast, Sokol'nicheskii [26] had small amounts of both living and useful space per capita. During the 1930s, parts of Sokol'nicheskii district had been included in Stalinskii district, a major site of industrial development. Two other important industrial districts, Taganskii [28] and Proletarskii [22], in the southeastern part of the center of the city, had average amounts of useful and living space. Historically, industrial or manual workers tended to live under more cramped conditions than non-manual workers, and apparently the pattern for residents in industrial districts to have less per capita living and useful space continued. In the central western districts, where there was little industry, amounts of living and useful space were higher than in the central eastern districts. This pattern repeated itself on the periphery. In the west, districts had more useful and living space per capita than in the eastern industrial districts. On the whole, however, more useful and living space per capita was found in the central districts than the peripheral districts.

Social Status and Housing Quality

Housing quality can be associated with the social characteristics of the population. In western countries, this has quite clearly been the case, but in the Soviet Union the links were much less clear. Unfortunately, very little information

Table 7

Association of social status with useful and living space per capita

Spearmans Correlation Coefficient *r*	Significance	Variable
0.69	.000	Total housing space per capita
0.75	.000	Total living space per capita

about the social characteristics of each district's population was available. There is some evidence to suggest a correlation between housing space and income. For example, a survey of 688 respondents in October 1987 found that people who enjoyed more living space per capita also had higher per capita incomes.[37] A study in Leningrad found a similar relation between per capita living space and income.[38] As one specialist concluded: "The differentiation in the level of housing provision among groups with different incomes testifies to the ineffectiveness of government housing subsidies: in general, they [housing subsidies] fall to families with high incomes, who have accumulated excess[39] living space."[40] Residents who could have better afforded to pay for their own housing actually received a higher implicit subsidy from the state, since they had more living space per capita.

Comparison of the relationship between useful and living space per capita, and the social status of each district, suggests that they were associated. Useful and living space per capita correlated positively with social status: districts with higher status residents are also those with more living and useful space per capita (Table 7). The correlation coefficients describing the associations between social status and useful and living space per capita are significant (p ≤ .01) and positive, with values of 0.69 and 0.75, respectively.

Housing Stock and Allocation

The final condition for residential differentiation is a housing allocation system that provides differential access for various social groups to housing of different types. We have seen that social areas existed in Moscow and that housing quality varied by tenure and location. Here I will explore how the housing allocation system, in part as a response to central governmental policies, contributed to existing residential differentiation. The central government considered housing to be both a right of every citizen and a privilege granted to certain members of society. The use of housing as a reward or incentive meant that some people had access to more and better housing, while others did not; the best workers, for example, received better quality housing sooner than less efficient co-workers.[41]

The Soviet leadership removed housing from the market shortly after the 1917 Revolution. Since then, low, standardized rents and a central allocative mechanism were the foundation of most of the housing sector. In principle, governmental and departmental institutions distributed housing on the basis of need, not ability to pay. In Moscow, at least theoretically, the city council and ministries allocated housing only to city residents, with rental rates tied to square meters of floor space. Rents, basically unchanged since the 1920s, did not vary by location, and accounted for the fact that housing expenditures consumed much less of a household's budget in the Soviet Union than in the west.[42]

The state supplemented its early commitment to shelter for all with a policy that sanctioned the use of housing as a reward. In the Russian Republic, the government announced a new housing policy in 1930, near the nadir of a serious housing crisis. Living space per capita in Moscow had fallen continuously from a high of 9.3 square meters per person in 1920 to 4.15 square meters in 1932. The 1930 policy remained in effect throughout the Soviet period, permitting the government to provide additional housing for certain categories of citizens. Elite workers in Party, governmental, and economic organizations, academics, Heroes of Labor and other recipients of honorifics, high-level military officers and artists were granted additional living space under the provisions of this policy.[43] These mutually contradictory policies suggest that municipal and ministerial measures were unlikely to have obliterated intraurban differences in the quality of the housing stock. Indeed, the allocative system itself may have perpetuated differentiation, albeit in a more muted form than existed before 1917, or than exists at present in western cities.

The housing allocation procedures adopted by the Executive Committee of the Moscow City Council at the end of the 1950s were designed to promote equitable, but not equal, treatment of all citizens.[44] The new rules stated that housing should be offered first to the most needy workers (*rabochie*), engineering-technical workers, and non-manual employees (*sluzhashchie*). Priority was also to be given to those who were good workers, active in society, i.e., involved in Party or Komsomol or other such official organizations, and had resided for a long time in Moscow. People already on the waiting list for city housing were to have preference in receiving departmental or enterprise housing. Families of people who had died in the war, demobilized officers, and families with very sick members were to have higher priority for housing; their names were to be listed separately on a special waiting list.[45] Theoretically, people listed on the special waiting list would receive housing more quickly than those on the regular list.

These rules created conflict and allowed for bias in the allocation of municipalized and departmental housing, since evaluating a person's attitude to labor frequently became a very subjective process.[46] As Khrushchev said:

> In construction and the distribution of housing we cannot think that just because someone is alive that we should give him a good apartment. It is necessary to consider what he does, what he gives to society. In our socialist society everyone should give something to the greater good of the people . . . only then will he receive the right to use the blessings of society, which are created by society.[47]

In other words, housing should be distributed as a reward to those who contributed most to Soviet society.

According to publicly enunciated policies, families[48] whose amount of living space per capita fell below a minimum level were able to join the waiting list to receive a new apartment from either the municipal or the departmental fund. In Moscow, the minimum standards for the two types of housing differed. For example, families averaging less than 5 sq. m. per person of living space could join the municipal housing waiting list; those averaging less than 7 sq. m. living space per person could join the departmental housing waiting list.[49] Thus, an individual's institutional affiliation could determine his or her eligibility to receive new housing at all. In theory, wait-listed families received new housing with not less than 9 sq. m. per person in order of their place on the list.[50]

The city council also maintained special priority waiting lists. For example, veterans, large families, people living in housing slated for demolition, KGB troops and "persons singled out by the government" were all eligible for priority waiting lists, and were to receive housing before other families on the regular wait list.[51] For people able to afford cooperative housing, which cost much more than socialized housing, the option was available to join a housing construction cooperative if they had fewer than 8 square meters of living space per capita.[52]

In 1990, 1.3 million people, or 15% of the Moscow population, had between 1 and 5 square meters of living space per capita, well below the norm of 9 square meters; 2.6 million people, or 30% of the population, had 9 to 11 square meters of living space per capita; and 187,000 people, or 2.1% of the total population, had more than 20 square meters of living space per capita. The latter were extremely well housed by Moscow standards.[53] As of January 1, 1988, a total of some 880,000 people were waiting for housing. The waiting list for municipal housing included 557,000 people and that for departmental housing totalled 528,000; about 200,000 people were on both.[54] Given that 1.3 million people were eligible to join the waiting list because they had less than 5 square meters of housing, large numbers of eligible people must have withheld their names from the waiting list.

The waiting period for housing varied significantly, from 1-2 years to 7-8 years, with 6-7 years the average. This variation stemmed, at least in part, from the way housing was distributed to one or another department, organization or enterprise. One enterprise might have received all of the housing it needed for that year, while another might have received none at all. According to the Vice-chairman of the Moscow City Soviet Executive Commitee (*Mosgorispolkom--*municipal government), in 1990 the city council was obligated to turn over approximately one-half of all housing built during the year (approximately 1.5 million square meters) to fulfill resolutions of the central government providing specific departments in Moscow with housing. Among such central governmental annual directives to provide housing was a 1986 resolution calling for the allocation of 1,200 square meters of useful space to the USSR Academy of the National Economy, which actually required one-half or one-third this amount.[55] One result of this dual distribution system for housing was that "people in leading organizations [got] better accommodation in more attractive locations."[56] Furthermore, departmental institutions themselves differed in the amount of housing they funded for their workers. During the tenth five-year plan (1976-80), nine times more housing was built per capita for workers in public transportation than for workers in the Main Moscow Repair Administration (*Glavmosremont*). The Administration of Water and Sewerage (*Upravlenie vodoprovodno-kanalizatsionnogo khoziaistva*) obtained twice as much housing per capita for its workers as did the public transportation authorities and eighteen times as much as did the Main Moscow Repair Administration.[57] Ministries or other organizations with extra housing were able simply to hold it vacant until they needed it instead of permitting it to be allocated to people waiting for housing.[58] Once again, the department/municipal housing allocation system affected the individual's housing possibilities.

At the same time, many people who were not on the waiting list received housing. Based on the results of its own investigation, the All-Union Central Trade Union Council concluded that one out of three apartments in the Soviet Union had been allocated unfairly (i.e., not in accordance with the rules for housing allocation).[59] In 1987, in Moscow, people on the waiting list obtained only 45% of all housing distributed (including cooperative housing).[60]

The central government's dual housing policies perpetuated some degree of residential differentiation. Policies designed to provide both more and better quality housing for certain categories of people meant different social groups received different types of housing. Special housing seemed to be concentrated primarily in the western part of the central city, which would contribute to differences in the social composition of districts. Unfortunately, measures of elite concentration, such as information about the location of recipients of honorifics, are not yet available. British geographer and Soviet specialist Anthony French described how his own visual inspection "suggests clustering of elite apartment buildings in a central wedge with its apex delimited by the building of senior party and government members on ulitsa Granovskogo from which the wedge continues outwards and westwards."[61] Soviet observers, too, described concentrations of elite buildings on streets such as Ryleeva (Leninskii district), Sivtsev Vrazhek (Leninskii and Kievskii districts), Kibal'chich (Dzerzhinskii and Babushkinskii districts) and Profsoiuznaia (Sevastopol'skii and Cheremushkinskii districts).[62] A number of embassies and foreign residences were also situated in these regions.

Under *glasnost* a series of accounts have emerged detailing the privileged positions of certain groups with respect to housing. It turns out that high Party officials are entitled not only to Moscow residency, but also to above average housing. According to A. Zharovyi, a deputy to the Moscow City Council, a secret agreement between the Central Committee of the CPSU and the Council of Ministers permitted certain categories of party and government leaders to receive both a Moscow residence permit and an apartment. Privileged groups generally moved into elite buildings, which had been built by organizations such as the Central Committee of the CPSU, the Council of Ministers of the USSR, the KGB, the Council of Ministers of the Russian Republic (RSFSR), the Moscow Party Committee of the CPSU (MGK KPSS), and so on. The elite who lived in these buildings frequently received much more space than the average Muscovite and their apartments had been more expensive to build.[63]

The denial of a residence permit to Ivan Polozkov, a member of the Politburo, may have marked the beginning of a new era in terms of the "entitlement" of certain privileged elites to Moscow residency. On November 5, 1990, the Moscow City Soviet's committee on housing and residence permit denied a request to provide Polozkov with an apartment for four people and a residence permit. The proposed apartment measured 125.2 square meters (80.8 sq.m. of living space) which would have provided 31.3 sq. m. useful space or 20.2 sq.m. living space per capita.[64] At the beginning of 1989, the average resident had 17.5 sq.m. of useful space per capita and 11.2 sq.m. of living space per capita.[65] The Central Committee's request to house Polozkov and to provide him with a residence permit was refused "for the first time in the country's history."[66]

Other Forms of Housing Allocation

Within the larger framework of the system for housing construction and housing allocation, it was possible for people to pursue their own housing preferences, although at a cost of time, money, or both. Legally, Muscovites could exchange one apartment for another, assuming that they could find someone with whom to exchange.[67] The Central Bureau for Housing Exchanges facilitated this process by registering people who wished to exchange apartments. The Bureau even published a listing of people seeking to exchange apartments (*Biulleten' po obmenu zhiloi ploshchadi*). Unofficial, but nevertheless legal, exchanges also took place among people who advertised informally on one of the many walls and bus stops that served as informal billboards, or who arranged exchanges among friends or acquaintances.[68]

A significant black market existed in housing. Bribes were paid to join a cooperative or jump the waiting list, apartments or rooms were rented for fees well above those legally permitted, and fictitious marriages to Muscovites were arranged. Those with connections frequently used influence (*blat*) to obtain housing.[69]

Evidence about the second economy in housing is anecdotal and remains incomplete. Gathering information about illegal activities in any society is difficult; in the Soviet Union, where censorship prevailed, information about illegal activities was virtually impossible to obtain. I did not therefore include information on the second economy sector in housing in this analysis. But one may hypothesize that individual housing transactions, legal or illegal, probably reinforced existing patterns and preferences. If some districts were more desirable than others, people would want to live in those districts regardless of which part of the housing economy they were in.

Conclusion

The evidence presented suggests that at the end of 1988 there existed in Moscow residential differentiation and that differences in housing quality were associated with variations in social status. Indeed the system of housing allocation contributed to the development of what might be termed "social areas."

A dual policy pursued by the Soviet government explains why living space was unequally distributed among different social groups. Officially the central government deemed housing to be both a right and a reward. But policies designed to provide sufficient housing for everyone were tempered by policies designed to reward the contributions of select social groups with readier access to more and better quality housing. Further, central government policies differentiated between "valued" workers (frequently the elite, active Party members) and ordinary citizens.

Western scholars have long assumed that Soviet housing policies and urban planning strategies did not result in equitable distribution. But empirical confirmation was lacking. The policy of *glasnost'* provided the conditions to allow scholars to examine the evidence with care.

In retrospect, 1988 may have been a unique moment in time for such an examination. As the process of privatization proceeds apace, the pattern of residential differentiation identified here will surely undergo substantial modification. It is important to have assessed the way in which social goods were distributed before 1989 in order to create a baseline against which to measure the impact of the market.

Notes

1. Paul Gregory and Robert C. Stuart, *Soviet Economic Structure and Performance*, 3d ed. (New York: Harper & Row, 1986); David Lane, *Soviet Economy and Society* (New York: New York University Press, 1985); Blair Ruble, *Leningrad: The Shaping of a Soviet City* (Berkeley: University of California Press, 1990); Jerry Hough, *The Soviet Prefects: The Local Party Organs in Industrial Decision-making* (Cambridge: Harvard University Press, 1969); Alec Nove, *The Soviet Economic System*, 3d ed. (Boston: Allen & Unwin, 1986); Peter Rutland, *The Myth of the Plan: Lessons of Soviet Planning Experience* (London: Hutchinson, 1985).

2. Donna Bahry, *Outside Moscow: Power, Politics, and Budgetary Policy in the Soviet Republics* (New York: Columbia University Press, 1987); Cameron Ross, *Local Government in the Soviet Union: Problems of Implementation and Control* (New York: St. Martin's Press, 1987); Jeffrey Hahn, *Soviet Grassroots: Citizen Participation in Local Soviet Government* (Princeton: Princeton University Press, 1988); Ruble, *Leningrad*.

3. William Taubman, *Governing Soviet Cities: Bureaucratic Politics and Urban Development in the USSR*, Praeger Special Studies in International Economics and Development (New York and London: Praeger and Pall Mall, 1973); D.T. Cattell, *Leningrad: A Case Study of Soviet Urban Government*, Praeger Special Studies in International Politics and Public Affairs (New York: Frederick A. Praeger, 1968); Ross, *Local Government*; Ruble, *Leningrad*.

4. Ruble, *Leningrad*.

5. Henry Morton, "The Contemporary Soviet City," in *The Contemporary Soviet City*, eds. *Henry Morton and Robert Stuart* (Armonk, NY: M.E. Sharpe, 1984), pp. 3-24; Hough, *The Soviet Prefects*; Ruble, *Leningrad*; Cattell, *Leningrad*; Rutland, *The Myth of the Plan*.

6. J.L. Abu-Lughod, "Testing the Theory of Social Area Analysis: The Ecology of Cairo, Egypt," *American Sociological Review* 34 (1969): 198-212.

7. Jeffrey Klugman, *The New Soviet Elite: How They Think and What They Want* (New York: Praeger, 1989); Michael Voslensky, *Nomenklatura: The Soviet Ruling Class*, trans. Eric Mosbacher (Garden City, NY: Doubleday, 1984); Mervyn Matthews, *Poverty in the Soviet Union: The Life-styles of the Underprivileged in Recent Years* (Cambridge:

Cambridge University Press, 1986); Mervyn Matthews, "Social Dimensions in Soviet Urban Housing," in *The Socialist City*, eds. R.A. French and F.E. Ian Hamilton (New York: John Wiley, 1979), pp. 105-17; Murray Yanowitch, *Social and Economic Inequality in the Soviet Union: Six Studies* (White Plains, NY: M.E. Sharpe, 1977).

8. Duncan Timms, *The Urban Mosaic* (Cambridge: Cambridge University Press, 1971); Abu-Lughod, "Testing the Theory of Social Area Analysis," pp. 198-212.

9. G.D. Andrusz, *Housing and Urban Development in the USSR* (London: Macmillan, 1984).

10. A.J. DiMaio, *Soviet Urban Housing: Problems and Policies* (New York: Praeger, 1974), pp. 122-23; S.S. Shatalin, *Tendentsii i perspektivy razvitiia sotsial'noi infrastruktury* (Moscow: Nauka, 1989), pp. 128-33.

11. For example, universities.

12. Lane, *Soviet Economy and Society*, p. 182.

13. Mikhailovskaia and Vozniak, "A Region's Socioeconomic Development and Unlawful Behavior," *Soviet Sociology* XIX (Spring 1981): 75-84; Walter Connor, *Deviance in Soviet Society: Crime, Delinquency, and Alcoholism* (New York: Columbia University Press, 1972), pp. 154-56.

14. A.Kh. Karapetian, *Dokhody i potreblenie naseleniia SSSR* (Moscow: Statistika, 1980); *Sem'ia i narodnoe blagosostoianie v razvitom sotsialisticheskom obshchestve*, eds. N.M. Rimashevskaia and A.Kh. Karapetian (Moscow: Mysl', 1985); Peter Wiles, *Distribution of Income: East and West* (Amsterdam: North-Holland Publishing Company, 1974); Matthews, *Poverty in the Soviet Union*.

15. *Obraz zhizni naseleniia krupnogo goroda: opyt kompleksnogo sotsial'nogo issledovaniia*, ed. A.S. Pashkov (Leningrad: Izd-vo Leningradskogo Universiteta, 1988); N. Kalinina and G. Ronkin, "Housing: Ownership, Control, Distribution," unpublished article (Moscow 1989); Timothy Sosnovy, *The Housing Problem in the Soviet Union*, ed. David Goldstein, Studies on the U.S.S.R., 8 (New York: Research Program on the U.S.S.R., 1954); Shatalin, *Tendentsii i perspektivy*; Matthews, "Social dimensions"; DiMaio, *Soviet Urban Housing*.

16. DiMaio, *Soviet Urban Housing*, pp. 122-23.

17. Laura Engelstein, *Moscow, 1905: Working-class Organization and Political Conflict* (Stanford: Stanford University Press, 1982), pp. 40-51.

18. Manual workers are defined as those engaged primarily in physical, not mental, labor and include workers in fields such as industry and construction. *Statisticheskii slovar'*, 2d ed., s.v. "Kategorii personala" (Moscow: Finansy i statistika, 1989).

19. The type of factor analysis used here, principal axis factor analysis, calculates the factor in such a way as to maximize the amount of common variance it explains; in principal components analysis the derived component is calculated so as to maximize the total amount of variance explained. R.J. Johnston, *Multivariate Statistical Analysis in Geography* (London: Longman, 1978), chap. 5.

20. For example, Bob Murdie used 109 variables to derive six factors in his classic study of the factorial ecology of Toronto from 1951-61. He used principal components analysis, which includes all of the variance into the analysis, not just the common variance. The six factors explained 72.2% of the variance in 1951 and 75.0% in 1961. No factor explained more than 23% of the variance. For descriptions of other factor or principal components analyses and the amount of variance explained by each factor or component see Timms, *The Urban Mosaic*. Robert Murdie, *Factorial Ecology of Metropolitan Toronto, 1951-61: An Essay on the Social Geography of the City*, Department of Geography, Research paper no. 116 (Chicago: Department of Geography, 1969), Tables 38 and 39.

21. In ascending order the factor scores are: Solntsevskii -1.92; Liublinskii -1.68; Krasnogvardeiskii -1.41; Kirovskii -1.05; Sovetskii -1.05; Zheleznodorozhnyi -0.98; Timiriazevskii -0.97; Zelenograd -0.78; Volgogradskii -0.69; Perovskii -0.69; Taganskii -0.50; Kalininskii -0.48; Tushinskii -0.41; Proletarskii -0.24; Pervomaiskii -0.16; Kuibyshevskii -0.07; Babushkinskii 0.02; Voroshilovskii 0.08; Kuntsevskii 0.14; Moskvoretskii 0.18; Sevastopol'skii 0.30; Baumanskii 0.31; Cheremushkinskii 0.47; Krasnopresnenskii 0.70; Sokol'nicheskii 0.77; Sverdlovskii 0.82; Gagarinskii 0.87; Leningradskii 1.05; Kievskii 1.07; Oktiabr'skii 1.28; Dzerzhinskii 1.59; Frunzenskii 1.60; Leninskii 1.84.

22. Because the Party and the government served together as the political leadership, in this study "central leadership" or "central government" refers to the top-levels of governmental and Party institutions, i.e., the Politburo, the Central Committee, the Supreme Soviet and the USSR Council of Ministers.

23. Ellen Hamilton, "Social Areas Under State Socialism: the Example of Moscow" (PhD diss., Columbia University, forthcoming 1993), chap. 3.

24. *Moskva entsiklopediia* (Moscow: Sovetskaia entsiklopediia, 1980), s.v. "Zheleznodorozhnyi raion."

25. *Ibid.*, s.v. "Sovetskii," "Krasnogvardeiskii," "Liublinskii," "Volgogradskii," and "Perovskii raion."

26. *Statisticheskii spravochnik: O zhilishchno-kommunal'nom (zhilom i nezhilom) fonde goroda moskvy po sostoianiiu na 1 ianvaria 1989 goda* (Moscow: Gorodskim biuro te inventarizatsii ispolkom Mossoveta, 1989).

27. Kalinina and Ronkin, "Housing: Ownership, Control, Distribution."

28. A cooperative apartment dweller must sell the apartment at a price determined by the amount originally paid for the unit amortized over the number of years of occupancy. Thus, cooperative housing cannot be considered as an investment in the same sense that housing in market economies is an investment. V.Z. Rogovin, "Sotsial'nye aspekty uskoreniia resheniia zhilishchnoi problemy," in *Sotsial'nye aspekty uskoreniia resheniia zhilishchnoi problemy*, ed. V. Rogovin (Moscow: Institut sotsiologii AN SSSR, 1990), p. 15; L.V. Babaeva, V.I. Grishanov, A.N. Krivoruchko and E.Ia. Nazarchuk, *Programma sotsiologicheskogo issledovaniia "zhilishchnye usloviia gorodskogo naseleniia"* (Moscow: Institut sotsiologicheskikh issledovanii AN SSSR, 1990), p. 9.

29. Shatalin, *Tendentsii i perspektivy*, pp. 100-101; A.K. Guzanova, "Otnoshenie naseleniia k povysheniiu oplaty zhil'ia," in *Zhilishchnyi kompleks SSSR: problemy i resheniia*, ed. O.S. Pchelintsev (Moscow: Institut ekonomiki i prognozirovaniia nauchno-tekhnicheskogo progressa AN SSSR, 1989), pp. 118-19.

30. G. Lappo, A. Chikshev and A. Bekker, *Moscow--Capital of the Soviet Union* (Moscow: Progress, 1976), p. 149.

31. Andrusz, *Housing and Urban Development*, pp. 37-39, 82.

32. Shatalin, *Tendentsii i perspektivy*, pp. 104-105.

33. Hamilton, *Social Areas under State Socialism*, chaps. 3 and 6.

34. *Kompleksnaia programma po obespecheniiu kazhdoi sem'i v g. Moskve otdel'noi kvartiroi na period do 2000 goda v svete reshenii XXVII S"ezda KPSS* (Moscow: Ispolnitel'nyi Komitet Moskovskogo Gorodskogo Soveta Narodnykh Deputatov, 1988), pp. 18-20, 60-61.

35. For the 33 districts in Moscow, Spearman's rank-order correlation coefficient is .98, which is significant at the .01 level.

36. *General'nyi plan rekonstruktsii goroda Moskvy* (Moscow: Moskovskii rabochii, 1936).

37. Unfortunately, as is frequently the case with Soviet survey research, the sampling technique, methodology, and so on are not described. In fact, the author does not even state where this survey was conducted; although I believe it was conducted in Kalinin (now Tver). Guzanova, "Otnoshenie naseleniia," pp. 116-17.

38. 5000 people were surveyed from 1984-1986 in Leningrad. For a description of the survey and the findings, see Pashkov, *Obraz zhizni naseleniia krupnogo goroda*.

39. I.e., above the norm.

40. Shatalin, *Tendentsii i perspektivy*. p. 100.

41. DiMaio, *Soviet Urban Housing*, pp. 122-23; Sosnovy, *The Housing Problem*, p. 112; Matthews, "Social dimensions," p. 107; Shatalin, *Tendentsii i perspektivy*. pp. 128-33.

42. In 1988, a survey of the family budgets of 2375 Muscovite families employed in industry found that housing and communal services (i.e., rent, heat, electricity) totalled 2.8% of the family's total income. Industrial workers earned more than many other workers, so most families probably spent a higher percentage of their income on rent, but the share of total family income devoted to housing was far less than in developed market economies. *Moskva v tsifrakh 1989* (Moscow: Finansy i statistika, 1989), p. 55.

43. DiMaio, *Soviet Urban Housing*, pp. 122-23; Sosnovy, *The Housing Problem*, p. 112.

44. Presumably this was not the case under Stalin or the Executive Committee would not have felt it necessary to announce new rules. The available evidence suggests that under Stalin better quality housing went to the new elite, but the evidence is circumstantial. Sosnovy, *The Housing Problem*; R.A. French, "Changing Spatial Patterns in Soviet Cities--Planning or Pragmatism," *Urban Geography* 8 (1987): 309-20.

45. S.I. Matveev, "Ustranit' nedostatki v obespechenii moskvichei zhiloi ploshchad'iu," *Gorodskoe khoziaistvo Moskvy*, 1961, No. 8: 16-18.

46. V.P. Semin, "Raspredelnie zhiloi ploshchadi--pod kontrol' trudiashchikhsia," *Gorodskoe khoziaistvo Moskvy* 34, no. 1 (1960): 13-15; N. Kalinina, "Housing and Housing Policy in the USSR," in *The Reform of Housing in Eastern Europe and the Soviet Union*, eds. I. Tosisc, J. Hegedus and B. Turner (New York: Routledge, 1992).

47. Matveev, "Ustranit' nedostatki," p. 17.

48. "Family" here means either an individual or several people related by blood or marriage.

49. Kalinina and Ronkin, "Housing: Ownership, Control, Distribution."

50. For a more detailed description see DiMaio, *Soviet Urban Housing*, pp. 116-31.

51. *Ibid*, p. 124.

52. Kalinina, "Housing and Housing Policy."

53. A. Rudakov, "Waiting for an Apartment (interview)," *Moscow News*, March 4, 1990, p. 19.

54. *Kompleksnaia programma*, p. 6.

55. Rudakov, "Waiting for an Apartment."

56. Matthews, "Social dimensions," p. 107.

57. S.N. Zhelezko, *Naselenie krupnogo goroda* (Moscow: Mysl', 1986), p. 84.

58. *Kompleksnaia programma*, pp. 60-61.

59. Rogovin, "Sotsial'nye aspekty," p. 12.

60. Bekker, Trifonov and Babkina, 49.

61. French, "Changing Spatial Patterns," p. 313.

62. S. Volkov, "Zhil'e po spravedlivosti." *Vechernaia Moskva*, Feb. 28, 1990, p. 2. My own observations confirm this concentration of apparently elite housing in the central western sector of the city. The number of non-Soviet cars parked along streets such as ul. Alekseia Tol'stogo and sporting license plates identifying their owners as private Soviet citizens astonished me during my visits to this area in 1991-92.

63. G. Valiuzhenich, "Na podzakonnykh osnovaniiakh," *Argumenty i fakty* 44 (Nov. 1990): 4-5.

64. A. Illish, "Moscow City Soviet Deputies Decide to Deny I. Polozkov a Moscow Residence Permit," *Current Digest of the Soviet Press* 43, no. 45 (1990).

65. *Statisticheskii spravochnik*.

66. This did not mean, however, that Polozkov will not end up living in Moscow. According to Maksimov, the chairman of the Moscow City Soviet's subcommittee on law and order: "Either officials of the Moscow City Soviet will deem it necessary to make an exception, overruling the Deputies' decision, or the CPSU Central Committee will install Polozkov in 'its' living quarters without following the legally prescribed procedures." Illish, "Moscow City Soviet Deputies Decide."

67. *Party, State, and Citizen in the Soviet Union: A Collection of Documents*, ed. Mervyn Matthews (Armonk, NY: M.E. Sharpe, 1989), pp. 183-84.

68. Henry Morton, "Who Gets What, When and How? Housing in the Soviet Union," *Soviet Studies* 32 (April 1980): 235-59; N.B. Barbash, *Metodika izucheniia territorial'noy differentsiatsiy gorodskoy sredy* (Moscow: Institut geografiy AN SSSR, 1986); D. Sidorov, "Perception of Variation in the Level of Living Among and Within Large Soviet Cities," Paper presented at the annual meeting of the Institute of British Geographers, Harrogate, England, January 1991; Andrusz, *Housing and Urban Development*, p. 213.

69. Morton, *The Contemporary Soviet City*, pp. 242-52.

Sovietology and Perestroika:
A Post-Mortem

Edward W. Walker

When Mikhail S. Gorbachev was elected the General Secretary of the Central Committee of the Communist Party of the Soviet Union (CPSU) on March 11, 1985, he became leader of one of two world superpowers. Internally, the Soviet Union was endowed with enormous natural wealth, the third largest population in the world, a massive industrial stock, a huge defense and internal security apparatus, and a well-educated, urbanized society that seemed less politically alienated than those of Eastern Europe. Moreover, having overcome numerous crises in its sixty-seven year history, the Soviet state seemed highly institutionalized. Indeed, as early as 1968 Samuel P. Huntington had argued that the Soviet state should be characterized together with the liberal U.S. and British states as "developed" because it possessed "strong, adaptable, coherent political institutions" including "effective bureaucracies, well-organized political parties, a high degree of popular participation in public affairs, working systems of civilian control over the military, extensive activity by the government in the economy, and reasonably effective procedures for regulating succession and controlling political conflict."[1]

Less than a year after becoming General Secretary, Gorbachev issued a call for "radical reform" to overcome a "crisis of stagnation," later winning approval for his program for restructuring (perestroika) the Soviet political economy at the January 1987 Central Committee plenum.[2] As Gorbachev described it, perestroika would entail not only a deepening of glasnost, but economic decentralization and a "*demokratizatsiia*" of the political system as well. In the six-and-a-half years of Gorbachev's rule, the Soviet state imploded. Contrary to Gorbachev's hopes, perestroika did not renew Soviet socialism but rather destroyed it. Serious ethnic violence broke out in the Transcaucasus in 1988 and anti-regime mass mobilization got underway shortly thereafter with the emergence of the "popular front" movements in the Baltics and the summer 1989 miners' strike. Between 1989 and 1991, Moscow's alliance system in Eastern Europe disintegrated, Article 6 of the Soviet Constitution guaranteeing the CPSU its monopoly of power was repealed, and a "parade of sovereignties," "a war of laws," and eventually a "war of Presidents" threatened to degenerate into outright anarchy. With the failure of the August 1991 anti-perestroika coup, the CPSU and the Soviet state were dealt their final death blow.

It does a disservice to the drama and wrenching pain of these events to suggest that perestroika and the subsequent *destroika* of the Soviet Union have their parallels in Sovietology. Suffice it to say that the period has forced a new generation of students of "Soviet" politics and society to ask very different questions from those of their predecessors. No longer challenged to explain order, stability, institutionalization, or the functioning of "the Soviet system," we find ourselves confronted by dysfunction, fundamental and disjunctive institutional change, rapid attitudinal and behavioral adjustments to an ever-changing structure of opportunities, anti-regime mass mobilization, ethnic violence, and the driving force of intense nationalism.

While daunting, these new explanatory challenges are replete with scholarly opportunities, crying out particularly for disciplined comparative treatment. Transitions are under way in virtually every Soviet-type regime, and new states are emerging in the republics and possibly in certain sub-regions of the former Soviet Union as well. Comparativists are thus presented with as close to a controlled macro-societal experiment as we are likely to see. Holding constant a similar institutional starting point, we will be able to observe the independent effects of social-cultural conditions, international pressures, and assorted "contingent factors" (e.g., the role of personality and leadership or various "acts of god" such as the Chernobyl nuclear disaster or the Armenian earthquake) on variations in process and outcome. The need to explain what these cases have in common (e.g., the collapse or abandonment of the *ancien regime*) and how they vary means that the new generation of "post-Sovietologists" will need to adopt different concepts and approaches from those of their predecessors.

Nevertheless, we should not ignore either the accomplishments or the failures of pre-Gorbachev Sovietology. Rather, there are important lessons to be learned from a careful analysis of Sovietology's record. This essay, which is written by a "post-Sovietologist" who has no record of predictions or arguments to defend, explores these lessons.[3] I begin with a review of some of Sovietology's more notable accomplishments, turning next to an analysis of its principal failures.

Sovietology: The Accomplishments

While there has been much hand-wringing recently about the failure to "predict Gorbachev," I believe most of this hand-wringing is ill-founded. In the first place, the charge is not entirely accurate. One did not have to be a skilled "Kremlinologist" to recognize when the forty-seven year old Gorbachev was brought to Moscow in 1978 to become Central Committee Secretary for Agriculture that he was worth watching. When he became a non-voting Politburo member in 1979 and then a full-member in 1980, he was widely seen as a strong candidate to become the post-Brezhnev generation's first General Secretary despite the fact that he was responsible for agriculture, the "Achilles heel" of the Soviet economy. Indeed, when it became clear over the course of 1982 that Brezhnev was dying, Gorbachev and the then fifty-nine-year-old Leningrad Party first secretary, Grigori Romanov, were identified as the two leading candidates from the younger generation, with Gorbachev regarded as being more open to liberalization. Nevertheless, both were seen as long shots in the immediate succession struggle.[4]

Gorbachev's political fortunes rose during Yuri Andropov's brief tenure--indeed, there were signs that Andropov was grooming Gorbachev as his successor.[5] When the appointment fell to Chernenko upon Andropov's death in November 1983, there was speculation about a deal between the old guard and the reformers under which Chernenko's victory was conditional upon Gorbachev's becoming second-in-command and heir apparent.[6] These rumors were supported when Soviet sources indicated that Gorbachev was chairing not only the Secretariat but also the Politburo, and then again when Gorbachev made his highly publicized visit to Britain in December 1984. Gorbachev managed to charm both the Western media and the conservative Margaret Thatcher, who stated that Gorbachev was someone she could "do business" with. Thus it was no surprise that when Chernenko died on March 10, 1985, the Central Committee chose Gorbachev as its new leader--indeed, it would have been a surprise had it not.

Ironically, subsequent first-hand accounts have suggested that Gorbachev's victory on March 11 was more precarious than outside observers realized. Rumors at the time that old-guard Brezhnevites were hoping to block Gorbachev by supporting the candidacy of Viktor Grishin, the long-time Moscow first secretary rumored to be deeply involved in Moscow corruption, were subsequently confirmed by the playwright Mikhail Shatrov and by Boris Yeltsin in his account in *Against the Grain*.[7] Both Gorbachev and Egor Ligachev likewise later revealed that Gorbachev's victory had been a narrow one--as Ligachev put it, "Everything could have been different" had it not been for his support and the support of several other members of the leadership then being attacked for their conservatism.[8] It may well have been that the absence of Vladimir Shcherbitsky, the first secretary of the Ukraine then in the U.S., and of Dinmukhamed Kunaev, the first secretary in distant Kazakhstan, allowed Andrei Gromyko to garner the support needed to present the Central Committee with the Politburo's "unanimous" recommendation of Gorbachev.[9]

Clearly, then, any Sovietologist who claimed to "know" that Gorbachev would be the next General Secretary would be claiming a knowledge that even members of the Politburo did not possess, including when Chernenko would die (recall the many Soviet "heirs apparent" whose political fortunes had rapidly declined and that Brezhnev, after suffering a debilitating stroke in 1975, managed to hang on as General Secretary for seven years), the success of the backroom maneuvering needed to secure his victory, the number of Politburo members who would be absent from the crucial Politburo session (or sessions), the Politburo members who would decide to support Gorbachev, and the opposition that might develop on the Central Committee to any Politburo "recommendation." Moreover, if by "predicting Gorbachev" one means "predicting perestroika," then one would have to assume not only that one could know Gorbachev's intentions, but that Gorbachev was himself aware of what he intended to do upon becoming General Secretary, an assumption Gorbachev and his colleagues would later repeatedly deny.[10] Thus the best that any Sovietologist could have done was to point out, as many did, that Gorbachev appeared to be the front runner in 1983 and early 1984 and that he seemed more open to liberalization than his colleagues.[11]

More important than the correct identification of Gorbachev was the fact that Sovietologists were well aware of the accumulating problems the Soviet Union was facing in mid-1985.[12] There was in the first place an enormous literature on the declining economic performance, with CIA statistics (which since have been criticized as too generous) showing a secular decline in growth rates beginning in the early 1960s and then accelerating in the last half of the 1970s. The CIA also estimated that the Soviet military burden was high (some 12-14% of GNP, or approximately twice that in the much wealthier United States) and relatively stable, that the rate of growth in investment was declining, that living standards (estimated generously at about one-third of those in the West) were essentially stagnating, and most ominously, that factor productivity was falling.[13] Moreover, there was virtual unanimity among Western economists that the downward trend in performance could not be notably reversed in the foreseeable future.[14]

Supplementing this grim picture of the Soviet economy was a considerable literature on intensifying political problems. For example, most Sovietologists agreed with Zbigniew Brzezinski that Brezhnev's victory had brought about a "rule of clerks" and "oligarchical petrification"--clearly, the Brezhnev leadership had abandoned any commitment to revolutionary transformation and had opted instead for consensual politics and commitment to the institutional *status quo.*[15] As a result, it was generally felt that the country lacked the leadership needed to overcome the growing malaise at the top as economic problems intensified, military and political pressures increased, and Brezhnev became ever more feeble. So, too, did many Sovietologists recognize the mounting pressures for generational change within the political elite. Brezhnev's commitment to "stability in cadres" had meant little upward mobility for an increasingly frustrated younger cohort within the political elite. Short of some sort of miracle of longevity, this younger cohort would inevitably come to power, and as both Seweryn Bialer and Jerry F. Hough argued, the new generation would likely be more open to change.[16] Taking a more ideational approach, Stephen Cohen likewise held that the "Children of the 20th Party Congress" and the "*shesti-*

desiatniki" (the 1960ers) who had supported Khrushchev's populism represented a reform wing within the elite that opposed Stalinism and bureaucratic degeneration and drew its inspiration from Lenin's New Economic Policy (NEP).[17] Cohen's arguments were borne out by the role in the early reform era played by the likes of Fedor Burlatsky, Georgi Shakhnazarov, Aleksandr Bovin, Aleksandr Yakovlev, and indeed by Gorbachev himself, as well as by the early effort to use the NEP to legitimize perestroika. Finally, other Sovietologists stressed the increasingly evident political corruption, elite privileges, and black market activity. "Soviet neo-traditionalism," as Kenneth Jowitt argued, was opening a growing gap between the regime's legitimizing myths and political reality, undermining in particular the claims to having established a superior form of "socialist justice."[18]

The conventional wisdom in the pre-Gorbachev era about the political attitudes and mood of the Soviet public has also stood the test of time. A tacit agreement, it was argued, had emerged between state and society whereby the state would offer order and material security for compliance and social support from below.[19] Nevertheless, survey research done on emigres (particularly the large Soviet Interview Project [SIP]) also suggested that this tacit agreement was slowly breaking down, and that Soviet society, and particularly Soviet youth, was becoming increasingly alienated politically.[20] Disgusted by the obvious hypocrisy, by the pervasive corruption, by the need to resort to bribery and illegal economic activity to make ends meet, by pressures to participate in largely fraudulent forms of political participation, and by the brain-numbing constraints on intellectual and artistic creativity, Soviet society was retreating from participation in public life into the private arena of friends and family. These conclusions were to be confirmed by glasnost-era Soviet descriptions of the general anomie and alienation of the pre-reform era, as well as by the very mixed (and changing) reaction of the Soviet public to perestroika. Thus Western observers picked up both the vested interests in the existing order as well as the growing pessimism and alienation.

Finally, those quick to criticize Sovietologists for stressing obstacles to change and sources of political stability should remember that these arguments have hardly been refuted by perestroika. Rather, the last six-and-a-half years have confirmed the extent of social support for regime norms and social opposition to liberalization (particularly in the economy), the difficulties posed by the multi-national character of the Soviet Union and the risks of genuine democratization, and the difficulties of a transition to a market economy.

In sum, Sovietologists can be credited with having recognized the growing pressures for change and the likelihood that there would be some sort of important break with Brezhnevism. Moreover, they were hardly surprised when Gorbachev succeeded Chernenko and then reinitiated Andropov's discipline campaign while allowing a limited glasnost over the course of 1985-87, including discussion of decentralizing economic reform. The real surprises, and the real failures, came later.

Sovietology: The Failures

With some exceptions, most Sovietologists were guilty of one or more of the following in the Gorbachev era: first, failure to anticipate both the multi-dimensional character of perestroika (particularly its non-economic dimensions) as well as how far Gorbachev would be willing to go along those dimensions; failure to identify the deep contradictions in Gorbachev's program; and third and most importantly, surprise at the brittleness of the core institutions of Soviet socialism.

In part, of course, these failures can be accounted for by the nature of the problem. One can reasonably doubt whether different methods or concerns would have made for significantly better predictions about perestroika and its consequences, particularly given the paucity of reliable information and the role of contingent factors in the dynamics of the transition. Nevertheless, debate would have been improved had Sovietologists had a better appreciation of the "main fronts" of perestroika. There are six factors that seem to have clouded vision in this regard: (1) vague and ambiguous language; (2) excessive focus on what the Soviets used to call "subjective factors"; (3) concept stretching; (4) misunderstanding or neglect of ideology; (5) failure to appreciate the mobilizing power of ethnicity and nationalism; and (6) ideology within Sovietology.

1. Vague and Ambiguous Language

In reading the Sovietological debate about the likelihood of reform in the period leading up to Gorbachev's arrival in power and his early years in office, one encounters frequent references to modifiers such as "systemic," "structural," "institutional," "fundamental," "radical," etc. Those who argued that "systemic" change, for example, was neither likely nor under consideration were usually opposed by others who anticipated "fundamental" reform. Unfortunately, it was usually unclear what was meant by either "systemic" or "fundamental." Just what the Soviet "system" was, what would qualify as "fundamental" change, or what was meant by its core "structure(s)" or "institutions" was usually left unspecified. The intent often seemed to be to equate these terms with some vague notion of "importance" without regard to the yardstick being used to evaluate "importance." One could infer, however, that at times the yardstick was the Soviet past, a standard that tended to promote exaggerated claims about the extent of change. In others, the yardstick seemed to be whether change would make the USSR like a liberal democracy, a more rigorous standard that usually led to a conclusion that "fundamental" change was unlikely. Finally, in a few cases the standard seemed to be the more interesting question of whether change would bring about the desired results, with "radical economic reform," for example, meaning sufficient to improve economic performance.

Along with this muddle over these "property concepts" was confusion and vagueness over the full intension and extension of "object concepts" such as "reform," "revolution," and "regime transitions."[21] Again, although used frequently, there was little attention to their semantic problems or controversial histories.[22]

This neglect of conceptual clarity not only makes it difficult to evaluate many of the assessments of the period, it seems to have contributed to fuzzy thinking.[23] Greater attention to semantics would have forced Sovietologists to give more disciplined attention to identifying the core institutions of Soviet socialism (e.g., state ownership of the means of production, central planning, the monopoly of political power by the Party, the domination of public life by the state) and to the structural pressures bearing down on those institutions (e.g., socio-economic modernization, changes in the balance of military power of the international economy, demographics, geological factors, etc.). It would also have facilitated debate over the truly *systemic* properties of the institutions of the *ancien regime*, raising questions such as:

(1) Does central planning require state ownership of the means of production?

(2) Is democracy compatible with fixed and centrally-determined prices?

(3) Does state monopolization of economic and political life require state monopolization of public discussion?

(4) How deeply rooted are the accumulating problems of the "pre-crisis," and relatedly, were policy (e.g., investment policy) or personnel changes likely to overcome those problems?

(5) What would the consequences be of different strategies of institutional change (e.g., economic reform without glasnost or political reform)?

(6) What would the consequences be of different sequences of institutional change (e.g., glasnost before economic reform)?

(7) What would the consequences be of partial institutional

       changes (e.g., democratization without democracy, or econ-
       omic decentralization without market pricing)?

Although there is no reason to expect that a consensus would have been reached on these questions, they were fundamental to the course and outcome of perestroika and should have served as the central issues for debate. Indeed, these were the very issues Gorbachev was asking Soviet social scientists to debate in the wake of the liberalization under glasnost.

2. Excessive Focus on Subjective Factors

At the watershed January 1987 Central Committee plenum, Gorbachev criticized Soviet social scientists for their "dogmatism," challenging them to do a better job of uncovering the roots of the "crisis phenomena" that had accumulated from the past. The explanations Soviet social scientists offered in response can be placed along a spectrum. At one pole were those stressing the "subjective" failings of the former leadership, while at the other were those emphasizing "objective" factors for which the Brezhnev leadership could be blamed only for failing to overcome. These differences in emphasis revealed differences over what needed to be done to overcome accumulating problems. Conservatives tended to stress subjective factors, arguing that the solution to current problems rested in replacing people, new policies, or a new ideological/propaganda line. In contrast, "radicals" like Gorbachev stressed the objective roots of "stagnation," arguing that only structural change would improve matters (hence the term "perestroika").

Implicitly, these same differences characterized the position of Sovietologists in the period leading up to and after the commitment to perestroika. Had these differences in emphasis been taken up with vigor, the ensuing debate would have been revealing and important. Unfortunately, the Sovietological debate tended to focus for the most part on the *nature* of subjective factors, ignoring considered analysis of the objective roots of what Gorbachev would call "the pre-crisis." Instead, debate focused on Gorbachev's intentions, his formal powers, and his authority; on elite preferences and the balance of political forces at the top; and on the extent of social support for perestroika.

These subjective factors were, of course, hardly unimportant. Nevertheless, they were difficult to monitor, both because of a lack of reliable information and rapid changes in beliefs and key actors. More importantly, focusing on subjective factors seems to have fostered the belief that they were what counted. It was as if all Gorbachev needed to do was convince his colleagues and the Soviet people to support his program and all would be well. This was far from the case, however. Even under the best-designed reform program and highly favorable initial conditions, transitions from Soviet-type regimes are painful and precarious: East Germany had the best performing economy in Eastern Europe, a skilled and culturally homogeneous people, extensive economic ties and a common language with West Germany, huge commitments of West German capital, and the contributions of scores of highly-skilled West German bureaucrats and professionals, and still East German society came under tremendous economic and cultural strain after the revolution of 1989. None of these facilitating conditions was present in the Soviet Union. The Soviet economy was in much worse shape, the Soviet regime had been in place for a longer period, and the USSR was as much of an ethnic conglomerate as Yugoslavia. Thus, even if Gorbachev's program had been coherent, economic collapse, a degree of ethnic violence, and the dismemberment of at least part of the Soviet Union would have been very likely.

Gorbachev's program, however, was deeply flawed. He repeatedly made clear that he wanted a perestroika that would bring (1) democratization but also the continued monopolization of political power by the CPSU; (2) economic decentralization and a "socialist market" but also state ownership of the great bulk of the means of production and centrally-determined prices; and (3) democratization but also the preservation of the territorial integrity of the USSR. All three were contradictory in principle or impossible in practice, and his efforts to carry out his vision made economic catastrophe, ethnic violence, and political collapse all the more likely. Moreover, his strategy for the timing and tempo of perestroika--e.g., the launching of glasnost and *demokratizatsiia* before a long process of piecemeal economic reform--was at best dubious.

Sovietology would therefore have been better served had more attention been paid to the objective contradictions and implications of Gorbachev's program. In particular, the structural and institutional roots of accumulating problems, the extent of institutional change needed to put the country on the path of "renewal," the consequences of different transition paths, and the result of a failure of perestroika should have been in the forefront of the debate. Put differently, Gorbachev should have been taken at his word, and the question should have been, Assuming he stays in power, what then?

3. The Pitfalls of Concept Stretching

Most pre-Gorbachev Sovietologists can be placed along a continuum. At one end would be those who held that Soviet-type political systems were totally different not only from liberal democracies but from other non-democratic regime-types as well. At the other end would be those who stressed that the politics and policies of these regimes were very similar to the politics and policies of many non-democratic regimes and democratic regimes. While most Sovietologists were located somewhere in between, the extent to which these camps dominated the field changed considerably over time.

In the post-war period, Western political scientists felt challenged above all to explain the failure of liberal democracy in inter-war Europe. As a result, these "traditionalists" tended to stress the evident similarities between liberal democracy's great challengers, fascism and communism, as well as the distinctiveness of these regimes from liberal democracies--hence the popularity of the concept of "totalitarianism."

But as political life in the "communist camp" changed after the death of Stalin and as variation between and within the self-styled Marxist-Leninist polities intensified, this consensus began to break down. Above all, the intense mobilizational methods characteristic of the interwar fascist and communist regimes began to subside in the Soviet Union and Eastern Europe (although not in China). Moreover, the battle for civil rights for African-Americans, the Vietnam War, the Watergate scandal, the oil shocks of 1973 and 1979 and stagflation, and other challenges to Western democracies gave added impetus to a growing "revisionist" perspective, this time symbolized by a generalized assault on the concept of totalitarianism. Initially, new conceptualizations of Soviet regimes were offered that suggested that Soviet-type regimes were only somewhat less different than the traditionalists had held.[24] One approach stressed the revolutionary-transformatory ethos of Soviet-type regimes. David Apter's "mobilizational system," Robert C. Tucker's "movement regime," and Charles Lindblom's "preceptoral system," suggested that Soviet-type regimes were similar to other "revolutionary" Third World regimes in their commitment to rapid and state-led socio-economic development.[25] Once revolutionary enthusiasm had dissipated, the implication was that Soviet-type regimes would be essentially similar to other non-democratic regimes. A second conceptualization focused not on transformatory intentions but on the extent to which the state monopolized public life. Allen Kassof's "administered society," T.H. Rigby's "mono-organizational society," and A.G. Meyer's "bureaucracy writ-large" and "USSR, Inc.," stressed not transformatory intentions and mobilizational methods but the extent to which the bureaucratic state penetrated and dominated society.[26] In Meyer's case especially, the suggestion was that the "communist" and liberal-democratic worlds were converging around large, hierarchical bureaucracies that would come to dominate public life.

By the mid-1960s, these conceptualizations were giving way to others that stressed similarities more explicitly. The earliest and most influential of these was the "interest group" approach to policy analysis. As originally articulated by H. Gordon Skilling and his colleagues, the argument was that the character of the decision-making process within the Soviet state was very much like the policy-making process within any large bureaucracy.[27] It was argued that interest group theory could help explain why political authorities in Soviet-type regimes made particular decisions about resource allocation, foreign and defense matters, or economic reform. More controversial was Jerry F. Hough's notion of "institutional pluralism," which was offered as an over-arching conceptualization of Soviet-type systems that captured what was essentially important.[28] Later, Valerie Bunce and John Echols borrowed from Philippe Schmitter and argued that Brezhnev's USSR was an "exclusionary corporatist" regime in which there had been a successful inclusion of major bureaucratic interests and "non-governmental elements" in the policy-making process.[29]

I should stress that these changing conceptualizations were being offered against a background of changing explanatory interest. No longer concerned with the failure of liberal democracy in the inter-war period or with the possibility of imminent collapse of what seemed to be a well-institutionalized polity, Sovietologists were now more interested in the functioning of the system as it existed at the time. Thus Hough, in his revision of *How Russia is Ruled* by the traditionalist Merle Fainsod (which he retitled *How the Soviet Union is Governed* on the grounds that like other modern societies the Soviet Union was "governed", not "ruled"), noted that while Fainsod had focused on "how the system as a whole, the regime as a whole" had managed to survive, his interest was, "given the existence of the system, how are within system questions decided?"[30]

While revisionism gained the upper hand by the late 1970s, it never dominated the field to the extent traditionalism had in the early post-war period. Rather, many continued to argue that Soviet-type regimes were different in decisively important ways and to resist the revisionist effort to stress similarities.[31] In addition, the revisionist-traditionalist debate also involved differences over choice of term, with Hough's use of "pluralism" being particularly controversial.[32] In part it reflected differences over empirical questions (e.g., the extent and character of the internal divisions within the Soviet elite, the nature of the policy-making process and the influence of various groups in that process; the degree to which particular state institutions actually represented the interests of their "customers," etc.). Most fundamentally, however, I believe it reflected a failure of logic. Conceptualizations were treated as contraries or even contradictories that were in fact alternatives. There was no reason one had to deny that Soviet regimes were fundamentally different from liberal democracies and other non-democratic regimes while at the same time agreeing that the decision-making process and politics within the state were in many respects similar to those within any large, bureaucratic hierarchy, particularly monopolistic and non-democratic ones. It was also perfectly understandable that those studying the policy-making process and the functional division-of-labor within the Soviet state would stress its multi-organizational character, its complex distribution of authority, and different preferences within the elite. This did not mean, however, that one had to ignore the fact that the state in Soviet-type regimes was not simply *any* bureaucratic hierarchy; rather, it was an enormous administrative apparatus that claimed privileged access to the philosopher's stone while monopolizing public life. Consequently, those interested in what might bring about regime change in the long run understandably focused on these distinctive institutional features. What was not understandable was that each camp had to deny the obvious insights of the other.

Nevertheless, it is also true that in practice where one stood on the "similar-distinctive" question correlated with where one stood on the most meaningful questions dividing Sovietologists in the pre-perestroika period (and indeed well into the Gorbachev era as well). These were (1) how serious and deeply rooted the pressures for change were; (2) what would the nature of any change be; and (3) could the Soviet regime overcome accumulating problems relatively painlessly. Revisionists suggested that change would be gradual and controlled and that a reform-minded leader would have a good chance of overcoming accumulating problems.[33] Traditionalists, in contrast, held that accumulating problems were deeply rooted and could be overcome only by discontinuous and disruptive institutional change.[34]

History has rendered its verdict on this debate. The six and a half years of the Gorbachev era have shown conclusively that Soviet-type regimes do indeed suffer from deeply rooted problems and that highly disruptive, discontinuous, and painful institutional changes are needed to overcome those problems. Moreover, while all large, modern states may be "institutionally pluralist," not all collapse, and the striking rapidity and near universality of the collapse of Soviet-type regimes makes it difficult to believe that their common institutional properties did not rest behind their failure--as the Soviets would say, it was hardly *sluchaino* ("accidental") that these regimes failed under very different international and societal conditions. Second, it is now clear that transitions from Soviet-type regimes are far more complex and problematic than "transitions to democracy" from authoritarian regimes. Not only do the former entail intricately related political and economic change, but they also require, *inter alia*, the development of entire bodies of law, the recreation of entire professions (e.g., law, accounting, managers of private enterprises), the reemergence of entire classes (entrepreneurs and capitalists), and, with few exceptions (e.g., the church in Poland), the reconstruction and re-legitimation of the institutions of civil society.

This brings me finally to pitfalls of "concept stretching."[35] The revisionists seemed to argue that integrating Sovietology into the social sciences required treating everything as equivalent. As a result, in many cases *terms* rather than concepts or explanatory approaches were imported--that is, the intension of a term was changed in order to make it applicable to the Soviet case (e.g., pluralism or corporatism). Cross-fertilization is to be welcomed, and borrowed concepts and explanatory approaches can be applied to different *explananda*; this does mean, however, that we need to treat cats as dogs.[36] Moreover, in rejecting the argument that Soviet political reality was decidedly different, revisionists tended not only to project Western political reality onto the Soviet

Union but to be much too sanguine about the prospects for the Soviet future.[37] For example, while pointing out that a multiplicity of state bureaucracies participated in the policy-making process, revisionists missed the *extent* to which the monopolistic Soviet state was particularly vulnerable to "departmentalism" (*vedomstvo*), or the autarkical and self-interested behavior of departmental officials and indeed entire ministries. Similarly, the notion that local Party officials functioned as "power brokers" and economic problem solvers interested in consensus, conflict resolution, and economic efficiency led many revisionists to miss the extent of "localism" (*mestnichestvo*), or the self-interested, dysfunctional, and corrupt behavior of party officials who were often more akin to a Boss Tweed or a feudal baron than to a French "prefect."[38] Much the same could be said of defenders of the notion of "corporatism." In suggesting that high politics in the Brezhnev era were characterized by "interest representation" by leaders of state bureaucracies, revisionists missed the extent to which these leaders and their subordinates pursued their own interests at the expense of ultimate consumers.[39] Moreover, the argument that the Soviet system under Brezhnev had evolved into a well-functioning, orderly, corporatist system with a leadership committed to incremental increases in resources for major bureaucratic interests was not only incorrect (there were important disagreements over resource allocation under Brezhnev), but it obscured the fact that those resources were not boundless and that declining growth rates were forcing tough choices on an indecisive leadership. Put bluntly, it made a difference that bureaucratic politics were taking place in the absence of open competition for public office and that budgetary decisions were being made against a background of state ownership and central planning of virtually the entire economy.

In sum, the "revisionists" of the 1960s and 1970s went too far. While correcting some of the exaggerated imagery of "totalitarianism," many swung to the opposite pole. Ironically, they thereby undermined their efforts to integrate Sovietology into the larger discipline of comparative politics by neglecting comparative control.[40]

4. Misunderstanding Ideology--The Key Subjective Factor

If the revisionists were wrong in suggesting that Soviet-type regimes were like any others and that they would continue to adapt successfully to a changing environment, most traditionalists were wrong in failing to understand the true importance of that fundamentally important subjective factor--ideology. While revisionists tended to ignore ideology, traditionalists assumed either (1) that the Soviet elite was deeply cynical and concerned above all with the preservation of their power and privileges, or (2) that the Soviet elite was ideologically fanatical. In both cases, it followed that the elite would never commit to serious reform that might threaten power and privilege or that smacked of ideological compromise.[41] Ironically, then, traditionalists were usually as sanguine about the long-run viability of Soviet-type regimes as revisionists, albeit for different reasons.

Perestroika demonstrated not only that revisionists were wrong in ignoring the importance of ideology, but that traditionalists erred in assuming that the elite was either universally cynical or fanatical. The deep opposition within the Party to the market, to private property, and to "bourgeois" democracy; the vigorous defense of Marxism-Leninism by people like Egor Ligachev even when political careers would have been furthered by an opportunistic abandonment of "communist principles"; and above all, Gorbachev's dogged commitment to Leninism and the "socialist choice" have demonstrated that Marxism-Leninism was not mere window dressing. There were, in fact, many "true believers" in "Leninism" if not "Brezhnevism" in 1985, and these true believers accounted for the great bulk of the supporters of perestroika in its early period.

The tendency to underestimate the importance of ideology made it difficult for traditionalists to explain the initiation of perestroika and contributed to their underestimation of the seriousness with which Gorbachev and his allies would pursue reform. Samuel P. Huntington once wrote, "Perhaps the hardest lesson to learn for governments sensitive to the needs of reform is the importance of introducing reforms from a position of strength."[42] The striking fact about the initiation of perestroika is that the Soviet leadership did begin perestroika from a position of relative strength, well before a genuine economic or political crisis had left it with no choice but to accept change. By contemporaneous statistics, both Western and Soviet, economic growth rates were respectable by international standards, there was no evidence of an imminent revolt from below, and there was no reason to fear imminent outside invasion. The real "crisis," then, was a subjective one.

Perestroika was launched not because the Soviet elite wished to protect its privileges or because it was fanatically devoted to a vulgar Stalinist Marxism. Rather, it began because it felt a need to restore its own confidence in socialism's historical destiny and its derivative belief in the legitimacy of its continued rule. Above all, the Soviet elite had concluded that socialism was losing its historic competition with capitalism: not only was poor economic performance making it impossible to deliver the material goods, but the mounting evidence of political corruption and widespread flaunting of regime norms was undermining the claim that Soviet socialism was providing a superior form of social justice. Gorbachev and his allies therefore launched perestroika in the hopes of "renewing socialism." Never did they intend it to undermine the founding principles of state ownership: central planning, the monopoly of political power by the Party, or the territorial integrity of the USSR. Moreover, ideological dogmatism accounted not only for Gorbachev's well-intentioned but naive belief in the possibility of building a Soviet socialism with a human face--

it also accounted for his prolonged and vigorous opposition to what he saw as opportunistic compromises.

Thus, rather than providing a driving force for an expansionist foreign policy or as means for brainwashing the Soviet public, the real importance of Marxism-Leninism rested in its contribution to the Soviet elite's belief in the legitimacy of its rule. The fact that most Westerners took these claims as self-evidently absurd says more about their own prejudices and assumptions than it does about the credibility of those claims to the Soviet elite before perestroika. Moreover, in focusing on the legitimacy of the *ancien regime*, Westerners erred in focusing on the extent of broad social support for the regime and paying insufficient attention to the credibility of the regime's legitimizing claims. As Martin Malia has put it:

> Instead of taking the Soviet leadership at its ideological word--
> that their task was to 'build socialism'--Western Sovietology
> has by and large foisted on Soviet reality social science
> categories derived from Western realities, with the result that
> the extraordinary, indeed surreal, Soviet experience has been
> rendered banal to the point of triviality.[43]

5. Euro-Rationalism and the Nationality Question

Not only liberalism and Marxism but mainstream understandings of the "scientific method" are all children of the Enlightenment, and all have contributed to a tendency for social scientists to underestimate the mobilizing power of ethnicity, nationalism, and religion. Indeed, not only Gorbachev but Sovietologists were surprised not only by the survival of ethnic/national consciousness and religion during the Soviet period but by the fact that mass mobilization during perestroika was structured by these "traditional" identities. Moreover, many continued to insist on the power of the centripetal pressures of economic self-interest (which were usually exaggerated) and fears of disorder despite growing evidence that not only the CPSU leadership and its allies but the Union itself had been thoroughly discredited by 1990. As a result, instead of hoping for and promoting peaceful divorce, democracy, and open economic borders, many Western governments and observers promoted and predicted the survival of the USSR, despite its enormous cultural diversity and incorporation of nations with long histories of mutual enmity.

It is difficult to believe that such an extraordinarily diverse country as the former USSR could have become democratic and remained united even in the absence of intense economic distress, a collapse of political authority generally, and destruction of an entire belief system. A shrinking economic pie, great redistributions in wealth and income, difficulties in securing property rights, the distributional consequences of privatization, and the need for scapegoats will create difficulties for democratic consolidation in societies taking the path of transition from Soviet-type regimes in the best of circumstances. For example, the ethnically homogenous countries of Eastern Europe (e.g., Poland and the former GDR), which after all could blame the Soviets for their problems, have seen a rise in anti-Semitism, attacks on Gypsies, hostility toward immigrants, etc.

In the former Soviet Union, however, the transition has been and will continue to be even more painful. Nor do people have to look very far for someone different to blame. In these circumstances, continued ethnic violence in the Transcaucasus, in Central Asia, and in parts of the Russian Federation is almost inevitable. The optimistic assessment by Westerners of all political persuasions that democracy and the territorial integrity of the former USSR were compatible is difficult to explain except by the influence of exaggerated and simplistic notions of "self-interest" and rationality.

6. The Motivational Fallacy

Finally, a word about ideology *within* Sovietology. Lurking behind the debate over the nature and future of the Soviet regime was an *ad hominem* "apologist-demonologist" dispute focusing on motives rather than substance. On the one hand, those who argued that Soviet-type regimes were viable and similar to other polities risked being called "apologists" for "the evil empire." On the other, those who stressed differences and intensifying problems risked being called "rabid anti-communists" or propagandists for the American government. In both cases, the implication was that pointing to similarities/accomplishments or differences/failures was an "ideological" move intended either to support or discredit Soviet socialism, and thus both were "non-scientific."

These "apologist-demonologist" charges were not only misguided but they had the unfortunate effect of deterring all but the very bold from taking up the performance question. Professionally, it was less risky to focus on the Soviet past, on the decision-making process, on the functions of the local Soviet in Sverdlovsk, or on the career paths of the Soviet elite than it was to ask whether the Soviet regime was performing well. As a result, Sovietology was slowly being reduced, as Alexander J. Motyl has put it, to the "deification of [mere] data" and "political journalism" at the expense of explanation and theory.[44] Performance, particularly poor performance, was in fact no more "ideological" or "non-scientific" a subject than any other. Rather, performance arguments were truth claims based on available evidence that could and should have been weighed against the legitimizing claims of the Soviet regime and universal human needs (e.g., decent homes). Moreover, changing performance indicators invited explanation: investigating the causes of achievements or accumulating problems could provide answers to questions about whether declining economic performance would continue, whether corruption would become ever more pervasive, whether social support for the regime would wax or wane, and what the elite would or could do about the country's many problems--hardly trivial questions.

Conclusion

There are important lessons to be drawn from the record of Sovietology for the study of new, post-Soviet polities. These are (1) the importance of careful use of language; (2) the pitfalls of concept stretching; (3) the need to give due consideration to the credibility of legitimizing myths; (4) the importance of "objective factors" and core institutions in limiting choice and shaping of outcomes; (5) the dangers of over-simplistic notions about "rationality" and "self-interest"; and (6) the pernicious effects of *ad hominem* charges about motives. By avoiding these problems, I believe post-Sovietologists will be better prepared to describe, explain, and even anticipate events in what promises to be a long period of turmoil in the former Soviet Union.

Notes

1. *Political Order in Changing Societies* (New Haven, CT: Yale University Press, 1968), p. 1.

2. Mikhail S. Gorbachev, *Izbrannye rechi i stati* (Moscow: Politizdat), Vol. 3, 1987, p. 181, and Vol. 4, 1987, pp. 299-354.

3. One of these lessons is not to ignore or distort the work of one's predecessors. For a discussion of the failures of "professional memory" in Sovietology, see A.G. Meyer, "Coming to Terms with the Past--And with One's Older Colleagues," *The Russian Review* 45, no. 4 (1986): 401-408; and Thomas Remington, "Fathers and Sons: The Dialectics of Soviet Studies," in *Politics and the Soviet System: Essays in Honour of Frederick Barghoorn*, ed. Thomas F. Remington (New York: St. Martin's Press, 1989), pp. 1- 11. For political science, see Gabriel A. Almond, *A Discipline Divided: Schools and Sects in Political Science* (Newbury Park, CA: Sage Publications, 1990), especially Part II, "Generations and Professional Memory," and Giovanni Sartori on "novitism" in *The Theory of Democracy Revisited* (Chatham, NJ: Chatham House, 1987), p. 505.

4. In addition to the eventual winner, Yuri V. Andropov, the other front runners were Konstantin U. Chernenko, Brezhnev's long-time aide-de-camp, and Andrei Kirilenko (see, for example, the discussions in William G. Hyland, "Kto-Kogo in the Kremlin," *Problems of Communism* 31 (Jan.-Feb. 1982): 17-29; Jerry F. Hough, "Soviet

Succession: Issues and Personalities," *Problems of Communism* 31 (Sep.-Oct. 1982): 20-40; and Sidney Ploss, "Soviet Succession: Signs of Struggle," *ibid.*: 41-52. For articles identifying Gorbachev as a likely General Secretary in the long run, see Jerry F. Hough, "Changes in Elite Competition," in *Russia at the Crossroads: The 26th Party Congress of the CPSU*, eds. Seweryn Bialer and Thane Gustafson (Boston: Allen & Unwin, 1982), pp. 43-44; and Archie Brown, "Leadership Succession and Policy Innovation," in *Soviet Policy for the 1980s*, eds. Archie Brown and Michael Kaser (London: Macmillan, 1982), pp. 240-45, and 269-70.

5. For an overview, see Michael J. Dixon, "The Chernenko Succession: An Initial Assessment," Congressional Research Service, The Library of Congress, March 7, 1984, esp. p. 3.

6. For an analysis of Chernenko's victory, see *ibid.*, and Mark Zlotnik, "Chernenko Succeeds," *Problems of Communism* 33 (Mar-Apr. 1984): 27-31.

7. Mikhail Shatrov, *Ogonek*, 1987, No. 4: 5; and Boris Yeltsin, *Against the Grain* (New York: Summit Books, 1990), pp. 138-39.

8. Ligachev, *Izbrannye rechi i stati* (Moscow: Politizdat, 1989), p. 278.

9. See Gromyko's account in *Memories* (London: Hutchinson, 1990), p. 341.

10. As early as the January 1987 plenum, Gorbachev was admitting that "perestroika has turned out to be more difficult, the reasons for the accumulated problems in society even deeper, than we had earlier imagined. The more deeply we are drawn into the work of perestroika, the clearer its scale and its significance becomes, the more clearly revealed are the unsolved problems" (*op. cit.*, Vol. 4, p. 300).

11. See Archie Brown, "Gorbachev: New Man in the Kremlin," *Problems of Communism* 34 (May-June 1985): 1-23.

12. See in particular the writings of Seweryn Bialer in the period, including, "The Harsh Decade: Soviet Politics in the 1980's," *Foreign Affairs* 59, no. 5 (Summer 1981): 999-1020. William E. Odom summarized Bialer's views at the time as follows: "Bialer's strong implication is that significant change in Soviet politics is bound to occur, although he does not venture to predict its direction" ("Choice and Change in Soviet Politics," *Problems of Communism* 32 [May-June 1983]: 15).

13. For an overview, see Laurie Kurtzweg, "Trends in Soviet Gross National Product," in *Gorbachev's Economic Plans*, Study Papers Submitted to the JEC, Nov. 23, 1987, Vol. 1, pp. 126-65, and the remainder of the articles in the volume.

14. See, for example, the conclusions of the econometric analysis in Abram Bergson and Herbert S. Levine, *The Soviet Economy: Toward the Year 2000* (Boston: George Allen

& Unwin, 1983).

15. "Victory of the Clerks," *The New Republic*, Nov. 14, 1964: 15-18; "The Soviet Political System: Transformation or Degeneration?," *Problems of Communism* 15 (Jan-Feb. 1966): 1-15. Brzezinski's use of terms such as "ossification," "petrification," "degeneration," "stagnation," "conservatism," "inertia," and "immobilism" became the most common terms applied in glasnost-era Soviet analyses of Brezhnevism (see, for example, Fedor Burlatsky, "Brezhnev: Krushenie ottepeli--razmyshlenie o prirode politicheskovo liderstva," *Literaturnaia gazeta*, Sept. 14, 1988: 13; Burlatsky, "Khrushchev, Andropov, Brezhnev: The Issue of Political Leadership," in *Perestroika 1989*, ed. Abel Abanbegyan (New York: Scribner, 1989), pp. 187-214; and Roy A. Medvedev, "L.I. Brezhnev: Nabrosok politicheskogo portreta," *Rabochii klas i sovremennyi mir*, 1988, No. 6: 142-61). Indeed, Brzezinski was also prescient in arguing in the above cited works that lack of institutional change raised the risk of the "degeneration" of the Soviet system. In a later work, he was to reiterate this argument, predicting a combination of "petrification" and "technological adaptation" in the 1970s followed by a shift toward pluralism in the 1980s, and he concluded that at some point "the political elite must decide to embark upon deliberate political reform" (*Between Two Ages* [New York: Viking, 1970], p. 165).

16. Seweryn Bialer, *Stalin's Successors: Leadership, Stability and Change in the Soviet Union* (Cambridge: Cambridge University Press, 1980), pp. 81-126; and Jerry F. Hough, *Soviet Leadership in Transition* (Washington, DC: The Brookings Institution, 1980). For slightly more skeptical views of the reformist tendencies of the new generation, see George W. Breslauer, "Is There a Generation Gap in the Soviet Political Establishment?," *Soviet Studies* 36, no. 1 (Jan. 1984): 1-25; and Mark R. Beissinger, "In Search of Generations in Soviet Politics," *World Politics* 38, no. 2 (Jan. 1986): 288-314.

17. "The Friends and Foes of Change: Soviet Reformism and Conservatism," in *Rethinking the Soviet Experience: Politics and History Since 1917* (Oxford, UK: Oxford University Press, 1985), pp. 128-57, as well as *An End of Silence: Uncensored Opinion in the Soviet Union*, ed. Stephen Cohen (New York: Norton, 1982).

18. "Soviet Neo-Traditionalism: The Political Corruption of a Leninist Regime," *Soviet Studies* 35, no. 3 (July 1983): 275-97.

19. See, for example, George Breslauer, "On the Adaptability of the Soviet Welfare-State Authoritarianism," in *Soviet Society and the Communist Party*, ed. Karl Ryavec (Amherst: University of Massachusetts Press, 1978), pp. 3-25.

20. The SIP results are reported in *Politics, Work, and Daily Life in the USSR*, ed. James R. Millar (Cambridge: Cambridge University Press, 1987). See also John Bushnell, "The New Soviet Man Turns Pessimist," in *The Soviet Union Since Stalin*, eds. Stephen Cohen, *et al.*, pp. 179-99, and Zvi Gitelman, "Soviet Political Culture: Insights From Jewish Emigres," *Soviet Studies* 29, no. 4 (Oct. 1977): 543-64.

21. For the difference between property and object concepts, see Giovanni Sartori, "Guidelines for Concept Analysis," in *Social Science Concepts: A Systematic Analysis*, ed. Giovanni Sartori (Newbury Park, CA: Sage Publications, 1984), pp. 79 and 91. In the former case, the reference is to a variable property of an object, while in the latter it is to the object itself.

22. There were some exceptions (see, for example, Timothy Colton, *The Dilemma of Reform in the Soviet Union*, rev. ed. [New York: Council on Foreign Relations, 1986], pp. 4-5). For an overview of the semantic difficulties with the concept of "revolution," see Christopher M. Kotowski, "Revolution," in *Social Science Concepts*, ed. Sartori, pp. 403-51. For analyses of the concept of reform, see Huntington, *Political Order*, pp. 344-96, and "Reform and Stability in South Africa," *International Security* (Spring 1982): 3-25, and Albert O. Hirschman, *Journeys Toward Progress: Studies in Economic Policy-Making in Latin America* (New York: Norton, 1973 [1963]), pp. 227-97, and especially pp. 247-49. On the language of regime change, see Giovanni Sartori, *Parties and Party Systems: A Framework for Analysis* (Cambridge: Cambridge University Press, 1976), especially pp. 217-43 and 273-323.

23. For example, how can one evaluate Jerry F. Hough's statement that the post-Brezhnev Soviet leadership would be forced to effect personnel changes and embark on a program of economic reform to maintain "the vitality and perhaps even the stability of the system" unless we know what was meant by "the system"? (*The Soviet Leadership in Transition* [Washington, D.C.: Brookings, 1979], p. 151).

24. For overviews of this debate, see the essays in *Pluralism in the Soviet Union*, ed. Susan Gross Solomon (London: Macmillan, 1983), pp. 4-36; Merle Fainsod and Jerry F. Hough, *How the Soviet Union is Governed* (Cambridge: Harvard University Press, 1979 [*How Russia is Ruled*, 1953, 1963]), pp. 518-76; the symposium titled "Pluralism in Communist Societies," *Studies in Comparative Communism* 12, no. 1 (Spring 1979): 3-38, with contributions from Sarah Terry, Andrew Janos, William Odom and Zvi Gitelman; and Gabriel A. Almond and Laura Roselle, "Model Fitting in Communism Studies," in Almond, *A Discipline Divided*, pp. 66-116.

25. David Apter, *The Politics of Modernization* (Chicago: University of Chicago Press, 1965), pp. 357-90; Robert Tucker, "On Revolutionary Mass-Movement Regimes," *The Soviet Political Mind*, rev. ed. (New York: Norton, 1971), pp. 3-19; and Charles Lindblom, *Politics and Markets* (New York: Basic Books, 1977), pp. 52-62.

26. Allen Kassof, "The Administered Society: Totalitarianism Without Terror," *World Politics* 16, no. 4 (July 1964): 558-75; T.H. Rigby, "Traditional, Market, and Organizational Societies and the USSR," *World Politics* 16, no. 4 (July 1964): 539-557; T.H. Rigby, "Politics in the Mono-Organizational Society," in *Authoritarian Politics in Communist Europe: Uniformity and Diversity in One-Party States*, ed. Andrew C. Janos (Berkeley: University of California Press, 1976); A.G. Meyer, *The Soviet Political System: An Interpretation* (New York: Random House, 1965), p. 472; and A.G. Meyer,

"USSR, Incorporated," *Slavic Review* 20 (Oct. 1961): 369-76.

27. See the essays in *Interest Groups in Soviet Politics*, eds. H. Gordon Skilling and Franklyn Griffiths (Princeton, NJ: Princeton University Press, 1971).

28. "The Soviet System: Petrification or Pluralism?" *Problems of Communism* 21 (March-April 1972). See also Hough's essays in *The Soviet Union and Social Science Theory* (Cambridge: Harvard University Press, 1977).

29. Valerie Bunce and John M. Echols III, "Soviet Politics in the Brezhnev Era: 'Pluralism' or 'Corporatism'?" in *Soviet Politics in the Brezhnev Era*, ed. Donald Kelley (New York: Praeger, 1980), pp. 1-23. I should note that it was never clear just who these "non-governmental elements" were, a tricky question in a country where the state was virtually the only employer.

30. *How the Soviet Union is Governed*, pp. vii-viii.

31. See, for example, William E. Odom, "A Dissenting View on the Group Approach to Soviet Politics," *World Politics* 28, no. 4 (July 1976): 542-67.

32. See, for example, Giovanni Sartori, "Concept Misformation in Comparative Politics," *American Political Science Review* 64, no. 4 (Dec. 1970): 1033-53. Hough later expressed regret at his use of the term "pluralism," adding, "The major differences between the Soviet Union and the United States today are not nearly so great in the degree of influence of establishment interest groups . . . as they are in the scope of governmental action and its restrictive character" ("Pluralism, Corporatism, and the Soviet Union," in *Pluralism in the Soviet Union*, ed. Solomon, p. 54). Indeed Hough would later defend the insights of traditionalist arguments about totalitarianism (see, for example, *Russia and the West: Gorbachev and the Politics of Reform*, 2d ed. [New York: Touchstone, 1990 (1988)], pp. 46-54).

33. See, for example, the writings of Jerry F. Hough, especially "Gorbachev's Strategy," *Foreign Affairs* 64, no. 1 (Fall 1985): 33-55; "The Politics of Successful Economic Reform," *Soviet Economy* 5, no. 1 (1989): 3-46; and "Gorbachev's Endgame," *World Policy Journal* 7, no. 4 (Fall 1990): 639-72.

34. For a traditionalist view, see R.V. Burks, "Reform in the Soviet Union," *The Washington Quarterly* 8, no. 1 (Winter 1985): 177-81, and later, Martin Malia ("Z"), "To the Stalin Mausoleum," *Daedalus* (Winter 1990), 119, no. 1: 295-344.

35. See Sartori, "Concept Misformation."

36. See Giovanni Sartori, "Comparing and Miscomparing," *Journal of Theoretical Politics* 3, no. 3 (1991): 243-57.

37. For example, Bunce and Echols argued, "First, [Soviet] corporatism has been successful, especially in terms of economic growth. What's more, it is plausible to suggest that the current growth rate of 3-5 percent per year can be maintained in the foreseeable future; even agriculture, despite popular notions, is hardly in dire straits. In addition, this economic growth can be brought under corporatism at little or no cost to any major sector" ("Soviet Politics in the Brezhnev Era," p. 20). And they added that "the logic of corporatism and its benefits to elites, groups, and masses are not insignificant. Brezhnev, therefore, seems to have been much more of an innovator than many scholars have argued; like his predecessors, he has ushered in a new system. But, unlike his predecessors, this system may even outlive its founder" (*ibid.*, pp. 20-21). I should note that Bunce would later modify her views in "The Political Economy of the Brezhnev Era: The Rise and Fall of Corporatism," *British Journal of Political Science* (Sept. 1984): 129-58.

38. See Jerry F. Hough, *The Soviet Prefects* (Cambridge: Harvard University Press, 1969).

39. Seweryn Bialer, in contrast, stressed the growing venal departmentalism, or what he called the "corporative orientation" of Soviet bureaucracies, in his *Stalin's Successors*, pp. 52-53.

40. Frederick J. Fleron and Erik P. Hoffmann have noted that the effort to "integrate" Sovietology into Western social sciences failed, arguing that this failure helps account for the discipline's unpreparedness for perestroika ("Sovietology and Perestroika: Methodology and Lessons from the Past," *The Harriman Institute Forum* 5, no. 1 [Sept. 1991]). They do not, however, concede that the fallacious assumption that borrowing methods, concepts, and theoretical approaches meant treating everything as alike contributed to this failure.

41. Thus Jeane J. Kirkpatrick, for example, argued that Soviet "totalitarian" regimes were different from other non-democratic regimes in that transitions from authoritarianism to democracy were far more likely (*Dictatorship and Double Standards: Rationalism and Reason in Politics* [New York: Simon & Schuster, 1982]).

42. "Reform in South Africa," *International Security* (Spring 1982): 17.

43. "To the Stalin Mausoleum," p. 298.

44. *Sovietology, Rationality, Nationality: Coming to Grips with Nationalism in the USSR* (New York: Columbia University Press, 1990), p. 3.

Index